BETWEEN 2 GODS

A MEMOIR OF ABUSE
IN THE MENNONITE COMMUNITY

TRUDY HARDER METZGER

eLectio Publishing

Little Elm, TX

www.eLectioPublishing.com

Between 2 Gods: A Memoir of Abuse in the Mennonite Community
By Trudy Harder Metzger

Copyright 2015 by Trudy Harder Metzger
Cover Design by eLectio Publishing

ISBN-13: 978-1-63213-087-7
Published by eLectio Publishing, LLC
Little Elm, Texas
http://www.eLectioPublishing.com

Printed in the United States of America

The eLectio Publishing editing team is comprised of: Christine LePorte, Lori Draft, Sheldon James, and Jim Eccles.

Publisher's Note
The publisher does not have any control over and does not assume any responsibility for author or third-party websites or their content.

Author's Disclaimer

The author has made every attempt to recreate events, locales, and conversations as accurately as possible, and where appropriate, based on her memories of them and having confirmed as many details as possible with individuals involved. Any discrepancies and inaccuracies are unintentional. However, in order to maintain their anonymity, in some instances, names of individuals and places have been altered. Additionally, some identifying characteristics, such as physical properties, occupations, and places of residence, have also changed.

I dedicate this book,

Between 2 Gods

to:

My husband,   Tim Metzger,
my faithful companion,   my best friend, and the
love of my life. He knows well the story that spilled
onto the pages of this book, and loved patiently,
always, in spite of my story. Not passing
judgement, he listened compassionately as I trusted him with it in
our early years together.
Thank you
!

Tim, you loved me to wholeness. Through you, God revealed His love and
brought redemption into my life! I give you my heart with deepest trust and
appreciation.

CONTENTS

Special Thanks To

My husband, Tim, and our children—Alicia, Nicole, Bryan, Toddrick, and Kordan—for your patience with me, as a wife, as a mother, and as an author. You have paid a price for my story, having suffered in the aftermath, and you have paid a price for my telling it publicly. There is no one in the world I love more, or to whom I am more deeply indebted.

Christopher Dixon, of eLectio Publishing, for giving my dream wings. You looked beyond the extensive editing my book needed, and saw potential to bring hope to "half the population of the world" by sharing my story.

My mother for many hours spent sharing stories of previous generations and your life with my father, filling in the gaps to my story. In all that was, and all that wasn't, I thank God for redemption. Thank you for blessing this project. It was hard living, and hard telling, for both of us.

My late father, whose struggle shaped my early life and brought me into deep conflict with God, forcing me to search for truth. Your desperate search for God inspired me in spite of the harshness and dysfunction of our relationship. Asking for forgiveness, before your death, meant a lot; you were a broken man, stripped of all but God's grace. RIP

My eight brothers and seven sisters, as well as my in-laws, for what each of you has contributed to my life. Where aspects of your story inevitably overlapped with my experience, I have tried to respect your privacy and not reveal your identities, especially in vulnerable situations. I wish you all God's best!

My nieces and nephews, who have paid a high price with their own experience, for the story written in the pages of this book and the way it shaped us as a family. I pray that God will restore in you what generational sins have stolen from us all.

Mrs. Wolfe for giving me a safe place on the most traumatic day of my childhood. You have a special place in my heart and my story.

Vanessa Grosset, my agent and cheerleader, who believed in this book, in its purpose, and in me, from day one. You are a God-send, with your rock-solid faith, passion for people, and determination to make this happen.

Eric Stanford, of Edit Resource, whose skill transformed my manuscript. Your magical touch with words, and your focus, made all the difference! You took the clouds, rain, and sunshine of my story and made a beautiful rainbow!

Family members and friends who encouraged me to tell the truth, regardless of cost or consequences. Especially those in conservative Mennonite settings, whose cries propelled me forward. God has not forgotten you.

Christine (Kuepfer) Shantz, who believed in this project for all its "twenty years in the making," and who read every attempt at writing my story with faith in the outcome, and encouragement for me to continue. A truer cheerleader does not exist. Words fail to express my thanks.

Friends who contributed to this project, in various ways: Boz Tchividjian, Cheryl Mason Thompson, Cindy Weber, Dale Ingraham, Elias Kanaris, Dr. Ike Reighard, Kelita Haverland, Marion Mills, Margaret Kuepfer, Monica Orr, Sheri Griffin, Sheri Gingrich, Tina & Richard Miller.

The late Helen Martin, who 'graduated' from this world on November 19, 2014, only weeks after helping me with my manuscript. You were an amazing woman of God, a true friend, and a warrior for the vulnerable and those of us fighting front lines. RIP.

The late Pastor Don Mills for believing in the "uncomfortable vision" God has given me for healing in sexual abuse victims. You encouraged me, and went out of your way to thank me and bless me, even calling me at work to offer prayer and encouragement.

My friend and fellow author, Ira Wagler, for offering support that can only come from one who has "walked this way" before. You have encouraged me to press on, knowing such vulnerability comes with a price tag.

Cousin Helen Knelson and friend Helen Reddekopp for unmatched support and a safe place to share, to weep, to laugh and be unbelievably crazy, when I needed to de-stress. I treasure our unique friendship.

Marlene Herford-Martin for stepping into my teenage trauma, and abandoning everything to be with me the night I emptied that bottle of pills in my hand. The story could have ended so differently, but God...

Howard and Alice Horst for daring to ask that traumatic and life-changing question: "Were you sexually abused...?" and then walking through the aftermath as all hell broke loose, even inviting me to live in your home. It was through you that I met Jesus in a most personal way, in the Mennonite church. The ripple effects of your love and care will impact many generations, and thousands today. We all thank you!

Most importantly, "the God who won my heart." You are a kind and gracious "Papa." Thank you for revealing Your great love to this very wounded soul, and making Yourself known so that I would see the other god does not exist. How I love You!

Foreword

Every life is a journey. Some begin their journey surrounded by love and support, while all too many start their journey alone, not knowing the meaning of those two incredibly important words. Trudy Metzger started her journey in a religious setting where "Godly" appearance and following the rules to keep God happy defined her world. Trudy Metzger's world was also one in which she was alone and had very little understanding of authentic love and support. She was a child who became all too accustomed to an abusive father and a family that preferred the horrors of silence over the liberation that comes from truth and transparency. Instead of accepting a journey defined by oppressive complacency, from an early age Trudy's life became all the pursuit of love and protection. A pursuit that had no use for an oppressive God who conditions his love and blessings upon obedience to the rules. This pursuit led Trudy to leave home at an early age (sixteen) and walk away from it all in search of the authentic love and protection she so desperately craved. Instead of getting better, Trudy found herself struggling through dark and painful valleys. Sure, there were some moments when light shone into the valley, but for too many years Trudy's journey was defined by valley after valley. Just when she thought a valley couldn't get any darker, she stumbled into another that was even darker. Where was the protection? Where was the love? Where was the hope?

In the course of my own journey confronting the darkness of abuse that is so prevalent inside of our faith communities, I have been immeasurably blessed to encounter some of the most amazing heroes. Trudy Metzger is one of those heroes. A hero who has struggled through a journey filled with painful valleys. A hero who has spent her life protecting and loving those she has encountered in the valleys who have given up hope. Whether she realizes it or not, Trudy Metzger is a beautiful reflection of a God whose very character is defined by love. A God who goes into the valleys to pursue people. A God who walked the dark valley of abandonment, isolation, and deep suffering. A God who understands. A God who grieves. A God who cares. A God who loves without conditions.

The journey of Trudy Metzger that is found in the pages of this book is nothing short of amazing. However, this journey is ultimately not about Trudy Metzger. It's about the God of Trudy Metzger. It is about a God who walked and suffered with her through each and every valley. It's about a God who never gave up on her even when everyone else had walked away. It's about a God who never let her go even during those moments when she had lost all hope. It's about a God who gave her the protection and love she had been looking for all along.

It is my prayer that as you walk this journey with Trudy, not only will you come to know and love this hero, but that you will encounter the loving God who turns everything upside down, and who will never let you go.

~ Boz Tchividjian ~

Basyle "Boz" Tchividjian, former child abuse prosecutor, currently teaches *Child Abuse and the Law* and several other courses at Liberty University School of Law. As a prosecutor for over eight years, Professor Tchividjian created the first "Crimes Against Children" division at the Office of the State Attorney of the 7th Judicial Circuit in Florida. As division chief, Professor Tchividjian was personally responsible for prosecuting hundreds of cases of child sexual abuse. Professor Tchividjian has spent over 17 years using what he learned as a prosecutor to train and equip prosecutors, investigators, social workers, and medical personnel in handling various aspects of child sexual abuse prosecutions. Boz is also the founder and executive director of G.R.A.C.E., an organization that educates and equips the faith community to correctly respond to sexual abuse disclosures, while also providing practical guidance to the Christian community on how to protect children. G.R.A.C.E. provides confidential consultations to churches, schools, and other organizations that are struggling with abuse-related issues, and assists institutions and abuse survivors by providing independent investigation services.

Preface

Earliest memories of my childhood are not of fairy tales, nursery rhymes, and storybooks. Nor are they the voice of a parent singing lullabies or "Jesus loves me...." No playing "pat-a-cake, pat-a-cake, baker's man...," or bedtime stories to calm the mind and bring sweet rest.

The stories I recall hearing at bedtime were shared in a dimly lit room, with family members seated around the table, the lantern flickering. I was barely more than a toddler when I first heard the horrific tales that were shared, from time to time, with us children.

Shadows danced eerily around the room like gleeful demons clapping their hands at the darkness. Oh, how I despised the stories! And yet, I was drawn in by the very thing that made me dislike them so much—the horror.

I could see the woman's body hanging on the apple tree, deep in the woods, as my parents told the graphic suicide story; a woman who had left her husband and disappeared one night never to return home. She was found some days later, body hanging in the apple tree, crows pecking at her flesh.

Some stories were told for the sole purpose of frightening us into listening to God—like the story of the young woman who repeatedly skipped church, choosing rather to spend her time in front of the mirror, doing her hair, trying to make herself look beautiful. One Sunday morning, after the rest of her family left for church, the devil just up and carried her away to hell, where she burned forever and ever. Such was the consequence for falling into the clutches of pride. We were admonished to never obsess about our looks, or try to be anything except plain and humble, lest we should succumb to a similar fate.

Other stories were of friends, relatives, or acquaintances—stories of violence, murder, and suicide. Yet others were old wives' tales passed down from generation to generation, with no particular purpose other than to horrify the mind, or create some perverse object lesson.

There was the woman who gave birth to a demon and was mauled beyond recognition immediately after giving birth. And another supposedly gave birth to a creature that was half human and half swine. Of course, some

xi

sin committed by these women had led to these unfortunate consequences. The first woman had engaged in an affair, only to discover that it was the devil himself, not another human, resulting in the demon-child. We were to learn from these tragedies and avoid similar outcomes in our own future.

Tragically, this is what my parents were taught, and, out of their own brokenness, they passed it on to us at a young age. I cannot hold them hard for it. They seemed sincerely to believe these things to be truth, telling them with great intensity and passion. In telling these horror stories, they functioned within accepted cultural norms to make us conform, and hopefully avoid hell.

Tangled into this web of confusion and emotional abuse was a bizarre blend of controls and manipulations intended to inspire obedience to the God of wrath so that, one day, we would stand before Him, justified by our good choices. It seemed hell in this life would prevent it in the life to come. And then there was the physical violence and sexual abuse...

Looking back, it is almost as though I am outside of my own body, watching a drama unfold, and yet, ironically, I am fully aware that I am the lead role in the play—it is my life, after all.

I am a confused little girl with flyaway blonde hair and empty blue eyes, standing on the steps leading to an old house. Inside, my mother wails, begging for mercy, but dad continues to whip and beat her, yelling in uncontrolled rage. I take another step closer, leaning in to listen. I want to go inside, to help mom.

An older sister, Anna, who is no more than eleven years old, but far more aware of the danger than I, whisks me away. She knows that if I get caught by dad when he storms out, I will get whipped for eavesdropping.

I was three then.

Other memories are lost in my subconscious, buried with the trauma that resulted from them, and are known to me only because family members shared them with me. One such story is of a time when, as a toddler, I and two siblings were in dad's machine shop and he believed we burned out the motor on a lathe. Upon his return, dad flew into a rage and gave each of us a terrible beating. They say that I went to mom, crying, with my arm outstretched and my hand hanging limply at the end of the limb. Dad had struck my hand so violently that I had no strength left in my wrist to hold it up. I have no conscious memory of this event but during physiotherapy in my late twenties, when I developed chronic wrist pain and weakness, the therapist concluded I had most likely suffered trauma to my wrist early in life. The body remembers what the mind cannot recall. This is true of physical abuse, such as this, and it is true of sexual abuse. There is the subconscious "knowing" that we are sexually awakened, that someone has taught us things... things that come alive in our dreams but are never acknowledged. And, without knowing it, we live out of that trauma, and its impact drives us until that day when we face it, and find help and healing.

All of these things—the spiritually confusing stories, the misrepresentation of God through religious and sexual abuses, and violence used to control family, all with religious justification—caused deep confusion. Starting in early childhood, my spirit was sensitive and keenly aware of God. I longed to please Him and *know* Him, especially when I learned that Jesus had died for me. This truth resonated deep within me, starting in Mexico, before age five.

As confusion invaded this innocent awareness of God's love, through experiences that presented a harsh God with a measuring stick—which He used somewhat recklessly to bring people back in line if they sinned—I lost that sweet connection. It was as if He walked stoically forward, carrying that measuring stick over His shoulder, ready to strike at the mere hint of sin with a broad and careless sweep, not even bothering to shift His gaze on offenders, to know their hearts. Consequently, I found myself caught between two—the God of childhood, whom I had loved innocently, and the mean, ruthless god of experience—and not trusting either of them. One was impossible to please, and the other too good to be true.

As a result, the first eighteen years of my life became somewhat of a tug of war between these two forces—both claiming to be God, both claiming to have my best interests at their core. With my heart torn between them, vacillating and convinced of neither, I turned my back on faith and looked to other things to give me a sense of identity and belonging. But my spirit remained restless, searching.

Finally, having travelled far and wide and tried almost everything to find meaning, I discovered that nothing could fill that void, and I was still left to contend with the God dilemma. I found myself at a crisis point in my faith when I was brought face to face with Jesus and realized *"He is God"*; Jesus— Emmanuel, *God with us*—and He is good.

That revelation awakened a deep desire to know again the God of my early childhood. But I was hesitant. Did I have it in me to leave everything and trust this God enough to follow through?

****

I share my story to give you the courage to tell yours, no matter how hard it is, and to tell you the shame is not yours to carry. I have listened to many victims, head bowed in shame, staring at their empty, sweaty hands, as they struggle to repeat the things that were done against them. Almost without fail I say, "Look into my eyes," and when they do, I say, "It is not your shame to carry. You are precious... You are beautiful... You are loved," or some such affirmation. And then I coach them through it, encouraging them to spill whatever repulsive, violating details they carry inside, in silent shame, and wish to get off their chest.

Having spilled the ugly truth of how they were made to expose themselves, how they were touched, or having to perform oral sex—or some other painful experience—I again look them in the eye, and remind them they are not what was done against them, and it is not their shame to carry.

In telling my story, on the pages of this book, I discovered just how difficult it is to share the blunt truth of those violations, and how deep that shame runs. But it is not my shame to carry, so I've told it with that in mind, and if the blunt telling of truth offends you, consider yourself fore-warned. I didn't write this book to avoid offence, I wrote it for the wounded who wish just one person would understand the horror of molestation, abuse, violence, bestiality—whether from experience or witnessing it—rape, and spiritual confusion. I wrote it for those who wish to understand victims caught in silent shame, and those who want to understand the impact of abuse in religious settings. I didn't write it for the religiously arrogant and the judgemental who have never walked this path, or those who refuse to

xiv

acknowledge the truth… or those who have no compassion and offer only pat answers and bible verses as quick fixes. I only offer what Jesus offered me: understanding, compassion, and grace. That is what brought me healing.

To the self-righteous who will buy my book for the sole purpose of finding fault with it—or more likely borrow, so as not to defile their pocketbook: You will find that fault. Particularly in my bold reference to various forms of sexual abuse. Be offended. I've not written it for that purpose, but offence must come in order for the truth of sexual corruption in religious settings to be exposed, and victims to find healing. All I ask is, when you have banned my book, held your bonfires and gossip sessions, and offered desperate prayers for my soul, that you be one hundred times more offended that I learned to do these things as a toddler, and yet more offended that I offered such sexual services in the parking lot of church by age seven. And grieve that many of your sons and daughters know how to do the things that will offend you so terribly before they ever reach puberty. Then, having been faced with just how repulsive it is, how violating, and how devastating, repent for choosing to turn a blind eye for the sake of religious pride rather than protecting children and fighting for truth. And then call your leaders to repentance and accountability. These things matter to God and "shy language" hardly tells the truth, exposes the wickedness, and offers the victims hope. Bold disturbing truth, saturated with God's love and grace, does.

Finally, I wrote this book for those of you who have turned your back on God because the church wounded you and did not hear when you tried to expose abuse. Because of fickle holiness, and valuing image more than truth, you met a false god and lost sight of the One who loves you. I didn't write this book to sway you back into faith, but to tell the truth: we are a messed up lot in desperate need of forgiveness, with shameful sins hidden in our pews. You are right about that. I am so sorry that we pretended otherwise; you deserve to have that truth acknowledged. Rather than hide our sin, we ought to have owned up and begged God for forgiveness, and thanked you for your courage. Instead, we swept our sins under the proverbial carpet, and suffocated the truth until the ghost of it tormented you to a point of retreat.

In this we, the Christian community, sinned against you, and our corruption drove you away from faith. Please forgive us.

****

Statistics indicate that approximately one in four girls and one in six boys are sexually abused, and as many as sixty percent of cases are never reported. That is a lot of victims. That is a lot of readers who will identify with my story, in one way or another. Sadly, most will carry that shame in silence, never daring to say out loud exactly what was done against them, or what they were asked to do for others. For this reason I am considerably more explicit in the content—though never graphic—than I would tend to be, by nature. Self-preservation would cause me to write with greater reticence than I have chosen to. I have shared the vulnerable truth so that you will know you do not need to carry the shame, and it is okay to say out loud what you have suffered, and break the power of silence and secrecy.

As you walk with me through the tragedies and the triumphs of my story, if you have suffered emotional, physical, sexual, or spiritual abuse, I pray that you will find hope for your journey, and healing for your pain. If there is one thing I have learned in life, it is this: We all have a story. We all have pain. And pain demands to be acknowledged…

BETWEEN
2
GODS

PART ONE

Chapter One

Seated in front of the old dresser that morning, December 26, 1987, I caught my reflection in the mirror. The heaviness of the preceding two years, on top of a childhood filled with torment, showed. My eyes, now dark and oppressed, reflected the state of my soul. For an eighteen-year-old, I looked old, almost haggard. Had it really only been two years and two months since I left? I felt as though I had packed a good twenty years' worth of living in that time.

I left home the month before my sixteenth birthday to "get away from it all" and start a new life for myself, away from the abuse, violence, and religious confusion. But everything I had tried to run from had pursued me. And all I could do was keep running. There had been no escaping it. Overtaken by the very darkness from which I ran, I had come face-to-face with reality, buried beneath the burden of my own sins, and the sins of those who had violated me.

Mostly I had managed to keep my mind busy while I was away, avoiding harsh realities and the memories of home. Now, temporarily back with my family, it had all collided deep in my soul. One song about love, one encounter with divine grace had unravelled me, shattered my defences. It was as though heaven had silently stormed my soul, long claimed by hell, the meeting erupting in a war within, as each vied for my allegiance.

I thought of who I had become, all that I had done, the life I had lived. Like the woman in that song, caught in adultery and brought to Jesus for stoning, I felt filthy. Ashamed. Dark. Helpless. Hopeless. Condemned.

Was it really possible that Jesus had spoken those words, not only for the woman brought to Him for judgement, but for me, Trudy? A runaway rebel? Would He really wipe it all away? Give me a clean slate, a fresh start? And even if He could and would do all that, did I have it in me to stay the course if I chose a life of faith again? I wanted desperately to believe that He would, and that I could commit and then follow through. I faltered...

Dodi... The thought of him tugged at my heart. For all the dysfunction in our relationship, I had invested my heart... deep. Could I turn my back on

3

him, break off the engagement, and return again to live among the Mennonites? The people where, eighteen years earlier, it had all begun... the abuse... the stripping of my soul... and the sweet faith in the God who whispered in the breeze and offered sunshine kisses...

****

It was November 22, 1969. Lamps cast a dim light in my parents' bedroom on the eve of my birth, a chilly fall evening during one of the coolest months in Fresnillo, Zacatecas, Mexico. Towels, blankets, and several homemade diapers lay by the galvanized basin of water, prepared for the midwife, Mrs. Jacob Peters, who sat with my mother awaiting my arrival. Not only was Mrs. Peters the colony midwife, she was also family. Her first husband had been my father's first cousin, and her second husband my father's second cousin.

In the kitchen the wood stove burned, keeping the house warm and the water hot, ready for my first bath, and to care for my mother in labour and delivery.

It was eight o'clock the next morning, after a long hard night for my mother, before I made my appearance. Placenta previa, a condition where the placenta is too low and, in my mother's case, delivered first, had prolonged the delivery and put both my life and my mother's life at risk.

Mrs. Peters caught me and held me in that moment when I gasped for air, on November 23, 1969, weighing just over six pounds, with blue eyes and blonde hair. I whispered the name of God with that first breath— "Yahweh"—followed by the cry that opened my lungs and offered me life outside the womb.

Though contentment, smiles, and laughter would define my personality, this entry into life was a sign—as perhaps is the entry of every life—of the pain and tragedy that lay ahead. A prophetic foreshadowing of the many times my heart would breathe the name of God, followed by a cry of agony. And in that desperate "gasping for life," my spirit would find hope in Him throughout the years, just as I now found life with my first breath.

My maternal grandparents, Grandma and Grandpa Wall, came for dinner and brought my mom's next younger sister, Margaret, with them. Aunt

Margaret would stay with our family and help manage household duties for several weeks to give my mother, who had haemorrhaged with delivery, time to regain her strength.

Almost two months after my birth, my mother was taken to hospital. The initial haemorrhage and ongoing bleeding had drained her of strength and prevented recovery. The doctor commented it was a wonder we didn't both die during delivery.

For my father this was déjà vu, having lost his first wife, Anna Martens, to postpartum haemorrhage only twelve years earlier, and his newborn son only months later. My parents had married six months after Anna's death. Since then, my mother had given birth to seven other living children, as well as several stillborn babies, making me the eighth living birth for my mother, the twelfth in the family.

From both parents I inherited strong Anabaptist roots that could be traced back to Holland, Germany, and Russia, but my mother's family had the unique distinction of carrying Jewish blood. Our pride, however, was solely established in the Anabaptist legacy and Mennonite name. Along with the Martyr's Mirror, my father kept a book of the writings of Menno Simons, in whose name the church was founded, and held them in almost as high regard as the Bible.

Stories of Anabaptist martyrdom were shared almost reverently by my father. He had an obsession with the suffering of our forefathers and spent much time reading the stories, and applauding the resilient faith of those great men and women. While this had merit—because many Anabaptists did suffer tremendously for no cause other than their faith, and showed unmatchable courage—there was another, much darker, side to that truth. And that side of the story was never told, exposing the wicked deeds done by some of the Anabaptists against the Catholics. "They were not true Anabaptists... not faithful" is the excuse, while completely overlooking that maybe all Catholics were not true Catholics either.

A study on Jan von Leiden, an Anabaptist leader, reveals the horror of the dark side of our religious heritage and the blood on our hands. For a man whose motto was *"Gottes Macht ist meine Kraft"* (God's power is my strength), Jan von Leiden relied heavily on military power to advance his own kingdom

5

with little regard for human life. In 1534, following the death of his predecessor, he declared himself to be King of Munster, and the successor of King David. After legalizing polygamy and enforcing a law that said a woman must accept the first proposal made to her, he took sixteen wives for himself, and lived extravagantly while many in his community starved. He maintained rule, using military force to protect the city, until he was captured and executed in 1535.

Obscuring sin and the pursuit of power in our history, all while furiously pointing fingers at the Catholic church for her sins, spilled into many areas of life over the years, and remains a curse we carry to this day, in many of our churches. It is as though we believe that our sins can be easily covered with cultural silence and the guise of forgiveness, as long as we look right, dress right, and talk right, while we condemn the world around to hell for the very sins we hide.

Though both were Anabaptist forefathers, Jan von Leiden's dark story stands in bold contrast against Menno Simon's testimony of simple faith and trust in God. A man who fought for truth, Menno called the church to lay down arms and embrace righteousness and Christian honour in every area of life. He held unrepentant sinners accountable, while offering grace and forgiveness generously to the repentant soul.

That is the conflicted religious legacy that I was born to muddle through, sorting the beauty that remains in the culture from the darkness hidden in the past and the present. More importantly, I would spend my life in search for the true God; the one who resides not in religious culture, but, rather, dwells in the hearts of all who love Him. A God who looks for heart relationship, not merely people who legalistically keep the letter of the law.

In our home, my father was far stricter than my mother about following legalistic rules. He enforced them with rage and fury, if that was what it took. My mother, on the other hand, seemed not to hold strict rules in high regard. When asking for my cooperation in them, they were always presented as a demand from the church or my father. Seldom do I recall her speaking of cultural beliefs and practices with any sense of personal conviction. My father, while passionately committed, obviously remained unfulfilled, always searching for something more. Having adamantly rejected the teachings of

6

John Calvin—the once saved, always saved doctrines—the Old Colony Mennonites held the belief that one could never know for certain of salvation. To make such claims was arrogant at best, and downright sinful at worst.

My mother's lack of conviction was not learned from her parents. Grandma and Grandpa Wall followed church rules with sensitive conscience, far more so than my mother. Grandma's hair was always done in neat braids wrapped up on the back of her head, in keeping with Old Colony Russian Mennonite tradition. In public, and during the daytime, these braids were carefully wrapped under a kerchief, so as not to be seen by any man other than her husband. Hair was a symbol of beauty, and within the culture, it was perceived to hold strong sex appeal. For this reason, starting in early childhood, hair was always modestly contained. To cut it or wear it down would have been a sign of rebellion and considered a serious sin, bordering on whoredom.

The veiling of hair also symbolized submission in women, and served to acknowledge God's order of headship and male dominance in the culture. Unlike many other Mennonites and Anabaptists, most Old Colony Russian Mennonites did not wear this symbol until marriage, as it was directly symbolic of submission to a husband, not God. And the less religious women did not always wear the kerchief at home.

For church services the older, more conservative, married women wore an additional headpiece under the kerchief. This piece started close to the hairline and sat several inches tall, tapering back under the kerchief. The raised piece, created with lace, was hand-stitched in fine pleats with intricate detail, and attached to a lace cap-type headpiece that swooped down just past the nape of the neck. The lace portion was carefully covered with a kerchief.

Traditional dresses boasted hundreds of perfectly pressed pleats, spaced an inch or less apart. Each dress also had a carefully pleated cape, for modesty. The cape served as a double layer across the front bodice, to hide a woman's breasts. An opening under the cape allowed nursing mothers to discreetly breastfeed, without exposing much, if any, skin. Older women typically wore dark fabrics with small prints, if any print at all, while younger women tended towards dark colours with large, brightly coloured flowers.

Many of the cultural beliefs and rules focused on modesty and external appearances—particularly in women—in an effort to protect the church's image, and keep men from falling into sexual immorality. Men had short, tapered hair and wore overalls, to make sexual immorality difficult, and not draw attention to their privates.

While this created an illusion of safety and sexual purity, in reality the excessive focus on the body, and covering it to such extremes, was counterproductive. Women were objectified in the process, and the obsessive teaching—regardless how well intentioned—kept the body constantly in the forefront of people's minds. It also instilled the belief that sexuality, in and of itself, was dirty and perverted. The result was a constant unhealthy and subconscious focus on sex, creating an unnatural obsession and curiosity with it, opening doors to evil that could have been avoided. High rates of molestation, incest, and child-to-child sexual exploration evidenced the dreadful failure of rules and modest attire to effectively protect children, homes, churches, and communities.

Rather than acknowledge that the system had gaps, leaders imposed more and harsher rules and discipline in hopes of getting it right. There was no understanding of the concept that similar methods would produce similar results, and the only hope of transformation was in changing how things were done, by recognizing that Jesus is the solution for sin, not rules and harsh discipline.

In spite of deeply rooted religious beliefs, my parents desperately longed for freedom and hope. But my father's sexual addictions, crimes, and ongoing violence haunted him, causing trouble with the church.

Bishop Ben Bueckart suspected my father of abusing his children, and wanted to remove his four oldest children, those birthed to him by his first wife, and place them in another home.

This threat angered my father, and he decided to leave the church altogether and take his family to go live among the Mexicans, away from religion. Frightened because she knew her children would be in an ungodly environment with loose morals and would not get a proper education, mom resisted. Besides, my father's immoral history with these women made the very idea of living among them upsetting for my mother.

When Grandpa Wall heard of my father's threat to leave, he wrote my paternal Grandpa, Jacob Harder, and asked for his help to intervene. After some communication between the two of them, Grandpa Wall approached my father and asked if he would consider relocating to another Christian community, outside of the Old Colony movement.

In August 1970, when I was nine months old, my parents did just that, and moved to Campo 83 in Chihuahua. Here they joined a colony of Low German–speaking Mennonites known as the "Kleine Gemeinde," which simply means "Small Congregation." A more liberal brand of Mennonites who had split off of the Old Colony group in search of spiritual life, they had abandoned much of the legalistic Old Colony church system, in hopes of establishing a more evangelical fellowship.

In this new church some of the traditions of the Old Colony group were viewed as prideful or unnecessary, and my parents found themselves making changes that directly challenged their cultural upbringing. Women were not required to wear capes on their dresses, and the intricate detailing of pleated skirts was altogether discouraged, being interpreted as vain. In fact, women who arrived in the Kleine Gemeinde with these pleats were encouraged to alter the skirts, press out all pleats, and return the fabric to a smooth, flat cloth.

Despite these new rules and guidelines, the teachings of the Kleine Gemeinde focused far more on freedom, and the truth of Jesus Christ, than on cultural beliefs and rules. Here my parents began discovering new hope and purpose....

Chapter Two

Almost one year later, in June 1971, we uprooted again and moved to Campo 82, a neighbouring Kleine Gemeinde group. The property we rented had two houses. We ate meals in the main house, and most of the family slept there, while older brothers slept in the second house.

It was here, not more than a toddler in my crib, that I vividly recall being asked for sexual favours. It was as if the bars that held me in that crib symbolized the bondage in which I would find myself for many years to come.

The little girl, only a few years older than me, crawls into my crib, pulls up her skirt, and pulls down her panties, positioning herself in front of me. The experience doesn't feel new or unfamiliar. I know what she wants, what to do, and simply do it with no questions or further instructions, as though it is the most natural thing in the world.

My heart feels tattered, empty. Each time I am used, it is as if a piece of my soul is torn, like a useless scrap of paper, and carelessly tossed in the trash, with no regard for it. And no one sees that these tattered edges bleed invisible teardrops that never fall from my eyes, yet never stop. They just keep bleeding, until my soul is dry... lifeless... alone.

That scene is firmly etched in my memory, in graphic and brutal detail, like fresh blood on white linen. I recall it now only with sadness that these things continue to happen, and lie unacknowledged, in Christian culture. Sad that little children are victimized and know such explicit sexual experience as should only be known and enjoyed in the safety of adult relationship, with mutual consent, in the confines of marriage. The little girl could not possibly have understood what it all meant and had, undoubtedly, learned the act from personal experience.

Things I witnessed are even more troubling and traumatizing than personal experience and leave the mind in complete shock. Scenes replay in my adult mind, forcing me to watch as children are brutally violated while I am helpless to do anything except weep.

On one occasion, visiting relatives with teenagers when I was three, several siblings and these teens headed for the barn, where they were going to play. I tagged along. Walking along the dirt path to the barn, one of the teens stopped me. "You have to stay here. You're too young to play our games," she said.

Curious, I followed a bit later to see what it was they "played." Confused, I watched as the teenagers—closer to twenty years old than to ten—used my siblings for sexual gratification. By pretending to be animals feeding their babies, they made oral sex appear as innocent play. I wondered if mommies and daddies really feed babies that way. But, being too much for my child's mind to grasp, I pushed the thoughts from my memory, without a word to anyone of what I had seen. And there the memories lay dormant, locked up in my subconscious for many years, resurfacing only in nightmares and one or two childhood conversations, before disappearing from conscious memory for several decades.

Oral sexual abuse and child-to-child interaction was the only form of sexuality I knew, consciously, and knew it well… I only knew it as something people do, not aware how wrong and devastating these acts were. Other than what I witnessed, always it was me doing what I was asked to do, performing favours, and it would remain this way throughout childhood as other children and preteens used me this way, over and over again.

At age twelve, I casually said to a brother while breeding rabbits, "I really wonder how people have babies." He answered as casually, "The same way." I glared at him in disgust. "Don't be stupid!" Immediately he erupted in laughter, humoured by my naivety. I couldn't grasp how people could do "that," when all that I had ever known and experienced had taught me something very different.

Redemption lies in the wonder that God kept my mind from insanity, and healed me from the accompanying trauma.

These secrets of childhood were not the beginning of darkness in our family legacy. In both my father's family and my mother's family history, dark secrets had left deep scars. Grandma Wall was only six years old when her father, Great-Grandpa Dyck, took his thirteen-year-old son Peter aside. He instructed Peter to push his mother down the metal staircase, attached to the exterior of their home, as they were in those days. "If you don't push her down, I will kill you," he had told Peter. Out of fear, Peter did as he was told and pushed Great-Grandma to her death. But her death was not instant, and she suffered from her injuries for one week before she passed away.

This set in motion a series of events that left Grandma Wall—then a young Anna Dyck—wounded and, in many ways, destroyed. The children were taken from their home and placed in foster homes. Grandma lived with numerous families, being bumped from home to home, and suffered everything from physical abuse and violence, to sexual assault and emotional abuse. Rumour had it she was raped at a young age, but some things simply were not talked about.

A scarred soul, she met Cornelius Wall, who married her when she was only seventeen, and gave her heart a safe place. Watching them, there was never any doubt that they loved each other. While public displays of affection were never shown, their tone of voice always communicated affection.

I never knew my paternal grandparents, but it is no secret that my father's upbringing was abusive and dysfunctional. The stories were never told in great detail, but my father's broken spirit was a testament to deep pain that had never encountered healing, and in times of distress, little snippets tumbled out in bitter anguish or anger. Yet, at times, the stories he shared held nostalgic appeal, indicating that there were also good times.

Contributing to the confusion in his parental home was Grandma Harder's psychological and spiritual distress. She had lost her first husband, Aaron Zacharias, in death, and later lost two daughters, leaving her with deep emotional scars. A disturbed woman, she engaged in strange and demonic behaviours, not the least of which were claims of communicating with dead saints. She was found one day by one of her sons, under the old apple tree, engaged in enthusiastic conversation with no one else visibly present.

"Who are you talking to, Mother?" he asked.

But she shushed him and told him not to interrupt. "I'm talking with Abraham, Isaac, and Jacob," she said, returning to her imaginary spiritual dialogue.

When it came to her relationship with Grandpa Harder, it was strained, at best, if not hostile, especially in their last years together. She insisted on her own bedroom, and, in her determination, she hammered together a ramshackle frame to hold a mattress. Eventually guests left her bed infested with bedbugs, and her sons chopped it to bits with an axe, much to their delight, hoping it would force her back with Grandpa. But that didn't stop Grandma Harder. She built another, not any better, and kept her own room to the time of her death.

Starting in early childhood, sexual confusion held strong influence in my father's life. He never shared what awakened him sexually but, to his credit, in a culture of silence about sexuality, he owned up to my mother about his past. He shared of sexual addictions and obsessions that began at age five. And, when confronted, he admitted that by age thirteen he had victimized several girls. He also confessed that, before marrying her, he had slept with numerous Mexican women, as well as one or two in the church. After marriage he continued to visit brothels in the city and used prostitutes, right up to the year we left Mexico.

Sibling rivalry reigned in his childhood home, with older siblings being given power over the younger, if for no other reason than because of cultural norms. Being the second youngest, with four of the older being boys and the eldest being a half-brother, my father was quite low in the pecking order.

In spite of my father's tough exterior, he had a sensitive and tender heart; a heart crushed by harsh circumstances and the bullying of older brothers, further contributing to his insecurities. Whether these older brothers held any unkindness in their hearts, or if it was my father's interpretation of circumstances, we will never know. Having observed his sensitivity, it would stand to reason that at times misunderstandings played a role, escalating normal sibling rivalry to abuse. With no one to buffer or stand in the gap for him, these experiences became deeply rooted in his identity and spirit.

My mother's family also had interesting sibling dynamics. Unlike my father, my mother was the oldest living child, giving her a place of authority over younger siblings. Her older brother had died in infancy, as had the son immediately after her, establishing a special place for her.

By all appearances, observing my mother with her family, the relationships among siblings seemed to be healthy and fairly close-knit. An element of this was real, while some of it was superficial pretentiousness. As was so common, silence and denial of evil that lay buried came into play. Sexual abuse and incest were blatantly present, with nieces and nephews being molested by uncles and aunts, but never acknowledged by most who engaged in these criminal activities.

There was never any indication that Grandma and Grandpa Wall suspected the abuse, or even that my parents had any idea about it. It was never discussed until my mother was in her late seventies.

****

As if the confusion and damage done by sexual abuse did not leave me scarred enough, especially in relation to my sexual identity, one unfortunate circumstance scarred my body physically, as if to leave a physical testament to the psychological scars I carried.

Wil, who was almost five, ran after me in our little game-of-tag-for-two. At three, I ran as fast as my little legs could carry me, trying to escape, but instead, I backed in between two beds with no way out. Trapped, I turned and backed away from him, giggling and completely oblivious to the danger behind me.

Earlier that morning my mother had removed hot coals from the woodstove and instructed an older sibling to take them outside and dump them into the garden, where they would eventually be worked into the ground. Instead the bucket had been hidden between the two beds, against the wall, with the intent of taking it out later. As I backed away from Wil, I landed in the bucket of hot coals, seat first, leaving my buttocks badly burned, especially my left side. My left leg was also burned badly, almost halfway to the knee, leaving my body in agony and putting me out of commission for a while. I spent several weeks, mostly on my back, being catered to by the rest of the family. That part was fun. For me. Not so much for my family.

15

If I craved candy and asked for it, my mother sent someone to the store to get it. That's the only part I really remember—lying on a blanket in the sunshine, eating candy out of a little brown paper bag.

But the treats didn't remove the evidence. My body was scarred for life, much the way my soul, mind, and spirit had been scarred by abuse. Good would come from my suffering, but the scars would remain.

Chapter Three

Being too young to understand the half, there is much I cannot explain, as supernatural forces worked in a real way in that community—both good and evil—and superstitious beliefs invited powers that not everyone has encountered in obvious ways. Because of those superstitions, some predictions were elevated to psychic insight when, in reality, they were merely logical deductions, or conclusions drawn from similar past experience. Reading into the natural environment, like a violent storm, for instance, adds to the mysterious sense of foreboding surrounding dark events. But the same storm would be nothing more than a violent storm with no spiritual significance, if life circumstances were different.

The skies grew suddenly dark and ominous. The wind tossed buckets and loose items across the yard, as the storm moved in. My mother scrambled to return clean, wet laundry into galvanized tubs and fill them with water, before draping sheets over them to protect them from the fast approaching dust storm. Be it because of the dark circumstance we were about to encounter, or because of heightened sensitivity, either way, there was a sense of foreboding before it even happened. It was early 1973, just over a year after we moved to Campo 82…

A whirlwind had spun open in the dust, earlier, and then disappeared. Watching it twirl intrigued me, and made me want to spin and dance just like the whirlwind, and make my skirt spin open like that. Sometimes I tipped my head to the sky, spread my arms, and spun around and around, until my head could take no more. It gave my spirit a taste of something I longed for… that feeling of being unrestrained… a freedom I didn't understand.

Mom said that an open whirlwind indicated an approaching storm and the wall of dust confirmed it. I loved the whirlwinds, but the dust storms left me breathless, as though suffocating me. I ran to the house, anxious for shelter. When her laundry was safe from the storm, my mother joined my siblings and me inside. We stepped outside from time to time to keep an eye on the developing storm. There was a knock on the door, but when we opened it, no one was there. A walk around the house produced nothing. This was interpreted as a spiritual sign.

Earlier, when mom was out washing laundry, rubbing it furiously on the old scrub board, our neighbour Peter Bauman had dropped in to see my father and take a look around the property. He hoped our landlord would consider selling, and, since we were tenants as well as friends, he wanted to discuss it with my father. But dad wasn't at home.

Mr. Bauman came by three times that day to see if my father was home, insisting that he needed to speak with him. Each time, my mother explained that he was away, and that she couldn't speak for him and the landlord regarding the sale of the property.

By the third visit Mr. Bauman was extremely agitated, making my mother uncomfortable and concerned for his well-being. Accustomed to dealing with my father's anger and threats, she quickly recognized that Mr. Bauman was not well, and potentially a danger to himself or his family. After he left, mom commented that she hoped he wouldn't do something foolish like commit suicide.

An older brother gasped, "You shouldn't say that! It's too gruesome!"

Suicide was a monster we had contended with, starting in early childhood. When my father became overwhelmed with life, he resorted to death threats, suicide threats, and violence against his family. I could usually tell by his walk whether he was safe or whether it might be best to go into hiding. One learns at a young age to recognize the signs of mental distress, so it was no surprise that mom sensed it in Mr. Bauman.

A dark pigeon, a neighbour told my mother later, had flapped violently against their window at about that time. This, too, was interpreted as another sign of something dreadful about to happen. A blend of superstition and other paranoia, along with the developing storm, was taken quite seriously, escalating tensions.

The skies turned greyer and the rain fell heavily on the dry dusty ground. With heavy storms we were forbidden to step outside until the worst of it had passed, especially with thunder and lightning. When the winds died down, we were allowed to venture outside, welcomed by the earthy smell of fresh rain on the dry ground. Where puddles had formed, the last of the giant raindrops splashed up as they hit the water, like little angels. I watched, mesmerized, imagining a sea of miniature angels dancing all around me, splashing in the water. How I loved the rain! And that heavenly scent!

It wasn't long before my oldest brother, Pete, broke the news to my mother. "What you said earlier... that is exactly what happened. Mr. Bauman committed suicide."

Mr. Bauman's family had also noticed his odd behaviour earlier, and when he disappeared, they had searched everywhere for him. Unable to find him, his sixteen-year-old son went in the barn—the one place no one had wanted to look—and found him hanging. His funeral was dark, and a heavy spirit lingered in the air. There were no sweet thoughts of heaven, comfort, and meeting again. It was a bitter and final farewell, as they presented it, with no hope of salvation for Mr. Bauman.

Because of my father's struggle with depression and the suicide threats and death threats, Mr. Bauman's death was that much more troubling. I heard my mother say, often, that she feared my father was possessed by the devil, and she felt, at times, as though she lived with the devil himself. What if he listened to those dark voices one day?

I felt sad. The barn must have been filled with demons telling Mr. Bauman to do it, and the eerie sound of those voices haunted me. Sometimes I thought I could hear their voices, and I was sure the dark spirits were coming for me. When I crawled into my bed at night I was afraid they might grab me from under the bed. What if they came for me in my sleep? I tucked my feet snug under my blankets and left only my face out, so I would see them. Sometimes, when I was too frightened, I pulled the blanket over my head.

Other memories of those years in Mexico play in my mind. Some are vague, as if lightly sketched in black and grey, and then smudged, so that it is difficult to make out the details. Others are painted in vivid colour—even animated—as they play out in graphic detail on the stage of my memory. A few make me laugh and long for childhood, while many are troubling.

****

19

"Today is your birthday," my mother said. "You are four years old now."

We never really celebrated birthdays, and didn't necessarily even acknowledge them every year, so her words held little meaning. "What is a birthday?" I asked.

"Your birthday is the day you were born, and came into our family. And you were born four years ago," she explained.

But, since time lacked definition, as one day blended into the next with survival as the focus, her explanation gave little enlightenment.

"Your father is out in the shop. Why don't you run out and ask him if he would give you a peso for your birthday? Then you can get a candy or little treat at the general store," she suggested.

I could almost taste the sweet candy and my mouth began to water.

I shook my head. "I don't want to go," I said. I didn't want to be alone with dad—not even for a peso. My tummy hurt a little just thinking about it. I badly wanted to go to the store for a treat, but not bad enough to go to the shop and ask dad for money.

"Well, why not?" my mother asked.

I shrugged. "I just don't want to."

There were no words. I didn't like being alone with my father. I was afraid of him, but I never questioned why. When I was alone with him, and when he was cross, I often had the urge to go pee, and my tummy felt like someone had tied it in a tight knot. But how could I explain what I didn't understand?

As far back as I can remember, when my father came into the house, I watched his body language. If he was friendly and in good spirits, it was safe to come out, but if his voice had an edge of tension or his eyes had that faraway look—a look I had learned from my mother to describe as "devil eyes"—then it was best to stay away.

When he was in good spirits, dad was a lot of fun, if I could get past that subconscious fear that something might trigger him. But, lost in a moment with him, he had a great sense of humour, a quick wit, and loved to tell funny stories. And then there was the rare moment that made my heart skip a beat, when he reached out his giant hand and gently took hold of mine, as I walked with him. My hand was lost in his. Even as an adult, though my hands grew long, when I held my hands up against his, they looked small. But when he was angry, those hands became weapons that terrified me.

There were times when interacting with him was inevitable, even if it wasn't safe. Like mealtimes. My father was absolutely religious about the family eating together. Anyone who was at home was expected to show up for meals. Each evening my mother would have a meal prepared and the younger siblings were ordered to find all family members and tell them it was dinnertime. Tardiness was not tolerated. My father believed that his time was not to be wasted and we learned not to hold him up at dinner. He didn't necessarily show the same courtesy to others.

Some meals were a loud affair with everyone chattering at once. Other times—like those times when someone was late—the table fell to complete silence as the rage in my father's eyes had us all wondering whether that meal would be their last.

There were mealtimes when my mother pleaded with my father about one thing or another, in a tone that was a strange cross between terror and manipulation, triggering his anger. It was hard to tell if she got the response she wanted, or whether she was surprised by his outburst. She seemed not to know who she was if dad wasn't angry.

When a child had done something wrong, either at the table or another offence that had come to his attention before mealtime, dad would at times pound his fist on the table and yell, usually announcing that he was very angry—as though his outburst wasn't evidence enough—or his eyes would darken as he rose in silence and stomped out the door. The second response was more likely reserved for anger at mom, and always more terrifying, because we feared he would return with a rifle.

Those meals typically ended quite abruptly and everyone who didn't have dinner chores to do scattered, leaving the older girls and mom to clean up the dinner mess.

Knowing all of this, it is odd that my mother didn't understand the fear I had of going out to the shop to ask my father for a peso. Was she so completely numbed by life? Did she believe the risks were not real?

Again my mother urged me to go, and once again I resisted. "I don't want to."

"Sure you do. Run along and ask him for a peso," she coaxed. "I think he'll give you one."

I walked to the shop and stopped not far from where dad worked.

A memory plays at the fringes of my mind of awkwardly trying to find words to tell my father that it was my birthday. Of him asking why I came to tell him that. Then, even more awkwardly, telling him that my mother thought he might have a peso for me.

And then it all stops. Like a song that never finishes playing, or a story that is never told... Everything just ends. Goes black. The curtain drops too soon. And yet that scene has a profound impact on my life, as the terror of approaching my father and asking for a simple gift dominates the memory of my fourth birthday. And that fear translated, for many years, into fear of asking God for anything unless I felt I first had something to offer him.

Even in good times my heart remained subconsciously guarded, numb, and fearful when I thought of interacting with my father. He showed no physical affection, and seldom showed it in other ways. The emotion he displayed consistently, in the day-to-day, was anger when things weren't right. I interpreted his body language as hatred on the one extreme, and aloof and apathetic in the other extreme. I believed I was a mistake—always in the way—and that he did not want me, or my siblings, for that matter. We had one purpose in his life: to make him rich when we were old enough to find work.

The longing to be hugged or held was never really there. Naturally the desire to be loved was, in a subconscious way—whatever "being loved" should have looked like in real life. Years later the grief of that loss would consume me and, for a time, threaten to destroy me, but that pain and loss was too heavy for my little heart to know or understand then.

22

Aside from a few glimpses of the tender side of his heart, which always stirred something in me I could not describe, I felt only fear and the determination to survive. Only when I saw him snuggle and play with an infant did I recognize the longing in my own heart to be special in my father's eyes. But even then it was a blend of fear and desire.

My father loved to play with babies when they reached the stage where they responded to his noises and clowning around. Seeing this brought a thrill to my heart, and I wished that for a few moments I could be that infant, to bounce on my father's knee or sit in his hand, and be held high above his head. He liked to blow on a baby's neck or tummy and make the baby squeal with uncontrolled delight. The baby's antics made my father laugh.

Once, when I saw him engaging with an infant in playful affection, I tried to get him to play with me, and pay attention to me. If only I could make him laugh like that, I thought. So I tried. I pranced in front of him, spinning, twirling, and bouncing—doing anything I could to have him acknowledge me. But when he finally did, I wished I had not tried.

He spoke sternly, in a condescending tone, as though I should know better than to behave that way at my age. "Shame on you! You shouldn't behave that way! Now run along!"

Utter rejection and condemnation. My heart squeezed tight in my chest, and it felt as though life drained out of me. I was so ashamed. Ashamed of not knowing better. Ashamed of having tried... Ashamed of the desire... Ashamed that I was not good enough...

And at that young age I made a vow: "Never again." And I kept that vow. Later in life I pursued my father's heart for his spiritual well-being, but the desire to seek his approval or affection was shut down. On several occasions he offered approval, but not because I reached for it.

I buried myself in shallow comfort... *At least I didn't get a spanking*.... I had seen him spank my siblings, and whenever I did something wrong, I feared I would get punished too. Yet, while my father was often a cruel and violent man, I remember few beatings or incidents of physical abuse directed at me. But one stands out...

It was not long after I turned four. I awoke in a grump one morning and wanted Anna, who was eleven years old at the time, to help me get dressed. She was responsible for overseeing breakfast and she was obviously busy as she scurried about the kitchen preparing food for the family. As a pre-teen she had the responsibility of the average sixteen-to-eighteen-year-old, because of mom's ongoing health issues and constant pregnancies. She had become a mom figure to me and I favoured her over any other siblings, much the way a child would favour a parent.

"Anna, will you button up my dress?" I asked, hopeful that she would set her task aside for a moment.

"Go ask Tina. I'm too busy making breakfast," she said.

"I want you to do it!" I said, going into a stubborn pout.

Tina tried gently to persuade me, speaking sweetly and telling me that she would be happy to button my dress. But, typical of a four-year-old, I insisted that it had to be my way, or no way. With a pout on my face and my arms crossed I stood there. I would wait all day, if need be, but I would have it my way.

When Anna insisted that I let Tina help, I threw a temper tantrum, and at just that moment my father walked in the door.

He bellowed, voice filled with rage and dripping of hate, bringing my fit to an abrupt end, "What is going on here?"

"I want Anna to button my dress and she won't do it," I said, the pout now replaced by desperation. "She says I have to let Tina help me, and I don't want Tina to help me! I want Anna to do it!"

My father marched across the room and retrieved the strap that hung on a nail against the wall, then turned and marched towards me. Terror shot through my heart as he dragged a chair in front of me. He bent my little body over that chair and began whipping me with such force I thought I would die. I tried telling him that I needed to go to the outhouse but only squeaks came out, no words. Warm, wet liquid trickled down my legs, stinging my skin. When my father yelled something about pissing my pants, I tried to stop but it hurt too much and the water wouldn't stop running.

24

When he stopped whipping me, he told me to be quiet. Unable to stop, yet too afraid to cry, my body continued trembling with sniffles and snorts, as I attempted to hold back the tears.

He turned, eyes glaring. "If you don't stop it, I will whip you again so that you have something to cry about."

Emotions were constantly suppressed in this way, and we were threatened with punishment if we didn't control and hide our feelings. As a result, most of us had buried anger and pain, waiting to explode. My siblings—particularly the eleven who were older than I—took the brunt of my parents' anger. And some of these siblings carry physical scars of the beatings and abuse they suffered, not only at the hands of my father, but also my mother. I witnessed violence from both, and received whippings from my mother so violent that I had welts for days.

However, what I saw and heard did far more damage than the few strappings I experienced. The screams I heard still torment my mind, as does the sound of "the strap" ripping into the backside of mom or one of my siblings, and their soul-rending cries as they begged for mercy. The image of mom or an older sibling emerging after such a beating or whipping, with shoulders slumped hopelessly, eyes downcast, and tears falling, will draw unimaginable grief from my heart until the day I die. The terror, the wild, panicked eyes, and the screams... Those scars remain forever embedded in my memory.

The harsh environment, the judgement and the rejection of those earliest years, made life empty, meaningless, and without purpose. I found myself thinking often about death... How I wished I could go to heaven. It must be a lovely place...

But life continued. And with it that longing to be significant also lived on.

****

With arms spread wide like the birds flying overhead, I ran across the hot sand. I tipped and leaned, just as the birds did, pretending to be as light and free.

A warm, gentle breeze blew over my body, as if God Himself was breathing on me. The hot sun kissed my face, leaving tiny freckles sprinkled over my nose and cheeks. One freckle on my left cheek was conspicuously larger than the others, the size of an oat flake. The sun had kissed too hard on that spot.

The landscape in Camp 82, Chihuahua, was beautiful. In the distance, within view of our home, the mountains called my name, inviting me to climb to the peak, daring me to know the freedom of standing on top of the world. At least the top of my little world. The mountains were beautiful against the bright blue sky—the colour of my eyes. I couldn't possibly know that for sure, having never seen my own eyes, since we had no mirrors, but people told me the sky was blue, and so were my eyes. I quite liked to believe they were as beautiful—the loveliest shade of blue I had ever seen.

One day, I would climb the mountain and touch that sky. How I wished I was old enough! When older siblings went on school trips, and talked of the climb and the view on top, my desire to experience it only intensified. At the top of that mountain, I was certain, I would be happy. Closer to God, who had made this beautiful place.

Those moments alone with nature were sweet. I felt God, then, more intimately than anyone could imagine. What no one had taught me about the Creator, I experienced with Him, and it stirred hope in my little heart.

Then suddenly He slipped away, lost behind the shadows of fear, survival, guilt, and shame. I stopped thinking of Him much, and feeling Him as intimately. And, though there were moments, the conscious awareness of His presence faded, as fear and anxiety over an angry God took their place.

It would be many years before I would again be so free. Many years before I would again tip my face to the sun, arms spread out, and feel myself soaring high above the "stuff" of life. Many years before I would be so close to Him that I would again feel His breath in the wind and His kisses in the sunshine.

Chapter Four

In 1974 my parents bought a piece of land, and we moved yet again. This time we stayed in the same settlement, but moved to the opposite end of the "darp," or community. For several months we rented space in David Hildebrandt's cheese factory, while my dad and brothers built a house out of handmade mud bricks.

Our time in the cheese factory was bittersweet. I loved the Hildebrandt family. Especially their daughter, Trudy, who was much older than I. She was intelligent and beautiful, and I tagged after her with great delight. If she thought I was a pest, I never caught on.

My siblings and I enjoyed wandering to the part of the factory where cheese was dipped in wax for preserving. With some help we were allowed, a time or two, to dip our hands in the wax and let it harden. To watch the liquid form into a solid around my fingers, turning my hand white, fascinated me. But, as always, there was a darker side to the memories. Again, the barn carries a dark haunting...

This time the memories are personal. I am not a distant observer. I am there. Close... I am with them, being used...

The girl is no more than eleven years old, if that. I am five. She raises one finger to her lips... "Shh"... and beckons with her other hand. I am to be quiet and come with her. Everything feels secretive. It feels wrong. And yet it feels special. She wants only me. No one else. In her arms she carries a large empty burlap sack.

We hide behind the wagon, where she places the burlap sack under it, and tells me to crawl in the bag first. I huddle in the bottom of the bag. The dust is suffocating.

She crawls in, pulls up her skirt, and pulls down her panties... As I have always done in the past, I follow orders and relive what I saw in the barn that day, even while my little heart screams a silent "no."

As the confusion of these sexual encounters grew stronger, combined with a lack of healthy understanding about my body, I started to resent being a girl...

I escape to the privacy of the outhouse. I hate my body. I want to be a little boy. I don't understand why they have one, and I don't. Why our bodies are different. I take a stick and try to force it inside my body; my first act of self-harm and self-loathing. It hurts and I drop it.

If only God had made me a boy...

****

Saturday evening was bath night. Mom filled the galvanized tub with warm water and lined younger children up for our bath, trying to get as many through as possible before the water got too cool or dirty.

Placed in the middle of the room, up on two chairs, in the wide open space for all to see, mom set me in the tub. And it never bothered me until that day, when I looked out the window to see a handful of my siblings, along with the Hildebrandt children and their guests, lined up as if I was on display at a local theatre or museum. They pointed at me and laughed, before running away.

"They're laughing at me!" I said.

"Oh, they can't see anything anyway," mom said. "You're still very little."

Regardless of her intentions, downplaying my vulnerability was a subtle message that little people don't need to be protected, and bodies can't be exploited until developed.

I crouched down in the tub, ashamed and upset that mom didn't cover me. What she didn't realize, and I had no way of letting her know—or even understanding myself, back then—was that it was sexual encounters that made me feel so vulnerable, at such a young age, to be seen by a few children.

Almost, mom caught a boy, not much older than I, when he exposed himself to me. I went to the outhouse one morning and, finding the door locked, stood in the shelter, waiting for my turn. When he opened the door and saw me, before he came out, he asked if I wanted to see his body. I said no, but he ignored me and showed me anyway. He was a boy. And men and boys are stronger, so I couldn't do anything about it. He asked me to come in and show him my body, but I shook my head, too afraid to speak.

Thankfully mom shouted from across the yard at just that moment, and asked what was going on. I said I was waiting for my turn, and that scared the little boy away, much to my relief. I knew better than to tell mom, fearing I would be spanked for seeing his body.

Evenings spent with the Hildebrandt family, now and then, were my favourite. If I caught them at the right moment, dad and Mr. Hildebrandt would do riddles and games with me. Other times I would watch them play games and listen to them do riddles, trying to outwit each other. These evenings were peaceful and pleasant. And these were the times I missed when dad and my brothers finished building our house and we moved into our new place.

It was a dark dwelling, with only one door, one small window, and a dirt floor. Though humble, to put it mildly, it was better than some my parents and older siblings had known. It was in a barn, with missing barn boards, where my mother had given birth to my sister Anna. With so many children, poverty was not surprising. We never had much in the way of earthly possessions, but still we were far more blessed than many. We never neared the point of starvation, though there were times when we had precious little.

"I just don't know what to make," mom fretted one particular day. The house was empty of ingredients, save a few basic items, so she made a soup-type dish out of flour, milk, and an egg or two. Literally translated, it was "lump soup" (klieta moos), with small grain-sized lumps of cooked dough in the milk-based liquid.

It tasted bland, but I willed myself to eat without grumbling. When a sibling grumbled or made fun of it, I felt sorry for mom, but being one of the younger children, I bit my tongue. To speak against older siblings was almost as disrespectful as speaking against parents.

Having watched mom wring her hands earlier, distressed and anxious, and seeing the panic in her eyes, drew compassion from me. As a child I wanted desperately to make everything okay, and assure her that we would not go hungry. It was a heavy burden to carry as a child, the feeling that I needed somehow to make mom's world a better place.

This poverty did not scar me. I am a better person for having experienced it. Because, in spite of personal struggle and family dysfunction, generosity was something my parents taught by example. It was another day, my mother having made a large pot of soup for her family, when a group of Mexican gypsies passed through our community, begging for food. There was a bit of quiet fussing, as mom vented her concern that she had not made enough, but still I watched as she dished some food for each one, and my heart was happy.

My father, too, had a generous side. In a state of personal poverty, he sent money on several occasions to siblings more destitute than he. As far as I know, he kept this knowledge between himself and mom, who didn't share it with me until after dad's passing.

****

They say that necessity breeds innovation. And poverty proved this to be true, bringing out creativity in us. Older siblings made corn husk dolls of many sizes, creating entire families of them, including little babies. I especially loved the babies.

If there are pleasant memories that stand out above the rest, and make me long for childhood, this creativity is one such memory. I loved watching Nancy, my sister next older than Wil, as her skilled hands shaped these dolls. Frustrated when mine didn't turn out, I begged her to make some for me, and sometimes she did.

Bathroom tissue worked well to design paper flower bouquets. Watermelon ends, once every drop of red flesh was eaten, served well to create scales to sell these items. Bottle caps and other bits of metal were the currency for purchasing items. Rabbit droppings, once appropriately dried, served many purposes, much to the horror of some adults. Bugs and other creatures were delightful pets.

These were truly the best times of my childhood. Wil, who was only eighteen months older than I, was my closest friend. When we played house, he was the dad and I the mom, if I had my way about it. Younger siblings were our children and dolls were our infants. I thrilled at bossing my little family around. When they didn't listen, I would pretend to spank them, and they would wail and holler in pretend agony.

Following a stern scolding or spanking, my "children" would ask for forgiveness, and our make-believe world would once again be loving and peaceful. I would return to cooking, cleaning, and ordering my family about.

I wanted those moments to last forever. But, unwelcome and unbidden, other realities always returned. Some harsh, some fun, and others bittersweet.

Chapter Five

The beautiful little girl in the pretty white dress lay perfectly still with her eyes closed and hands folded neatly across her tummy. I wondered if the angels were already playing with Martha or if she was still sleeping and waiting for Jesus to wake her up and tell her she could run through the fields of flowers and play with the angels and the other children. I tried to imagine what it must be like.

Martha's death was sudden, unexpected. She was only six years old when she developed a rash over her body and wasn't feeling well. Her older sister gave her a bath to soothe her discomfort, and then tucked her in bed. Later, it was determined that Martha had the measles and within a short time she died. People speculated that she may have survived if she had not had the bath, saying that the chill from getting out of the water was too much for her sick body.

The funeral was sad, in a way, but the thought of Martha in heaven made me happy. I wanted to go back and see her again and again in the little white dress and imagine her in a happy place. If only we didn't have to die to live in a happy place.

In a culture that prided itself on simplicity, the dead were dressed in beautiful white gowns for burial. Even the men were covered in white shrouds that, in my little mind, looked purely angelic. The Bible says we will wear white gowns in heaven and the people wanted to make sure the dead were already dressed for that awakening. If only I didn't have to die completely to have one. It would be fun to have a pretty dress and have everyone walk by me in the coffin and say nice things, and then later I would get up and play again.

If only the people didn't drop you in the ground like that and cover you with dirt. I didn't like that part. Everyone cried and seemed so sad even when they talked of the children going to heaven, where I knew they would be with Jesus, in a happy place. It was altogether confusing, but I was sure they were right about heaven. I wanted to go.

Around the time of Martha's death, a series of tragic events took place in our community and a neighbouring colony. They all seemed to happen at once, the memories spilling into each other so that I constantly observed death at work around me. A little girl, around the age of two, had died not long prior to Martha's passing. I couldn't help but wonder about many things... *Why do children die? Who will be next? Will it be my turn soon?* Secretly, I hoped so.

Soon after Martha's funeral, my two older sisters, Anna and Tina, walked home from school with our neighbours' thirteen-year-old daughter, Catherine Friesen. With arms linked together, they chatted as they walked. My mother and Mrs. Friesen, Catherine's mom, when they observed, commented that the girls were walking unusually slowly. As they approached one of the mothers asked what they had been discussing so intently.

"Catherine said she hopes she gets to wear a pretty white dress just like Martha's when she dies," one of my sisters said.

That evening began like any ordinary evening in our community. My father owned a generator that produced electricity for all our neighbours, and every evening he signalled that he was about to turn off the electricity, by flickering the lights three times. After the warning he allowed fifteen minutes for neighbours to wrap up their tasks and light their lanterns before shutting down the generator for the night.

On that calm summer evening, this ordinary routine turned into a life-changing nightmare for our community...

A tall barbed wire fence—the standard way of marking property boundaries—separated our yards, but not our lives. Catherine's family had almost as many children as our family, and we often played together during the day. Evenings, however, were spent at home with our own families and occasionally as families visiting together more formally. That evening each family was home with their own children, and, as always, my father flickered the lights to give the warning.

Catherine's family was behind schedule and rushed about lighting lanterns. Catherine sat on the floor beside her older sister, Lena, and helped

34

light the second lantern. Then, as Lena stood to her feet, she bumped a burning lantern and watched in terror as the oil burst into flames, catching Catherine's clothes.

In seconds Catherine was ablaze. Screams coming from their home sparked a flurry of activity in our family. Dad ran, adrenaline surging through his body, and without hesitation leaped over the fence separating our properties, and raced across their yard to help.

Engulfed in flames, Catherine's body was badly burned from head to toe. Only her hair remained untouched. Her parents made a bed in the back of their station wagon to make Catherine as comfortable as possible for the long ride to a hospital in the city, where they hoped to get help for their daughter.

Over the next several days we ran often to the road, looking for some sign of the station wagon, praying Catherine would be okay. My mom and sisters recalled her wish to wear a white dress like Martha's and feared her time had come too soon. When we finally spotted the brown and beige station wagon, it moved slowly, reverently. Before they arrived, we knew our worst fears had become reality.

A pretty white dress was ordered—just like Martha's but in a bigger size—and our families banded with the entire community for yet another sad good-bye. I dared to watch Mrs. Friesen as she prepared Catherine's body for the funeral, something the family always did in a time and place where there were no funeral parlours, or money to afford them.

Skin hung loosely from Catherine's burned flesh. Her mother gently rubbed her body with salt water to remove as much as she could. Each touch, a tender blend of love and grief. It was a harsh life. I stood not far from the rough wooden bench that had become the temporary resting place for Catherine's body. Now a lifeless corpse, she lay there almost naked in the sun, her body a raw, blotchy red where skin had been removed, and parts that looked charred. A linen cloth covered her much like a bathing suit would have, tucked carefully between her legs and spread over her, reaching just above her breasts, protecting her dignity even in death. I closed my eyes and tried to remember the Catherine who laughed and played with us. I couldn't see her. I tried to imagine her in heaven. Heaven… it seemed so far away and yet so near…

I walked away. An empty black hole filled my mind, so that I wouldn't see her body like that. It was best to not think about it. Best to not remember anything.

****

Strangely, these were not all bad times for me. Sometimes I imagined I heard angels singing and whispering sweet things. And I wasn't alone. One day, sitting behind an old barn in our neighbourhood with Wil and Nancy, resting our backs against the wooden boards, we swapped stories about the voices we heard and the dreams we had. Some were sweet voices and pleasant, others dark shadows of sinister murmurings.

Whether the voices were real or imagined, or if the dark forms were merely our expression of inner fear, what stands out is how vulnerable I felt as I shared these thoughts. At that young age life had already taught me to survive, and survival meant not letting anyone inside those secret places. To share the secret places, be it voices, dreams, or fears, was to risk being made fun of, and thought a fool. And nobody wants to be a fool. I had shared a dream once and was immediately shamed into silence, teaching me not to speak in the first place.

"Children your age don't have dreams, and they definitely can't remember them in the morning. You're making it up," an older sibling had said, laughing at me and mocking my dream.

But that day with Wil and Nancy was different. With all the deaths in our community, we felt things we couldn't explain, and questioned life in a new way. Mingled with the sweetness of imagining these children in heaven was the memory of Mr. Bauman's tragic end the previous year. As we chatted we moved from the sweet voices of angels and children in heaven, to the looming darkness of his death. It gave me the shivers. I could almost feel it as a tangible presence, that darkness, when I thought too long about it, and I felt as though I would suffocate and never breathe again.

At night these fears and other tragic experiences blended into terrifying nightmares, overwhelming my little mind.

****

It was dusk and I was tired. I looked around, confused. Everything seemed so unfamiliar. Tables of goods were set up as if it were an open market. Had I met these people before? Who were they, and why was I in this crowd alone? I looked around for a familiar face, but found no one.

I walked as fast as I could. I had to get home before dark, but I didn't know who to ask. These people wouldn't know where I lived.

Then I saw him. The dark silhouette of a man, or was it the devil, lurking behind the people, obviously following me. He took a pair of socks from one of the tables and continued after me. I ran faster, darting between the people, finally breaking away from the crowd and into the dark night, the devil-man after me.

Breathless, I arrived at the old outhouse. If only I could get inside and lock the door, I would be safe. I opened the door, dove in, and tried to lock it. But I wasn't fast enough. His strong hands tore the door open just as I was about to latch it.

He stepped in and covered my mouth with his giant hand, then reached into his pocket, pulled out the pair of socks, and stuffed them into my mouth. I was suffocating. I could feel my eyes bulge. I struggled to break free.

"You must never tell anyone," he said. When he released me, I looked into his face for the first time. "You must never tell," he said again.

I awakened from the nightmare, trembling. Why did the man in my dream look so much like my father? Why did I have the dream? What was I not supposed to tell?

Chapter Six

As a Mennonite family we interacted predominantly with "our people." Social life consisted of getting together with other families in our colony and occasionally friends at neighbouring colonies. These were pleasant times, filled with food, laughter, and fun. Games of tag, prisoner's base, shadow tag, and many other interactive pastimes filled these events.

While I enjoyed our social connections, there were few children my age in our community, and I didn't have many playmates. This made it easier when my parents announced we were moving to Canada.

As my family made plans to relocate to a new country, I overheard snippets of adult conversations. Life in Canada would be better, safer. I felt hope rise inside of me. Having never known another life, I didn't know what I longed for, but I remember that glimmer of hope—the thought that life would be better.

Dad, too, was filled with hope; the hope of making a lot of money by sending his children to work in fields. They would pick strawberries, cucumbers, peppers, and tomatoes—whatever was in season—all summer long, and in the winter they would have other jobs as soon as they finished grade eight. His eyes sparkled as he spoke of it.

For mom it was the dream of being safe that gave her hope. In Canada, she said, there would be police officers who would protect us from the violence, though that "protection" came with cautions and warnings. We were told that Canadian police officers were allowed to shoot children on the spot, no questions asked, if children were not polite. They were to be feared and treated with utmost respect. For example, if a child would spit on an officer, even if it was by accident, the officer could shoot the child.

I resolved that I would always be on my best behaviour around them. In turn, they would keep me safe. How I looked forward to our new life.

Excitement spread through our family as we made preparations for the exodus from Mexico to Canada. Hope stirred. Dreams formed.

Dad built a wooden lining for the cap of our Ford pickup truck, leaving enough room to pack the walls full of books and "family treasures." We could not afford to pay duty on these items and he was not willing to leave them behind.

Having taken care of all the necessary details, we set out for our "land of promise" with eleven kids crammed in the truck.

I loved city lights at night, and how they sparkled from a distance, and all the brightly lit signs as we traveled through towns or cities. The dark had always been frightening, as far back as I could recall, but the lights made even the darkness beautiful. I couldn't see, back then, how true this would be in my life with time, and how the dark night of my life would shine with hope one day.

In Detroit a woman in a bikini stood on her balcony, hanging out laundry. Dad poked fun at her, making a degrading, yet religious, comment, and several brothers chimed in. I didn't understand why they would make fun of her, if it was so wrong. I felt sorry for her.

Not long after we crossed the border into our new country, two women in a car behind us caught my attention when they waved at me. I waved back, hesitantly.

What if they planned to kidnap one of us? Many times my parents warned us about strangers kidnapping children, and how careful we needed to be. A group of Mexicans had attempted to lasso several of my siblings with a rope as they walked home from school one day, so I knew it was real. I feared adults in Canada might kidnap children too.

The back door of the cab-over was tightly closed, but still I imagined them getting in some way and taking me away from my family. I walked away from the door for a while. When I returned, they were still there.

My fears eased when we took an exit and they no longer travelled behind us. At the overpass I looked down and saw them one last time. I was safe.

June 2, 1975, we arrived at Grandma and Grandpa Wall's small grey shingle-siding house. After hearty handshakes all around, and much fussing about who everyone was, and how old, and how much we had grown, aunts showed us around.

Aunts scurried about, preparing food for our large family. I soon picked a favourite single aunt—Aunt Margaret. She liked to tease, and paid attention to children. I liked that quality in adults.

"Do you want bread with peanut butter and syrup?" she asked, standing behind me at the table and leaning over my shoulder. I nodded.

She took a slice of Grandma's fluffy white homemade bread, cut extra thick, and spread it with peanut butter. And then came that magic moment when she stuck a teaspoon into a green and white tin bucket, with pictures of clover and bees on the side. She dipped into the corn syrup, lifted the spoon and twirled it quickly to keep a thick coating of delicious liquid gold on it, then held it over the bread and let it drizzle. I was mesmerized as it swirled in a circular motion onto the bread. I had never seen anything like it.

I sank my teeth into the bread and chased it down with a cup of cold milk, fresh from the fridge. It was all too good to true!

Later that day, I climbed up a ladder to a loft area and dropped my head on a nice soft pillow, followed by one of my aunts tucking blankets around me. It was the perfect ending to several long days on the road.

Maybe the life my mother hoped to find in this new country really existed.

****

We didn't stay long at Grandma's. Our first home was an old wood siding building, with fading red paint. Several large windows were nailed shut with particle board, and inside, old plaster walls crumbled apart here and there. Lilac bushes beside the house provided shade. It was home and, though simple, it was extravagant compared to what we had known in Mexico.

Behind the particle board that covered the windows, bees had made a home, affording us hours and hours of excitement. We quickly learned that if we ganged up and tossed large rocks against the boards, the bees would come swarming after us, and we had to run for dear life to get away. The adrenaline rush was always worth the risk of being stung.

The kitchen area had only one small cupboard and sink. Two old tables stood end to end, with a bench against the wall and chairs around the ends and other side, creating enough room for our large family to all sit together for meals.

A long set of wooden stairs that led up to the bedroom area worked perfectly as a playground. We used them as slides by carefully tucking our skirts between our legs, so as not to lose protection on the way down and to create speed. Then, raising our legs slightly and leaning back, we would go bumping all the way down on our seats. The boys had the advantage of long pants, and no skirts to contend with, but dress fabric was much more slippery, giving us the better ride as we bumped down on our rumps, time and time again.

That was not enough adventure for Nancy, who preferred using a cardboard box as a sled and flying full speed down the stairs. She was always the more daring one when it came to things like that. I enjoyed adventure and risk, but tended toward more caution. Besides, even if I had wanted to try some of her shenanigans, things were usually brought to a grinding halt before I had a chance, if mom was nearby or a sibling tattled.

The bedrooms were simple. Like the rest of the house, they had wooden floors, some with thin, worn-out carpet or peeling paint. The walls, apart from the plaster falling off, were decorated with scribbles and sketches.

It was here, in our first home in Canada—a place to which we would return, summer after summer, for the next four years—that my father set his "get rich quick scheme" in motion. It was the reason he had wanted such a large family, and the reason he had come to this land of plenty. He kept that no secret, sharing freely his hopes and dreams, as he did quick math on how much money he could make if he had each son and each daughter employed and bringing in money until age twenty-one.

Starting that first summer, my siblings worked in the fields, picking whatever fruits or vegetables they could. I was the oldest sibling to stay at home with mom. My role was to help her with whatever tasks she needed done, and to play with younger siblings.

Wil and I did everything together when he was home, but with him in the fields I spent more time alone, or playing with younger siblings. But it just wasn't the same without him.

Eva, who was three at the time, and Martha, who was two, were inseparable. Sometimes they played with me, but more often than not, I was off on my own while they played together. David, who was ten months old, was a sickly child, not gaining weight properly, and stayed pretty close to mom.

For a short time after we moved to Canada, life improved somewhat. During the first year or so, in this "land of promise," the fighting between my parents seemed to die down.

***

On a hot summer evening, my father walked in with brown paper grocery bags under his arms and announced he had a treat. We gathered around and watched as he took out boxes of Chapman's ice cream, and ice cream cones. It had been a rare treat in Mexico, when the ice-cream truck came around, so to have dad bring it home from the store was almost surreal. One by one, dad called our names, as he stacked the cones with the number and size of scoops he thought we could manage.

The Neapolitan looked so pretty, stacked on a cone. I took a lick, running my tongue across the cold sweetness. Mmmm.... The rich chocolate was my favourite, and vanilla almost as good, but the strawberry was a bit disappointing. Apart from that, the experience was a little taste of heaven. More and more, I loved my new country and all it had to offer.

That fall we moved to Corinth, Ontario, where my father had purchased a house. Located a ten-minute drive from Aylmer, it was a small hamlet in a friendly neighbourhood.

The day before I was to start kindergarten at Straffordville Public School, mom took me aside and told me I would need to wait one more day to start school. I was upset. I had been excited for school ever since my one-day visit in Mexico before we moved.

Seeing my disappointment, mom explained, "I talked to one of our neighbours, Mrs. Henry Guenther, and their son Kenny will be in your class if you wait one more day." She told me that he was a native boy, adopted by a distant cousin, making him my fourth cousin, and it would be better for me if I knew someone in my class.

I resigned myself to it. The next morning I walked proudly to the bus stop with my siblings and waited for the big yellow bus that had swallowed them up the day before, leaving me at home, lonely and bored. This was my day for adventure.

I didn't know any English yet, that first day, and wasn't able to communicate with other students or my teacher, so I took my cues from watching other children and doing what they did. There were so many new things to explore, books to look at, and exciting toys to play with!

When the children all formed a circle on the floor, I joined them. Ms. McDonald, the pretty teacher with short curly hair, took a book from her shelf, joined us on the floor, and started to read to us.

The bell rang and the teacher said something I didn't understand and the children scurried to where we had our coats and lunch pails. I put on my coat and grabbed my lunch box, assuming the day was over and it was time to go home.

Ms. McDonald came over and spoke kindly, all words I couldn't understand, and put my lunch box back. She pointed to the other children, who were going out to play, and her antics told me what I needed to know. It wasn't time to leave yet, and I was glad for that. I liked it in class. Slightly embarrassed, I made a mental note to be more careful. And from that point on I watched other students more closely, and did what they did.

I learned the new language quickly, and soon English was my language of preference. I loved the stories Ms. McDonald told, and enjoyed interacting with other children. With peace at home, friends at school, and a teacher I loved, it was the best year of my life.

Chapter Seven

As suddenly as life had improved, the violence started all over again. Our world returned to the same old hell. Had it ever really changed? Had I just missed it, been too caught up in this new world with its new language and new culture?

The summer after we moved, the last shred of hope and the final bit of trust in dad were ripped from my heart. There had always been fears, threats, violence, and abuse, but the worst of them—the death threats—had always remained empty threats with no actions to substantiate them in my mind or memory.

I had heard mom discuss the death threats with older siblings, even describing how she fled the property as dad fired gunshots behind her. I had heard her scream in agony, and watched siblings get beaten or have their heads smacked around, but I had never seen violence that endangered lives, or heard gunshots directed at human beings. I had never heard dad utter death threats; it was always third-party information, and never quite real.

In one moment, that innocence was taken from me.

My older siblings were out in the fields, picking cucumbers, when I awoke to dad gently rocking my shoulder and saying my name, in German.

"Trutje... Trutje..."

I opened my eyes, rubbed them, and sat up, squinting against the morning light as I tried to focus.

Dad was not a man to waste his footsteps. He wasn't a lazy man, but he made good use of the booming voice God gave him. If he was to wake us up in the morning, he did so by yelling from the bottom of the stairs so loudly that he jump-started the whole family's hearts all at once. This particular morning is the only memory I have of dad waking me using any other method. His voice was calm and steady, gentle and persuasive. It was all so strange.

"Go to the neighbours and tell mom to come home," he instructed.

Our summer sleepwear consisted of a homemade slip-type nightgown. In the morning we simply pulled our dresses over them. Dad helped me get into my dress and buttoned it down the back. Whatever our exchange as I got dressed, the details of the conversation are swallowed up by the nightmare that day would become.

"Now go very quickly," dad said again, speaking with the same uncharacteristic gentleness, "and tell mom to hurry home." And with that I ran out the door.

At the neighbours' all curtains were drawn, even the little one on the front door. When I knocked, Mrs. Wolfe pulled back the curtain a tiny crack and peeked out.

Why did everything feel so wrong? And why was everyone acting so weird?

On any ordinary day, Mrs. Wolfe's door was open and she was as likely to be found outside, feeding her cats some leftover gravy from a jar, in the little shed outback, or trimming her rose bushes, as to be indoors. And always, if she trimmed rose bushes and I happened by, she cut one especially for me, carefully removing every thorn so that I would not get hurt. Other mornings she invited me in to watch cartoons, which was a special treat since we had no TV. Summer mornings, on several occasions, she set up a tea party out in her yard, with a little table and chairs and a pretty tea set. She served us a drink and Cheerios, or "donut seeds," as she called them, even convincing me to plant some and see if a donut tree might not grow from it.

That was the Mrs. Wolfe I knew. This thing of peeking out windows was completely out of character. Mrs. Wolfe removed the deadbolt and pulled me in the door quickly, almost roughly. Immediately she dead-bolted the door again behind me.

"Dad said that mom is here and I am supposed to tell her to come home," I explained.

Even as I spoke, Mrs. Wolfe led me around the corner to the sitting room. It was the TV room, where we were occasionally granted permission, by my reluctant and conservative parents, to watch cartoons at Mrs. Wolfe's invitation. I loved those mornings.

This morning there were no cartoons. Mom was huddled in the farthest corner on a sofa, wringing her hands, with my next younger sister, Eva, sitting beside her. Mom looked an unhealthy grey colour. As I took it all in, Mrs. Wolfe explained that mom had been making bread when dad announced he was going to get his rifle to shoot her. He then planned to shoot the children who were at home, before going to the field to shoot the rest of his family.

"We have to wait here until police officers come and make sure it is safe for you to go home," she explained. I sat down on the couch beside mom and Eva, and waited.

The officers arrived some time later. The older officer, with greying hair, explained that they had talked with dad, calmed him down, and had removed all weapons from our property. They believed it was safe for us to return. The younger officer smiled, patted my head gently, and chatted with me for a moment before they left. I felt safe. Protected. As soon as they were gone, we returned home.

Dad wasn't a drinking man, more than an occasional beer. But that day he found comfort in a bottle of whiskey, drinking himself to oblivion, and then took to belting out gospel hymns in drunken irony. Half the neighbourhood could hear his deep, albeit slurred, baritone, as he sang, *"Ich geh' den schmalen Lebensweg..."* The English equivalent, being roughly translated, would be, "I go the straight and narrow way." And in his state, taking the lyrics literally, neither straight, nor narrow, would have been a successful walk, had he been asked to attempt such a thing. Spiritually he wasn't in much better shape.

At one point he staggered into the house long enough to vomit all over the kitchen on his way to the bathroom. He left mom to clean up after him— as though she didn't have enough to do with five of us children at home, ages six and under.

I manoeuvred carefully the rest of the day, watching around every corner, determined to stay a safe distance from him. This worked well until mid-afternoon. I tiptoed through the abandoned half of our house; what had once been a store of some sort and a post office. It had become our creepy hide-and-seek space, where boxes of musty clothes and hand-me-downs

47

were stored. Garbage bags upon garbage bags of clothing filled one small room, piled in a heap. These clothes were donated by sympathetic neighbours, wanting to help my mother dress her dozen or so children who still lived at home. With many rooms to hide in and old furniture sitting here and there, it lent itself to many delightfully terrifying moments as we competed to "out-scare" each other.

For that reason alone, this part of the house had me on edge and moving quickly, yet cautiously. We never knew where another sibling might be waiting to jump out and grab us. And even though I knew my siblings were in the field, the fear associated with the space was profoundly present.

As I neared the halfway mark, listening closely for any creaking of floorboards, or footsteps, with heightened sensitively, there was a sudden loud snort—a snore gone very wrong.

I froze, standing there as if in a tableau vivant. To my left, passed out on the couch, lay my drunken father. Fearing that any movement on my part would awaken him and earn me a beating, I remained motionless for what seemed an eternity, until his breathing returned to the deep laboured breathing of his drunken nap. Only then did I start breathing normally again, tiptoe to safety, and then run for my life.

The day blurs and blends into many shades of grey and black, a surreal collage of mental images and deep feelings forever etched on the canvas of my memory.

That day I became as strong on the inside as I was weak and vulnerable in body... maybe stronger. And from that day forward I took care of myself, relied on myself, and rushed the day that I would leave my family. That day was filled with "learning" that would take the rest of my life to be undone, in layers and stages.

Dad's violent and unpredictable outbursts rocked our world. Without warning, their impact created lasting scars.

****

A simple, faded barn-board bench sat outside the old red house. We had returned to the old "beehive house," as we called it, for another season of picking tomatoes. As in previous summers, with Wil gone, I was left to entertain myself, and spent much of my time daydreaming on that bench. On one occasion I grew tired and fell asleep, and the next thing I knew, I awoke to the "strap" ripping into my backside and across my legs.

I stood to my feet screaming, reaching back with my hands to protect myself, only to feel the strap rip across my hands. Through blurred vision I saw dad, hand raised, ready to strike… again… and again… and again. For no particular reason.

My heart shut down in steps and phases throughout childhood. That day was a big step. Initially, after the rude awakening, I felt numb. Physically I felt searing pain, but mentally and psychologically I felt nothing. The shock left my mind reeling.

Gradually, as the shock wore off, I felt hopeless and depressed. I found a secluded place in a corner of the house, on an old mattress, and cried myself to sleep. Each time I awakened, I closed my eyes to the world, willing myself to sleep, and praying I would die.

Another day, another trauma, another broken trust that left my heart shattered, strewn on the ground, trampled... Another death, as one more phase of innocence gasped its final breaths…

Would my heart ever be truly alive again? All I could think about was my desperate desire to die. Why had God not taken my life in early childhood, back in Mexico? How I had longed for that little white dress and a coffin. Sometimes I felt angry that God had not allowed it. Other times I felt sadness and deep grief. He could have spared me this. He didn't.

Maybe if I would hold my breath long enough… Maybe then the pain would stop...

****

Intertwined with the violence in our home, the strong religious teachings and beliefs continued, adding to the confusion and deeply rooted fear. I've heard it said that we live out in our day-to-day lives what we believe about God in our hearts and minds.

In our home this was true. God was viewed as a harsh judge, not a gentle and loving "Daddy," or "Abba Father," as Jesus called Him. God's hatred for sin translated into hatred for sinners. No one would ever have said it, in so many words, but actions proclaim loudly what words fail to communicate, or even deny. And God's commandments, written to protect us, became the measuring stick for our success or failure to please Him. The terror my parents had of Him was transferred to us, evoking within us an unholy terror of our parents, as well as God.

Dad's violent threats and outbursts could stop me dead in my tracks and make me muster up every ounce of self-control to prevent me from wetting myself, a battle that remained consistently part of my life until I left home at age fifteen. It returned from time to time, even in adulthood, when faced with disapproval from leaders or employers.

Only that once, when dad whipped me at age four, did I lose that battle, landing me in a puddle on the floor.

Emotionally we were abandoned, and rarely did I see either of my parents show much compassion, affection, or tenderness to a child past the age of about seven or eight, though, for the most part it was lost long before that. There were moments, but they were the exception.

The lack of love and affection at home made it awkward to receive love outside of our home. But that didn't stop God from sending people into my life who loved me shamelessly, reminding me that He was still there—a truth I would recognize many years later.

In our little community of Corinth everyone knew who everyone else was. There were seldom new faces or strangers in town, except to visit friends and family. So, when I saw the little girl of about eight years old, just slightly bigger than me, curiosity drew me to her.

We waved to each other across the street and soon started chatting, as young girls do. I discovered she was the granddaughter of an elderly couple who lived in an old faded-wood house, with pointed gables, and a garden patch in their back yard—a property that was slightly overgrown with vines, plants and gnarly old trees. It always reminded me of storybooks and fairy tales of long, long ago that I loved to read from the school library.

Immediately I loved Christa. She was the princess who came to visit the little old couple in the "fairy tale house."

From the start, Christa was an unusually affectionate friend. No one ever hugged me—it wasn't culturally acceptable—but when she stopped by, I didn't lack for hugs and kisses. I was almost embarrassed by her overt displays of affection and the fact that she didn't care if there was an audience, or who that audience was. I accepted it, but never returned it.

Secretly I liked it and looked forward to times when she visited her grandparents and we could play together. Christa seemed to look forward to spending time with me as much as I looked forward to time with her.

But the relationship was bittersweet. There were times when I was excluded from neighbourhood tent parties and ordered to stay away. It was always when Christa went to visit her "boyfriend" that I wasn't allowed to join them.

The rejection hurt, but I was relieved when she told me they "kissed and stuff" in the tent. I could only imagine what that "stuff" might be, and if I was right, I didn't want to do that. Still, it hurt to be excluded.

While she never said that they engaged in anything inappropriate, the perversions I had seen in my short life had triggered my imagination. Either way, the affection she offered was innocent and sweet, filling a void in my life, and making the memory of that relationship one of the best things that happened to me in those years.

In school I had a group of friends who mostly accepted me. I wasn't popular and, again, was excluded at times because the other children did things they didn't think I would want to do. On several occasions when I walked into the bathroom I saw them exploring each other's bodies inappropriately, and heard them talk about what they had done at a birthday party sleepover with the boys. It all reminded me of the things I had seen and done in Mexico. Things I didn't want to remember.

Chapter Eight

Mentally and psychologically we were stripped and violated in many ways, as children, on top of the physical and sexual abuse. Being called everything from evil beasts, to the German equivalent of sluts and whores, I lost all sense of value and identity at a young age. These things shut down my heart, even though I did not comprehend the meaning. In silence I carried the wounds, unable to speak about it with anyone, and not understanding fully the damage.

It would be many years before their haunting would reveal the depth of pain I carried as a result of words spoken. While taking deep root in my spirit and warping my identity, with so much energy consumed by survival, the impact of this emotional trauma was secondary to the violence and death threats.

At night, when the stairs creaked, fear gripped my heart with such force that I thought it would strangle me to death. Sometimes I held my breath until I was left gasping for air, just to make sure I didn't miss a sound, just in case he was coming for me. Just in case dad would open the door and come with a knife or a gun, or with the intent to violate me in some other way. When I could hold my breath no longer, I would lie in the dark, panting as quietly as possible, my heart pounding.

Shadows in the doorway haunted me, night after night. I lost much sleep watching those shadows, and wishing I could cry out for help. Longing for someone, anyone, to keep me safe and protect me from the evil that lurked all around. There in the dark I would lie motionless, alone. It was up to me to survive. There was no one else. Or was there?

My awareness of God was limited to what we were taught and told at home, and things like relationship, protection, and "presence" were not familiar to me in human experience. I could not grasp a relational God, or even a kind God. Other than begging for mercy when we sinned—in hopes that God might forgive us—and religiously adhering to cultural rules, God was not someone we were taught to "know." In the face of death we were instructed to plead for mercy, and hope that maybe God would find it in His heart to grant forgiveness, if we had some unknown or hidden sin. But to befriend God, and know Him intimately, was unheard of, and to engage in a loving relationship with Him was scandalous.

All but forgotten were the days when I felt God in the wind and the sun, back in Mexico. Faded into my subconscious, these memories had been replaced by a distant awareness of His existence and yet a powerful presence of His wrath and judgement.

At moments I felt God's presence, like when Ms. Harms, the Bible teacher in grade three, told bible stories. I kept track of the days until her next visit, and made a habit of waiting for her. When her car pulled in, I ran to meet her.

"Hi, Ms. Harms!" I greeted, as she got out of her car.

"Hi, Trudy," she said, always with a smile.

"Do you have something for me to carry in?" I asked. Always I wanted to be her little assistant, and always she found one thing or another for me to take in or do for her.

I loved her stories, told with great enthusiasm and conviction, but I especially liked the story of the prodigal son. As she moved the characters across the felt board, it came alive in my imagination. A father who loved his disobedient son, waited for that son to return, and watched for him every day, on a little bench in front of their house. The son, having taken the money his father gave him, spent it carelessly on parties and frivolous living, while his father's heart broke in grief at home. Then, when the son had nothing left, he worked on a pig farm, eating pig feed. One day he remembered his father and decided to go home, and see if his father would hire him. His father, who still sat on that bench waiting, saw him a long way off and ran to meet him.

Ms. Harms took the "sitting" father, replaced him with a running father, and bounced him toward the son. The father hugged the son and then threw a big party, so happy to see him again, in spite of the terrible things he had done. She explained that this is how God waits for His children to come home, and accepts them no matter what they have done.

At the end of class Ms. Harms handed out little red Testaments to anyone who wanted one. I raised my hand. If it had stories like that, I wanted it! I read the note at the back of the Testament and carefully signed my name. I didn't understand it, but I hoped one day I would.

I took the Testament home and started to read it immediately. I wanted to find and know this God. I vowed that I would read it as religiously as my father read his songbooks, and his big fat German Bible.

Often I heard him in his bedroom at night, reading mournfully, as if doing penance for his sins. It made me sad to hear him. If only God would listen, and help him. He desperately wanted to know God, but it seemed He always stayed just beyond reach.

I understood at a young age that my father was very wicked, and wondered if he had been too evil. Had he done things God would never forgive?

Yes, I would read my Testament as faithfully as dad, but it would be happy, not sad and mournful. I wanted to know more stories like the one about the prodigal son. Those stories made me happy. And so I began, that first night, with Bible reading.

I stumbled through the genealogies of Matthew. Long, boring, unpronounceable names. Lifeless. It just wasn't the same as the felt board, and I soon lost interest.

The sweet, innocent connection I had with God in early childhood had returned for that one brief moment in the classroom, lingered a few days, and then it was gone, lost from personal experience. Lost for many years, behind the teachings and rules of religion and culture that soon invaded my life, and the energy it took to try to live up to those expectations and be acceptable.

****

After arriving in Canada, my parents again attended the Old Colony Russian Mennonite church, returning to the church they had left when I was nine months old. While they attended on Sundays, somewhat consistently, as well as on religious holidays, we children did not. "Bad things happen to children in Sunday School," I overheard one of them say.

My siblings and I stayed home to help with tidying and food preparations. My older sisters did cooking and I got stuck with peeling potatoes, on occasion, as well as other tasks like sweeping. If we were naughty and didn't do our tasks, or if we fought, older siblings measured out whatever discipline they felt appropriate.

One Sunday morning, when I didn't do my task and got into mischief, Anna and Tina teamed up and marched me to the most dreaded of consequences. In the hallway leading to the kitchen, under the staircase, was a closet. Together they pushed me in, and blocked the door to lock me in.

There was nothing more terrifying than sitting in that blackness, wondering what dreadful creatures or demons might be hiding in there, waiting to kill me. Time stood still the moment that door closed, as immobilizing fear enveloped me. Each moment was an eternity, and though they didn't keep me in long, it seemed forever. When my sisters were ready to negotiate my release, I was relieved.

"Are you going to do what you're told?" one asked.

Without hesitation I agreed to be good and do whatever they asked, and not fight with my siblings. And with that it was over. But the nightmares lived on in my nights for many years, even continuing into my first pregnancy.

About eight months after arriving in Canada, and two years before that "moment" with Ms. Harms, things changed on Sunday mornings in our home. My parents, who still searched for purpose and meaning, began visiting other churches and took us with them. At the Gottes Gemeinde—the Church of God—in Aylmer, I experienced God's kindness in the people, and wished we would stay and put down our roots. I loved Pastor Joseph and Mrs. (Sonia) Jakobsh, and their daughter, Doris. They always greeted us warmly, and Doris always acknowledged me personally, and made me feel special.

One Sunday evening in particular stands out in my memory. The moment I entered the back of the church, Doris chatted enthusiastically with me. Though I loved the attention, I felt a bit shy, and soon made my way to the front of the church and seated myself for the song service. I followed along in the songbooks and tried to sing, even if I didn't know the songs well, teaching myself to read German in the process.

When the leader chose songs I knew, I sang at the top of my lungs. Especially when we sang *"Jesus nimmt die Sünder an...,"* which, translated, is, "Sinners Jesus will receive."

Off to the left, in his chair on the platform, Pastor Jakobsh smiled at me and nodded in approval. I was never so proud in my life as I was in that moment. A pastor—the most important person in church—noticed me. My feet didn't quite reach the floor and in my excitement I swung them back and forth, hardly able to contain the thrill.

But too soon my parents decided it was not the church for us. They were far too worldly and believed things that my parents were not comfortable with. I heard criticism about the cut hair, and clothing that was not conservative enough. I didn't understand all of that, but I had seen a glimpse of God in the people around me; a welcoming God, and I wanted more.

But soon after that experience in Ms. Harms' class, our family attended a direct-market cookware sales party at a cousin's home near New Hamburg, Ontario. There we met Elmer and Ella Grove, a couple from the Conservative Mennonite Churches of Ontario, a white-bonnet Mennonite church, as we called them in German.

At school, over that time, we studied pioneers and had gone on a school trip to a pioneer village, only weeks earlier. When I saw these Mennonites, I was delighted, certain that we had stumbled upon some real live ones.

Immediately Elmer and Ella took an interest in our family and asked if they could visit us and have church in our home. Dad was quite taken with Elmer, who instantly won his trust, and agreed to let them come, along with others from their churches.

Ministers from several Mennonite congregations took turns coming to our home, along with some of their wives. They spent time with us, singing, praying, and preaching. The preaching was over my head, but I will never forget some of the songs. "My sheep know my voice and they come at my call, and a stranger's voice do they not know....," or "Standing on the promises of Christ my King..." and many other songs and hymns, like, "When Peace Like a River" and "How Great Thou Art..." Some tunes I recognized as songs we had sung in German, others were completely new.

One Sunday Elmer and Ella invited our family to their home for dinner. We loaded up our van and visited New Hamburg Conservative Mennonite Church. My brother Wil proudly wore his new jeans with a Spider-man stitched on the back pocket.

When we arrived at church, Wil set out to find Bishop Elmer, excited to show him the Spider-man. Bishop Elmer smiled graciously and indulged Wil with some acknowledgement. We would later learn that such worldliness was strictly forbidden.

The service started with adults and children alike congregated in the auditorium for several songs and devotions. After a prayer, the song leader dismissed children from the main service, and we walked out while they sang another song. We followed the other children downstairs to an assembly area. Here we sang a few songs and then took up the offering while singing, "Dropping, dropping, dropping, dropping, hear the pennies fall, every one for Jesus, He will get them all!"

Girls reached in their purses, and boys in their pockets, pulling out coins. Embarrassed that I had no purse, and no coins, I felt out of place. A little girl noticed and slipped me a few coins so that I could join in.

An adult introduced me to a little girl my age, Charlotte Good, a pretty girl with the loveliest hair I had ever seen. The top was neatly combed back into hair bobbles, then divided into two braids. The colour, hard to define, was a cross between ginger and auburn, and her eyes a beautiful hazel brown. Cheerfully she guided me to my class.

Charlotte opened her purse, which revealed pretty pens, notebooks, and a variety of other items. I couldn't imagine what it would be like to have those things. She shared with me and even slipped me an orange Tic Tac when the teacher wasn't looking.

When classes dismissed, children rushed back upstairs for the main service, which lasted an hour or more. Teenagers congregated on benches near the front, while younger children sat with their fathers or mothers, since families didn't sit together. Segregated seating was intended to help the church stay pure, sexually, by avoiding close contact with the opposite gender.

That first morning a most unusual thing happened that impacted me for life. One row behind us, and off to my left, a beautiful young woman, with black wavy hair, stood to her feet and through tears spoke to the congregation. She held a little girl in her arms, and two little boys sat on either side of her. I didn't understand the meaning of it all, but she asked for prayer for herself and her children, because their daddy had left them.

Tears threatened to spill from my eyes. I had never heard of a daddy just up and leaving his family like that. Ours wasn't very kind, and he left for short periods of time, but to leave and not come back was foreign. I peeked over my shoulder at the cute little boys, who watched their mommy with big eyes. How could a daddy leave them?

Moments later, as the mommy sat down, the youngest boy pinched his finger and started to cry. He held it up to his mommy's face, big tears splashing on his shirt. Her own tears hardly dried, she took his finger, blew on it, and kissed it. Instantly his tears stopped. Like magic. She smiled past her own pain, reassuring her son.

I sat, dumbfounded, having never seen such a thing in my life. How could one little kiss heal a hurt, I wondered, and what made this mommy so kind, even when she was so sad? I would have to remember about the kiss when I was a mommy.

After the service we drove to Elmer and Ella's for dinner, an experience unlike anything I had ever had before. The smell of roast beef cooking greeted us as we entered, but it was the sight of her dining table that left me spellbound.

At home two mismatched tables sat end to end so that we could all eat together. An odd assortment of mismatched dishes and flatware were set, somewhat haphazardly, on the table in a last-minute rush before mealtimes. There was seldom, if ever, a table cloth or any other special fuss. Mom and my sisters were good cooks and, though quite poor, we always had good food since moving to Canada.

I walked into Ella's dining room almost reverently, as though God himself had made the arrangement. A pretty table cloth covered a long wooden table. Beautiful china decorated the table, all perfectly matched, and complemented by silverware neatly placed on a serviette. Each place setting had two drinking glasses; a tall one filled with water, and a small one for juice. Every second place setting offered tomato juice, and the other apple juice. The food didn't disappoint. The meal went on and on and on, with meat, potatoes, salads, bread, and finally, blueberry pie and ice cream. I thought my tummy would pop, it was so full!

After dinner we played games—a whole closet full to choose from—and chatted with Elmer and Ella. I had never been happier in my life. The time to leave came too soon.

Dad asked Elmer where to find a gas station. We would need gas to get back home. Elmer explained that it was best not to buy gas on Sunday—that should be saved for emergencies—and told dad to drive the van to his gas tank. He would fill it up at no cost and save dad having to buy on Sunday.

With time the Mennonites suggested we move closer to one of their churches, rather than organizing services in our home. My parents agreed to relocate, so several of the churches appointed individuals to find a suitable home for our large family. God's will would be determined by whoever could find a place first, within our price range.

The search committee from the little church near Bayfield soon found a large stone house on a seven-acre property, perfect for our family. This was disappointing, as the church had no children my age, except one boy, and only several other families had any young children at all. I had hoped we would move to New Hamburg, where Elmer and Ella would be our ministers. Not only were they kind to us but Elmer also had a way with dad, and when he was angry, Elmer could reason with him and get him grounded.

Besides, I had wanted to go to church with Charlotte. Soon after I met her she had invited me to her house. Her kindness reminded me of Christa and I was sure we would be great friends. How I longed to have one true friend to spend time with. I wanted desperately to go to Sunday school with her and hear more Bible stories, and sing the Sunday school songs.

That dream would not become a reality.

Chapter Nine

In May 1978, we moved to Clinton, Ontario, to a lovely country property. A collage of colours blended together to create the stunning stone structure that greeted us; our new home. The dilapidated main porch looked in need of some love, and the red lean-to shed-type structure was like a poorly planned afterthought. These features didn't do anything for the aesthetics, but all around it had my approval.

That property and house lent us many a good memory—some of the best of home life—in the years that followed.

A hill at the back of our property led into a woods to a big river just behind our property, offering a different heaven altogether. Here we spent much time exploring, always in search of some unique creature… salamanders under rocks, birds of many kinds, frogs, coloured turtles, snapping turtles, snakes, and mice. It was a wildlife heaven.

Mesmerized by the clear water, chattering cheerfully as it rushed over rocks in the river, I sensed God, if only for a moment. In the sacred quiet of His creation, with the bubbling water, interrupted occasionally by a bird's song or the scurrying of some small critter, my spirit came alive. Here, sitting on the bank of the river, or on the gigantic rock at the river's edge, I felt at peace. Nature offered a sanctuary for my soul, as it had in childhood, and as it would throughout my life, in times of distress, discouragement, and depression.

Ironically the rock that brought me so much comfort, I would later learn, was the scene of trauma for one brother who was sodomized there. A trauma forever engraved in the mind of the witness who stumbled upon Bruce, as he used my brother. A trauma that, when I finally learned of it, finally made sense of my brother's health issues and kidney problems in those years. Yet, not knowing of this, the rock was a haven; a place to which I escaped when I wanted to leave the world behind and know only the serenity of sunshine and nature. Or connect with the Creator who had set that world in motion long before I discovered it.

The house also offered many interesting memories involving wildlife. Mice were a given in an old house like that, and when they kept to themselves, they were little trouble. But in the middle of the night, when their gnawing and scampering disturbed us, it was war. And more than one battle with these invasive creatures led to excitement and laughter.

"Trudy, are you awake?" Nancy whispered.

"Yes," I said.

"Do you hear that?"

"Yes," I said again. The gnawing of a mouse had awakened me too, and I was ready for battle.

Quietly, we came up with a plan, whispering, so as not to scare the mouse away. We would get up, turn on the light, and immediately stuff something in front of the door to our room, and to the closet, to block any escape. Then, item by item, we would move furniture until we caught the little rascal.

And that is just what we did. It wasn't long before we caught a glimpse of it, scurrying from one hiding place to the dresser. We tiptoed in pursuit and moved the dresser, ready to stomp on the little critter.

By this time we both fought giggles. Tension has always made it difficult for me to contain my giggles. This was true in church, when I knew I dare not giggle during prayers—making the thing in my mind that much funnier—and it was true the time my mother threatened to spank me with a shoe. And it was most definitely true chasing a mouse in the middle of the night, when the house was perfectly quiet and noise would not be tolerated.

Still, in spite of the threat of giggles, and the occasional snicker, forcing us to pause a moment and collect ourselves, it had gone quite smoothly, with minimal noise. But we had not accounted for one detail: our long nighties.

As we moved the dresser, fully prepared for the attack, the mouse darted out, under Nancy's nightie, and ran up her legs.

Nancy's feet flew in panic as she grabbed her nightie, shaking it violently and shrieking in terror. In an instant I lost complete control, exploded in a fit of laughter, and doubled over, holding my sides, helpless to help her.

It all happened so fast from that moment on, and moments later, having conquered, we stood at the top of the stairs with a dead mouse dangling from one of our hands. Downstairs dad bellowed at us, as we tried to compose ourselves. "What is going on up there?!"

We didn't need to explain when he saw the mouse. The limp offering said it all and, to our relief, dad seemed slightly amused. He immediately calmed down, told us to throw it out and get back to bed. Back in bed, sleep evaded us, as we kept breaking out in giggles.

There was nothing in the world like the adrenaline rush of the chase, and the laughter that ensued as the tension of the risk that the creature might attack, increased.

But the best memory at that property took place on a summer Sunday afternoon, and involved only mom and dad. Following a rainy morning at church, and thunder showers into the early afternoon—during which time my parents had a nap—the sky cleared and a rainbow spread across the sky.

When mom and dad awakened, they stepped out into the freshly washed world. Together they walked down the porch steps and across the driveway, until they came to the edge of the corn field. Here dad held mom's hand as they walked along the grass.

For the first time in my life, and the only time ever, I saw my parents enjoy a moment of affection. And in that moment I knew what marriage should be, and the friendship that was possible.

And then the moment slipped away... But the promise represented in that rainbow lived on, leaving me with only one desire and expectation for my own marriage: to know joy and friendship.

****

Immediately after the move, we started attending Lakeshore Conservative Mennonite Church. It was a little white building situated near Lake Huron. The church had a private school, some country blocks down that same road, where I completed the last month of that school year and attended until grade nine. Again the little glimmer of hope that we had when moving to Canada appeared. Maybe, just maybe, this would be the "miracle" that would heal dad and make our world safe.

Instead, bullying and abuse added to our confusion. During recess one morning, I walked into the school basement to see several teenagers with their heads together, whispering. They looked up at my sister, then burst out laughing. I caught just enough of what they said to know they were making fun of Margaret, who stood by herself across the room, looking hurt and angry. Being four years younger and new to the school, I pretended I noticed nothing, and kept walking.

At home later, Margaret flew into a rage about some little thing that had nothing to do with the bullying, but ended with her venting about being made fun of at school. This became commonplace in our home, that we paid the price as a family for bullying at school, and not only with Margaret, but other siblings as well, as we struggled to fit into this new environment.

To the Mennonite children, we dressed oddly when we first arrived. We wore "worldly" dresses, not homemade ones, and didn't know that things like sandals and certain colours of shoes were also considered "worldly." This led to a lot of mocking, and marked our family as rejects in this new culture. Again I flew under the radar. I suffered little to no bullying from classmates, but what my siblings went through troubled my mind, and made me a misfit in both worlds. I couldn't identify with my siblings' suffering, but neither did I "fit the mould" of church and school culture.

In spite of these negative experiences, there was much about our new culture that I loved. More than anything, I loved studying the Bible, whether at school or in Sunday school, and learning more of the stories.

Janet Gingerich, one of my first Sunday school teachers, was always meticulously put together, with every strawberry blonde hair perfectly in place, and dresses fitted to her figure. She pronounced her words with the same detail, and spoke with confidence. Content of a lesson was not overly important; watching her was more fascinating than anything she had to say.

Besides, she dated my favourite song leader, Owen Brenner, and that alone made her famous in my mind. Owen was a charismatic leader, whose enthusiasm inspired a response from the congregation. When it was his Sunday to lead the traditional two pre-sermon songs, I immediately sat up. It would be a good morning. Better yet, when he did an entire evening song service.

And then the unthinkable happened. The air was heavy at church the Wednesday night it was announced. Owen was being excommunicated for living in sin. Just what that sin was, was not mentioned, but his parents, Elda and Morton, who was the lead minister, were clearly heartbroken over their son's fall from grace.

I heard rumours of what he had done, but couldn't believe he willingly risked everything in his world, including his future with Janet. What if the other man used him, coerced him… possibly even forced him? Did anyone ask? Were the rumours true at all? And, if they were true, did anyone try to understand him, hear his heart, and love him back?

It broke my heart and brought chaos, confusion, and devastation into my world. Lakeshore would never be the same without Owen. As with song leading, he was my favourite Sunday school superintendent. He spoke with passion and authority, stirring something to life deep in my spirit. All of that was gone, in one moment. How I missed Owen!

In the span of a few years, the church excommunicated, or put on probation, eleven members for bad attitudes, watching TV, listening to radio, all the while hiding sexual abuse and indiscretions in their own homes. Unless, of course, if that sexual sin was found out by the public—as in the case of Owen—and thereby presented the risk of ruining the religious image or family name. Then it was dealt with swiftly, and harshly.

To keep their hands on the church pulse, bishops and ministers made "house calls" to each member. They arrived with little black books in hand, ready to take notes and record all the sins that were confessed—or "reported"— to them. But the sins of some of their own sons and daughters were conspicuously overlooked, as were their own sins.

When Bruce, the minister's son, violated numerous youth to varying degrees, myself included, he was carefully protected from public exposure. Meanwhile the aforementioned sins of others were broadcast and announced from pulpit to pulpit of sister congregations across the province of Ontario.

More and more the harsh God of my childhood—a God who loathed humanness and loved perfection, a God whose love and grace were as consistent as a yo-yo in the hands of an amateur—was the God I saw at work in our new culture. Just like our parents, who punished us for every little offence—whether deliberate or unintentional—while condoning sin in their own lives, leaders showed partiality and misrepresented God.

What made it most confusing was the presentation of kindness and care, while functioning in this inconsistent manner, and caring more for image than people's hearts. On the one hand, I desperately wanted the approval of leaders. Having someone with that level of position and power offer a stamp of approval was appealing—the ultimate sign of "worthiness." But on the other, I feared their judgement, knowing I would never measure up or be "acceptable," and at a moment's notice could be met with harsh disapproval if I failed to perform or they received a false report from a "reliable source."

While some leaders represented God well for the most part—like Peter Steckle, a gentle-hearted middle-aged man, who seemed sincerely to know God—others, not so much. More and more, God became a confusing and inconsistent force who could not be trusted, and yet demanded our allegiance.

I wanted to make that commitment at age nine, but it was unheard of in the culture for a child to accept Jesus, and my father was especially against child evangelism. I was taught that children had to wait until they were old enough to fully understand their sinful condition and need for salvation before making such a commitment.

From the time that I had an awareness of needing a Saviour, the thought of dying before I was old enough troubled me. I was ten years old, when I was alone in the barn, and a violent thunderstorm hit. Fear choked my heart with such intensity that I could hardly breathe. My body trembled.

"Dear God," I prayed frantically, "please don't let me die in this storm… let me live until I am old enough to become a Christian." I added a silent promise that I would talk to someone. Maybe my Sunday school teacher, Susan. When the storm passed I went into the house and wrote in a little notebook:

> Dear Susan,
> Could we talk sometime? I would like to become a Christian, and there are some things I really need to talk to someone about.
> Sincerely,
> Trudy

I folded it in half three times, and created a tiny envelope with another piece of paper, then wrote *Susan Brenner* neatly on the front and taped it shut so no one could read it. I prayed for the courage to give it to her, but never found that courage.

Terror of God's wrath haunted my dreams as violently as they tormented my waking thoughts, and nightmares were no longer limited to running from dad and his guns and knives, or escaping from sexual abuse and demons. Grasshoppers, hidden in walls, spoke to me in those dreams, telling me I would go to hell if I didn't live for God. I would wake up and lie there, trembling and terrorized.

Not only did fear of God haunt my dreams, sometimes it prevented me from even falling asleep. They called it "conviction"; I call it torment. If God was no more forgiving or just than the people in my life, and if His rules were as inconsistent, then there was little hope of pleasing Him or being accepted. In my angst of being rejected by Him, I suffered in silent depression. No one noticed, or entered that frightening world.

At night I awakened after dreaming about God, my heart pounding, body trembling, consumed by that same debilitating terror that dad's violence triggered in me. The awareness would eat at my mind, like cancer... *I will die one day...*

And with that realization came an even more terrifying one that God might, regardless of my best efforts, rule me unfit and toss me in hell. What was worse yet, this God already knew my outcome and for every cry of my heart and every desire to be with Him, had the right to reject me and leave me to rot in eternal fire.

When I could stand the silent trauma no longer I crept out of bed, perched myself on the deep window sill of our old stone house, and wept. I sat there, staring into the night and wondering about life... about death... about eternity...

Many a wordless scream rose from my soul to this cosmic Being who held such ruthless power. If only I could know my final outcome... If only I could know for sure that I would make it to heaven... or hell, as the case may be...

If only....

If only I could know for certain that I would be okay in the end—that this God would welcome me and not cast me aside.

And then the thought would strike me with such force that I could hardly bear it, that knowing I would go to hell would extend it into this life and I would have to live with that knowledge. The thought of it took my breath away, fear suffocating me.

If only I had known that a loving God does not torment the mind with fears and trauma, but rather invites us into relationship. Terror is the work of the devil and his cohorts, some of whom are spirits, while others are power hungry leaders, described in the Bible as "wolves in sheep's clothing," and ruthless fathers who misrepresent the tender Father-heart of God. But no one told me these things, so night after night, I battled terror. And day after day I awakened to the same hopeless existence.

On the worst days, dad's violence greeted us with vengeance. When he yelled, my heart froze. But when his rage took on a calmer form, his voice was more vile and demonic than anything I have ever heard. And that is the sound I heard, soon after I awakened to him bellowing at mom that summer morning, almost two years after we moved to Clinton.

"Well, then I will have to kill everyone," he shouted, his voice dripping blood.

I sat on the edge of my bed, trembling, when two younger sisters, Eva and Martha, came to my room, just as frightened, and looking for comfort. We strained to make out dad's words. The front door opened and slammed shut, followed by silence.

"I think he said he's getting a gun," I said. Together the three of us fell to our knees beside my bed, visibly trembling, and praying that God would keep us safe and not let dad kill us. I learned later that dad had held a knife to mom's throat early that morning and had, indeed, threatened yet again to kill his family.

Over the years his threats ranged from cutting us up with sharpened knives, to shooting us, or saying we should all have our heads chopped off with an axe. This graphic violence was easy to imagine. We witnessed animals being slaughtered when we butchered. Dad's rifle took out a cow or pig with a single shot, and his knives were always obsessively sharpened, especially the butcher knives that were used to cut up the animals.

And when it came to using an axe, I knew its capabilities. I preferred to help chop off the heads of chickens, ducks, and geese over other parts of butchering—like plucking feathers. How I despised that job! By my preteens I had the process down to a science, and often did the chopping single-handedly. We hammered long nails into a large block of wood or a tree stump, positioned just over an inch apart. Directly below the bird's head, I positioned the neck between the nails, with the wings and legs firmly grasped my left hand, and pulled slightly to ensure the bird could not lift its head and escape. With a good aim and a sharp axe, one swing severed the bird's head and I held the body upside down to bleed out.

I had witnessed all of these things since early childhood and knew dad's strength could easily do something this horrible with his children. And the way he walked through the kitchen sharpening knives forced the mind to go places and visualize things that no human should have to contend with.

Thank God that in the middle of this hopeless existence, there were saints in our church who loved the real God. Saints who showed me His heart in ways that I would only see clearly, many years later.

"Grandma" Mary Steckle, an elderly woman in the Lakeshore church, seemed to know the real Jesus, from what I could tell. On Sunday mornings, having no friends at church, I would make my way to her side, knowing I would be loved. Her eyes always twinkled when she saw me.

One Sunday morning, after the women greeted each other with the Holy Kiss, Grandma Mary kissed my cheek—a gesture reserved only for church members in good standing—and said, "I think Trudy needs a kiss too!"

In the winter I helped Grandma Mary put on her coat, and wiggle the rubber "over boots," with furry trim, over her shoes in the winter. Grandma Mary had a place in my heart that only Christa and Charlotte had found previously, and anything I could do for her, I did with love. Though we were decades apart in age, the unconditional love and acceptance I felt from her offered a safety that brought out the best in me.

In every dark place, I found God hiding in the hearts of those who cared for me without judgement. Grandma Mary loved the bubbly chatterbox I was. She was just like I would have wanted God to be; she seemed quite perfect to me.

There were others, like Grandma Mary's son, Peter, and his wife, Rita, who were kind to us, though I wasn't sure our family was good enough for them. Their life seemed so wonderful. Rich. Together. Always "good," the image of perfection that we could only dream of, but never attain.

Then there were the three Gingerich families. Lorne and Bernice, Lenis and Marjorie, and Alvin and Erla. Lorne and Bernice were both vertically challenged, to say it with political correctness. Having no children of their own, they took great interest in us younger children and found our nonsense quite entertaining. Lorne was a bit of a rule breaker as well, and ended up in trouble with the church for having listened to the radio, which was strictly forbidden. Church discipline was applied quickly, both to bring him to repentance and to serve as a warning to others.

Lenis and Marjorie were quite proper, and always kind. While I never spent much time with their family, I appreciated them, especially Marjorie's thoughtfulness toward my older sisters. Our family didn't know about hygiene in the sense of using deodorant, body sprays, or that sort of thing. We took a bath once a week when we were youngsters, and more frequently as teens, but beyond that good hygiene was not taught. For their birthdays or Christmas, Marjorie always gave my older sisters gifts that included items like deodorant and body sprays. One Christmas, after church, Anna and Tina each carried a gift, wrapped in pretty paper, to the van. Our family seldom gave gifts, other than a few from our parents at Christmas, but we never wrapped them. I was happy for my sisters, and secretly longed for someone to do something like that for me.

"Wow! …What's that?… Who gave it to you?" We all asked questions at once, our curiosity getting the best of us.

"It's from Marjorie," Anna said. She unwrapped her gift, pulled a beautiful red glass cardinal from the box, and held it up. How I wished I was an adult and I could have one! The removable head concealed a little screw-on lid, and inside was the loveliest perfume from Avon. Charisma, it was called. I hoped they still had it when I was a grown-up.

Alvin, the church deacon, and his wife, Erla, had "wild" youth who never seemed quite able to toe the line of church standard. They made their dresses a bit shorter. A bit louder in colour and print. A bit fancier. And they veered from the traditional plain cape dress and added some fancy design of scallops—like those on a cowboy shirt—or gathers and other pretty details. And they were so much fun! The best times were summer nights when Alvin and Erla dropped by to see our family, and we played various lawn games, or did skits and pranks indoors.

My favourite skit was "The Cobbler." A sturdy kitchen chair, laid on its front legs with the backrest sticking out, was the makeshift cobbler's bench. It was completely covered with a blanket, and an unsuspecting participant would be recruited to be the client needing to get a shoe fixed.

The cobbler seated him or herself on the legs of the chair, to hold the bench in place, and the assistant welcomed and seated the client on the backrest. The client was invited to place the foot that wore the shoe needing repair on the cobbler's knee. When the unsuspecting client's foot was raised, and had no support, the cobbler would say, "I need to get another tool, I'll be right back," and rise abruptly, sending the client sprawling across the floor as the "bench" lost its support and tipped.

There were other times when we played card games and board games, but no matter what we did, times spent with the Alvin Gingerich family were always fun. Erla was always prim and proper, her clothes perfectly in place, her hair neatly tucked in her head veiling, and her heart was kind. Alvin, the church deacon, cared much for people, even their health. He knew his vitamins, and for every ailment he had a recommendation. Everyone in church knew it and made fun of him for it, and I could never tell if it was meant to be unkind or not.

Alvin and Erla's daughter Flo, though judged harshly by the church, was beautiful, inside and out. From high cheek bones and perfectly shaped eyebrows, to pretty lips and sparkling eyes, her face looked stunning. Her quiet laugh made a room sparkle, and her boisterous one exuded confidence; a declaration that she was comfortable in her own skin. And whether she had gained a bit of weight, or if she had tried some new diet and lost a lot of weight, made no difference. But the thing that made her most beautiful was her ability to love everyone and connect with anyone, regardless of age, class, or gender. And being a charismatic communicator who passionately pursued God, she inspired me and showed me a relational God.

And then there was Viola Martin. I loved her as much as I loved anyone. She was short and round. Very round. Most people said she was fat—she even said so, and she was funny about it. But, in spite of her weight, she could run. The first time I saw it, when I was eleven, my jaw almost hit the ground. Rumour had it that she weighed nearly three hundred pounds, but to me, none of that mattered. All that mattered was that I seemed to have a place in her heart.

Oh yes, and I mustn't forget, she had no teeth. It was most fascinating to watch her eat an apple. Her gums had toughened over the years and, after gumming her way through the peeling, it made no difference whether she had teeth or not. She told me that she had dentures but they were too uncomfortable and she decided she'd rather do without. Some people made fun of her, but I loved her. She had a heart of gold.

Viola invited me for holidays and sleepovers, sometimes for two or three days at a time, and spent time doing things with me. Sometimes we baked "Bachelor's Button" cookies or some other goodies. Other times she took me to see her neighbour, Gerty, who always gave me treats and thrilled at me being her "namesake." We both did not use our given name—Gertrude—something I preferred not to admit to anyone, ever. (And here I am writing it in a book!)

On one visit Viola did my hair in two braids, with it parted in the middle, like she had with her daughters in the Old Order Mennonite church, and sent me off to school that way. I quite liked it, until I got to school and the children laughed, not to be rude, but because it was different. I felt suddenly self-conscious, and wished I had insisted that she pull it back into a separate hair band at the top, before doing braids. Even so, it had been special that she wanted to make me look like I was one of her girls.

I also shared a birthday with Viola's husband, Seranus, and that was something she always remembered and celebrated. Even many years later, when I was married with children, Viola invited our family for a joint birthday party.

One night, when I was about eleven years old and visiting their home, a violent thunderstorm hit. I slept upstairs in their house, all alone, and would have slept through it, but was awakened when I felt the bed move. It was Viola, worried that I might be frightened by the storm. She explained that she didn't want me alone and afraid, and asked if she could crawl in bed. It was fine with me. I trusted her. Moments later she was sound asleep next to me, snoring loudly. Unable to go back to sleep, I lay awake, listening to the snorts and rumbles, and wishing the thunder would drown it out.

At length, she woke up again, sat up, and announced she was returning downstairs and I should come with her. I told her I would be okay, but she insisted I go with her. Reluctantly I followed her. She crawled in with Seranus, in the middle of the bed, and told me I could have the side. Even as I did so, wearing the most modest of pajamas, I resisted the urge to laugh. It was completely ridiculous!

Seranus, though smaller than Viola, was not a small man. And there was I, thin as a toothpick, in their bed, hoping they would not roll over me in their sleep. It was all perfectly safe and discreet and I never feared any harm or ill intentions, even for a moment, but it was awkward.

No sooner were we all tucked in, than a discordant duet of snores filled the room. I lay awake one more time, listening, wishing I was upstairs, tucked in bed, and sleeping through a thunderstorm, but I lacked the courage to escape.

Bizarre as that night was, I knew Viola cared for me and I could not have been in a safer place. Whatever issues their home had, whatever quirks and dysfunctions, it was one of my favourite places on earth.

I vowed I'd never tell a soul about that night. At eleven the thought of friends knowing was much too embarrassing, and I'd never live down the teasing! I could only pray that Viola, who said almost anything that came to mind, wouldn't blurt it out, especially in front of my friends. And there would be plenty of opportunity, since she drove school children daily.

Viola and Seranus lived north of our home, and Lakeshore school was southwest of us. Attending private school was an important part of the Conservative Mennonite culture and, if not enforced, it was strongly recommended.

This posed many problems for my parents. The cost of sending us and the challenge of getting us to and from school would have made it impossible without the help of the church. As a result, each morning found us in Seranus and Viola's station wagon, headed for Lakeshore Christian School, often singing, talking, or laughing, and occasionally fighting.

In many ways the church carried the weight of responsibility for us, where my parents lacked the resources or ability to do so, especially with the cultural expectations.

Even Morton, the lead minister who showed up with the little black book, and his wife, Elda, showed great kindness to our family, in many ways. When my mother was hospitalized after a vein burst in her leg—spraying blood up to the ceiling in their bedroom—the church helped with meals, and Elda personally came to check on us, giving some of us hugs and kisses. "Those are from your mom," she said. Though I highly doubted that, since mom never hugged or kissed us, the affection felt good.

This mixed message, offering kindness in practical ways, in contrast with the spiritual control in other ways, entangled with protecting their own families while dealing harshly with others, added to my confusion. On the one hand they were our "saviour"; on the other they robbed us of life and hope. Because they held so much power, prestige, and popularity, and we were the underdogs, we constantly reached for their approval.

As a result, it was nearly impossible to discern good from evil, right from wrong. Appearing well-meaning and kind, while misrepresenting and blurring the image of God, they warped what it means to have a relationship with Him.

It was here, in these years of confusion with God and religion, that an old struggle resurfaced. Men had all the power, and seemed always to abuse it, and women were sex objects, meant to be appropriately covered to prevent men from sinning, and with nothing to offer outside of marriage. And in marriage they made babies, kept their homes, and helped with farming. But, by all appearances, their voices were silenced, with nothing of value to offer from the heart or spirit.

Again I resented being female. I slipped into Wil's jeans one day and stood there asking God if He couldn't still make me a boy. I was certain He could, if He felt so inclined—being the Creator and all—but wasn't sure if He would want to.

Still, I felt as though there was something in me that had purpose. A destiny. And if He wasn't going to turn me into a boy, there had to be something else for me. Bishops seemed to be the ones with influence...

"Maybe God will make me be a bishop's wife, one day," I mused out loud.

Chapter Ten

School was a highlight during my years at Lakeshore. I loved to learn, but more than that, it was an escape from home. Whatever wasn't right in the classroom, for the most part, still felt safer than home.

Many factors played into making a school year good, or not so good, but the teacher was the strongest influence. I liked most of mine, most of the time, and some of them all of the time.

Viola Martin's daughter, Sister Laurene, taught me for the first two years at Lakeshore. Though quite strict, she exercised self-control even when she was cross, and had a good sense of humour. When she laughed, her eyes twinkled, as if they had their own little dance party happening.

Each morning, being a Christian school, we started with devotions and a time of prayer. During prayer I had my own secret routine. While everyone else prayed, I ducked my head down and looked up at Sister Laurene while she prayed, and watched her lips move, upside-down, creating my own private cartoon show. I never got caught, and I didn't do it to be naughty, but, however irreverent, it was entertaining.

My favourite part of the day with Sister Laurene was story time after noon recess. When she read, stories came to life in my mind and imagination, and she always knew where to stop to create a sense of anticipation for the next day. The best was when she glanced at the clock and knew it was time to get back to work, but instead she would surprise us by reading a few more pages.

Nonetheless, my report card, starting that first year in a Christian school, changed dramatically in tone from public school. Every report card prior to Christian school described me as a friendly, pleasant, and good student. But the day I set foot in the Christian school I was a misfit. While some teachers were more gracious than others, every one commented on my lack of self-control, my immaturity, and my desire for attention.

It was all in perspective. The same personality traits that had made me a good student in public school made me "bad" in my new surroundings. I didn't fit the mould, and I needed fixing, in their minds. At age ten Sister

Laurene wrote on my report card that I needed to "learn self-discipline in being sober-minded, diligent, and to 'act her age' in general." She went on to say that my nonsense was designed to attract attention from other students.

While she may have been right, it was simply me being "me," and I suddenly realized being "me" wasn't acceptable. The following year was similar, with a few more corrections, including the need to "control her emotions."

These emotions were usually, if not always, laughter and giggles, albeit at all the wrong times. When something struck me funny, all the tension from home life that was looking for release gave way into giggles. It started somewhere deep inside, at the tiniest hint of a funny thought, and I would find myself shaking with giggles, or laughing out loud. Occasionally it came out in anger, but not often. And in either case, it was not acceptable.

In this way the life was snuffed out of certain temperaments and personalities, as each child was shaped into an ideal, relatively emotionless creature who was to think a certain way, look a certain way, and most definitely act a certain way.

Brother Paul Zehr, whom I had next, taught the older grades and served as the school principal when I was in sixth grade. A tender-hearted, compassionate man, he was an excellent teacher. Only on one occasion do I recall being kept in at recess for disobeying him and breaking some rule. He said little that recess, but the little he said cut to my heart.

Accustomed to being yelled at, or beaten, and even fearing for my life if I did wrong at home, had made me tough and strong. But not tough enough to withstand the gentleness I encountered in Brother Paul that day. He wasn't angry. He didn't raise his voice. Instead, he spoke calmly, his voice filled with sadness and genuine concern for my well-being. He wasn't done with his few sentences before I began to cry. I apologized and made a silent vow to be good. And try I did!

His report card showed the same gentleness, and reflected precisely what I experienced that day. "...Her conduct was not always good, but is easy to bring to contrition. She will need to be controlled and guided."

Each of these teachers taught me something of God that played a role in opening my heart to Him. Sister Laurene brought the stories of the Bible to life in me, and Brother Paul's response to my failure gave me a glimpse of a God who might truly love His children and offer grace.

****

In November 1981, shortly before I turned twelve, I attended revival meetings where a dynamic "hell-fire and brimstone" preacher, Paul Ebersole, spoke at our "sister church" in New Hamburg. You could say he "scared the hell right out of me" that night. There was no way I was going to burn for eternity, separated from God.

At the end of the "invitation," as they sang "Only Trust Him," my heart began to beat wildly in my chest. I stared at my shoes, fighting a torrent of emotions. If I stood, my father's rage would resurface and only God could tell what he might do. His rage, only days earlier when Wil had made this decision, was vile and terrifying. What if my decision escalated it? What if he killed us?

But I had waited long enough. I had prayed that God would spare my life until I was old enough to accept Jesus, and He had. If I was old enough to count the cost of accepting Jesus, and conclude that even death was worth it, then I was old enough. At the end of the song, when I was certain I was willing to go home and die, if that was the outcome, I stood to my feet, weeping.

Having fought tears through the entire song before finally making that decision, it felt as though all the trauma of the years burst like a dam and spilled from my soul.

I went to the prayer room afterward, where one of the ministers, Aaron Martin, and his wife, Nancy, greeted me. They were kind and gentle. With the purest of intentions, they led me to a quiet Sunday school room downstairs for a one-on-one session. In gentle tones, Aaron read John 1:9. "If we confess our sins, He is faithful and just to forgive us..." and then, together, Aaron and Nancy questioned me, just as gently. Why had I stood? What sins had I committed? What did I need to repent of?

I was stumped. I didn't know of any major sins in my life. I was eleven. I just knew that my heart had cried out for something for years already, and I really hoped they could help me understand it. But I didn't know how to say that, so I searched deep for any sin I might be able to confess to fill that empty place in my heart, and somehow make my inside right with God.

"I cheated in school once or twice," I said. I had already apologized to the teacher, but it was something; a sin to confess. I couldn't think of anything else of consequence. I acknowledged not always listening well and obeying authority and said I would try to do better in that. They prayed with me, asking God to forgive me for my sins, and we parted ways.

I wasn't sure if the thing I had hoped for had in fact happened, but I felt a new boldness and courage rise up in me. Even if only temporarily. I had read countless stories of people who had sacrificed their lives for their faith in Jesus, and that was what I longed for, that nothing would ever stand between me and Him.

After my time with Aaron and Nancy, I went out to the van, to see if my family was ready to go. My father was not there yet—having himself asked for prayer, and met with another leader—but my mother and younger siblings were waiting. I jumped into the back seat, seeking solitude.

"Trudy, what have you done?" my mother asked, as soon as I was settled. Her voice was airy and tense—just as it was that day when I was six, and found her at the neighbour's house. My heart sank just a little.

"I did what I had to do," I said matter-of-factly.

"But what if your father is angry and kills us?" she asked.

"Then I would rather die knowing Jesus," I answered.

"When we get home, you will go see your father, when he goes to our bedroom, and you will tell him you didn't mean it, that you just felt bad about some things," she instructed.

"I will talk to him," I said, "but I will tell him the truth." And that is just what I did. I knocked on their bedroom door when I heard dad reading his Bible, and asked if I could come in. He didn't look me in the eye, but he listened.

When I had said, the best I knew how, that I wanted my life to be God's, he responded with, "Then go live it." And the conversation was over.

We were taught that "being good" was the proof of salvation, so I tried, from that day forward, to live up to the expectations of the church, the school, and my father. I tried to become soft-spoken and a quiet-kind-of-sweet young girl, obeying all the rules and being "meek." That is what good Christian women do and are. But, try as I might, life and my personality constantly got in my way, and I fell short.

Rather than losing their grip on me, my father's rage and control toyed with my mind more than ever, after that November night. More than before, I feared that he would act on his threats to murder us. Or me, specifically.

Numerous times, when older siblings made the decision to accept Jesus, dad had become angry. It was years before I understood that his reaction was fearing the loss of control over his family. The church was structured in a way that it made him feel powerless as a father and when children made that "faith decision" it placed teens in direct accountability to the church, and allowed the church to overrule a parent's authority. Not understanding this, I was confused as to why he hated us for choosing the faith he also professed to embrace.

One of my most haunting fears, after that November night, was that my father would shoot me "accidentally," pretending to hunt birds—a sport he engaged in often.

This fear gripped me so powerfully that I could hardly walk from the house to our barn. Whether it was broad daylight, semi-darkness, or the dead of night, that walk terrified me and I usually ran as fast as my legs would carry me, and arrived panting at the other building. Sometimes, in an effort to conquer the fear, I would force myself to move more slowly and sing hymns as I walked, trying to chase away the demons that haunted my mind.

Dad's ongoing violent outbursts didn't help. The sound of his booming voice when he flew into a rage had a way of sending electrical currents all the way down to my toes. And the instant that passed, my own anger at the injustice would rise to the surface, intertwined at times with a debilitating blend of hatred and compassion. I felt sorry for him, for the bondage he was in, but wanted the violence to stop.

On two occasions Wil physically restrained me when I threatened to call the police. I was sure the police would take dad away and never let him hurt us again. I've learned a lot about law enforcement since then. I know now that they usually take them away, right after they kill someone. That is, if they haven't already killed themselves. But, in my naivety I truly believed our world would be safe if I made that one call, and Wil assured me it would end my suffering forever, when dad got hold of me. When the heat of the moment passed, I was secretly thankful he had stopped me because somehow I knew he was right.

As siblings our conversations about the violence were limited to moments of outburst, panic, or some anger muttered in disdain. There were occasional discussions, but most of these were older siblings and mom talking, and younger children were quickly silenced and shooed away.

There was one occasion where Wil, Nancy, Margaret—who was next older than Nancy—and I sat down to devise a plan to rock our father's world and make him repent. Dad was quite fearful of the spiritual realm, and of ghosts and spirits in particular, and we saw that as an opportunity. We would get up in the middle of the night, when we were certain he was asleep, and give him a ghost encounter.

To accomplish this we would need a galvanized tub, some rope, and a white bed sheet. One of us would be the ghost and, with the sheet draped over us, would be lowered in the galvanized tub, out of Wil's window, which was directly over my parents' bedroom window. The other three would hold the ropes to lower and raise the "ghost." When directly in front of dad's window, the ghost would rap three times, in slow succession, before speaking to dad in German, on a first-name basis, with the same deliberate slowness. We sat there and practiced, with our most haunting voices, as if auditioning for a play:

"Peita..." (pause)... "Peita..." (pause)... "Peita." Our voices grew in volume, intensity, and firmness, each time we spoke his name, and faded each time. We imagined him sitting up in bed, terrified and confused, then continued planning what we would say next. There was some debate as to what would be most effective, but we concluded we would need to confront how he treated his family, and urge him to repent. We imagined it as a "forever" turning point in his life, bringing love and peace to our home.

We laughed and planned a long while, but never carried it out. The whole thing was too risky. If anything made him suspicious that his children had done this, it would be our end.

As my longing for freedom grew more desperate, I took to praying a morbid prayer. I asked God to make my parents repent and then let them run into a bridge or die suddenly some other way.

That solution seemed, from my vantage point, the most merciful thing a loving God could do. I didn't want my parents to suffer in hell for all the horrible things we had suffered at home, but neither did I want them to be my parents anymore. I was afraid that even if they acknowledged the evil, and repented for their sins, they would slip back into it and we'd all be back to where we started. An immediate death upon repentance seemed the perfect "seal" for their eternal well-being, and my freedom.

Every time things were going good, and they started functioning in a healthier way, it seemed some hell would break loose and disrupt life. This made it impossible to truly love even the good moments. And sometimes the smallest things did it. In hindsight, having had some life experience to fall back on, I see that my father was a fearful and insecure man, and that insecurity triggered his responses. But as a child there was no way to understand or process that. Nor should a child need to.

And some outbursts were caused by innocent misunderstandings. One evening, for example, dad told a funny story and in the story a dog walked around the corner of a house. But, in telling the story, dad jumbled his words and said, "the corner of the house walked around the dog."

Abe, who was seven, and quite a little mischief—not to mention the baby of the family and accustomed to attention—interrupted dad to repeat the mistake, followed by an outburst of laughter.

You could see the adrenaline surge as veins and eyes bulged and dad's face turned red with rage. "Did you just make fun of me?" dad asked. And before Abe could respond or defend himself he added, "Go get the strap. This you will only do once. You will learn not to mock your father."

The colour drained simultaneously from every face at the table, especially Abe's. And almost in sync, each one pushed their chair back and left the room. Dinner was over. No need to stick around and watch the beating. Even mom disappeared.

I found myself standing there alone, at age thirteen, wanting to pick a fight with dad, just to distract him. I never fought with dad, at least not willingly. This was different. It was my baby brother who had meant no harm. I would take a stand against dad's violence.

I began clearing the table—not a task I typically helped with. My chores were in the barn, working with animals and all the fun stuff that goes with that. It was one of my favourite places in the world. When it came time for dishes, I scattered and preferred not to return until it was all done. The house, and keeping it, was my least favourite thing in the world. Cleaning stalls in the barn, and shoveling manure, was far more fun. But not that night. That night the kitchen was my priority. I made a silent vow that if dad beat Abe, I would pick up the phone and report him, or take matters in my own hands. I had held his rifles when he wasn't around, just to see if I had it in me, should the need arise. One way or another, it would be his last act of violence in our home, if I could help it.

I stopped clearing the table long enough to look him in the eye. The warning look that says, "If you do, there will be a price." It's a look most parents use—especially moms—though without the threat, when a child is crossing a line. A look I should not have had to use on my dad.

He looked at me. "Well, what are you staring at?" he asked.

He had taken the bait. Fear surged through my body, deeper and harder than I anticipated. I pushed it down and said nothing. Picked up a few more plates. Stopped, now and then, and looked at him. But I never spoke a word in confrontation.

Abe returned with the strap, fear in his eyes. I recognized it—that terrible feeling I had experienced a few times with whippings. I had seen it in siblings, what seemed like a thousand times or more. It probably was.

Dad looked at Abe. He looked at me. He took the strap and held it. He never raised his hand to strike. He simply talked to Abe sternly for a moment about respecting his elders and not making fun of his father.

Abe promised never to do it again, asked for forgiveness, and was released to go.

I continued clearing the table. Dad rose from his chair and went out to the machine shop to work on some project he had on the go. We never spoke a word about our interaction. It was a silent exchange that made me realize he had a weak spot. He was not as strong as he appeared, and if only we dared to stand against the evil, we could make a difference. It empowered me in a strange way, but immediately after our silent confrontation, I had a lot of fear and trauma to deal with.

The moment dad was out the door, my body began to tremble and that inner anxiety rose to the surface. I had to find a way to get it out of my system, and talking was my outlet. I chattered incessantly, to any unsuspecting audience who might listen, adding an occasional nervous laugh, as I de-stressed. Eventually my body stopped trembling, and my mind stopped racing.

The truth settled deep: I had stopped dad, and spared my brother a beating.

While my father's temper was usually a threat to his family, and we suffered the consequences, there were times when it ran him into trouble as well. Wil and I were in the barn one Saturday afternoon, cleaning out the manure, when it happened. Over time we had collected an impressive heap in the large open area of the barn, where it stayed until we could load it on the manure spreader to take out to the fields.

Dad rarely did anything in the barn, which was just as well, because his temper with animals was ungodly, at best, on a good day. But every now and then, he would go on a mission to "train" a particular creature, as was the case that day.

He tied one end of a rope around a heifer, intending to "tame" it and teach it a lesson, probably for breaking through the electric fence, or some such offence. He wrapped the other end securely around his hand.

Dad was a strong man who could typically control a beast with what seemed little effort. He showed us how to grab a cow by the horns and flip it, simply by twisting the horns a particular way. At will he could make a creature do a summersault that way, landing on its side, with him in charge.

That was my expectation in the barn that day. He had the added adrenaline and strength, thanks to his temper, and the heifer wasn't as large as other animals he had mastered. But all situations are not equal. When he lost his temper and yelled, the startled creature took off so abruptly, it took my father off guard.

In an instant my father took off running behind the heifer at a rate of speed I had never seen him travel before. Especially not in confined spaces. With the rope still wrapped around his hand, so that he could not simply let go, he had little choice but to dodge cement pillars and try to keep up with the creature.

He managed to dig in his feet at one point, to slow things down, but the heifer outsmarted him and ran over the manure pile. Timing is everything. The heifer flipped dad onto the manure pile and dragged him through it, flat on his belly. Somehow he kept his face up.

Wil and I, who were to "watch and learn" and maybe help a little, suddenly scattered, dodging out of sight. I ducked behind a cement partition, torn between laughter and tears. It was the funniest thing I had ever seen, but if my father caught me laughing, I would get thrashed. And, truth be told, I felt sorry for him.

There was something about seeing him stripped of all dignity that tugged at my heart. I managed only to snicker quietly, while choking back tears, before composing myself enough to come out and act concerned.

****

In all the violence, chaos, and confusion, there was no safe place to turn at home, even when my father wasn't there. While I spent little time with my mother, and therefore had little personal experience with her violence, I saw enough to know she was not innocent.

Summers at home were the hardest, day after day, in a home with so many children and not enough love to go around. Whether canning, butchering, or gardening, or out in the fields picking cucumbers again, like we had when we first moved to Canada, it was hard slogging to get through those weeks.

While aspects of these tasks were enjoyable, the inevitable spats and threats cast a dark shadow on everything we did. My mother, who was exasperated with us, overwhelmed with life, and surviving a hopeless marriage merely out of a sense of duty and lack of alternatives, took out her feelings on us.

I walked into the kitchen one hot summer day and caught mom and one of my sisters in the middle of a fight. Both in a rage, one threatened to throw boiling water over the other, and the other threatened to do some vile thing in return. My vivid imagination saw it all play out as if it were already happening. I shuddered and left the house, frustrated with their immaturity. Frustrated that my sister didn't respect mom, and mom didn't control herself, and reach out to her hurting daughter.

I had seen mom, when I was about six years old, hit Tina across the face with a hairbrush, and then, when I was about eight, my second oldest brother, Jacob, had come for a visit and she got in a fight with him, and chased him with a rolling pin over her shoulder. He backed away slowly, his arm raised in defense. And I had seen her many times giving merciless whippings to siblings and had even been the recipient of a few.

Having those images branded on my memory, I could visualize the threats as if they were reality, and it was all too much. Outdoors, and in the barn, my world was safe with the animals. No fights. No threats. And no grumbling.

Grumbling was the one thing that prevailed, when there was no fighting. And listening to mom grumble about dad was the worst. I hated it. It was so wrong, in my mind, for me to need to listen to this. Their marriage was not my problem. Dad's rage and hatred for mom was not my problem.

I had felt only compassion as a child, but by my late preteens and early teens that compassion had dissolved into resentment. It felt as if mom used me, and drew me into her trauma by making me feel sorry for her.

****

87

It was a beautiful summer day. I was happy. The world was perfect. When mom asked me to help her hang up laundry, I cringed. This meant standing there, bored out of my mind, and mindlessly handing clothes pins to her. A perfect waste of beautiful weather. But I had no choice.

No more were we into doing laundry, and the grumbling started about dad. The way he treated her. His anger. His disrespect. How terrible a man he was. How evil…. This continued until I could bear it no longer. My tolerance meter dropped suddenly to zero, and I turned, silently walking away and into the kitchen.

When mom realized I was no longer there, and she was talking to herself, she became angry and started after me. Inside, she got the strap and met me in the kitchen. I saw her coming and got a few steps ahead of her, walking around the table, making sure to keep a good distance between us. When I made it back around to the door, I walked out, leaving her with the strap over her shoulder.

"Trudy, get back here! Right now!" she called from the porch.

I kept walking. Only a fool would go back for a ruthless strapping.

"Trudy!! Right now!!" she yelled again. When I still didn't respond, she added, "If you don't, I will tell dad when he gets home."

That got my attention. I stopped, turned, and looked her in the eye. "And then I will tell him that you were grumbling about him, and I will tell him all the nasty things you said. So go ahead!" She turned then and walked into the house, and never brought it up again.

It is one of only a few times I remember being boldly disrespectful to my mother. My father was strict about respect. Even though he wasn't particularly respectful to mom half the time, his expectation of us was that we respect and obey mom. If ever he caught us being anything less, a good thrashing was the likely outcome.

And mostly I didn't have a hard time with treating mom respectfully, and liked doing special things for her, now and then. When we made crafts at school for Mother's Day, I did so with great pride. I liked the way she laughed and lit up at seeing the things we gave her. It was in those moments when life was, in my mind, what it should be.

Chapter Eleven

As if all the drama and trauma of home life was not enough, along with the emotional baggage of buried memories of childhood sexual victimization, stress started in other areas of my life.

At school there were several abusive incident in grade seven, with Brother Elmer Martin, Viola's son, as my teacher. While a delightful teacher, in some ways, he had one weakness—his temper. For all the instructions I had been given to control my emotions and exercise self-discipline as a student, the same would have done him some good, rather than reacting.

A favourite of his was rapping students on the head if they didn't meet his expectations. Elton, a student from a Native reserve in Northern Ontario, started school at Lakeshore that year, having been placed in one of the church's homes, and he knew how to push buttons. When Brother Elmer rapped him on the head one day, he blurted out, with his eyes crossed, "Noogeee!" and the whole class erupted in laughter.

Pinching ears was Brother Elmer's other punishment of choice. If students didn't focus on their work, or were caught monkeying around in some way, he would sneak up behind them and pinch their ears aggressively.

I was the recipient of this on at least one occasion. And it made me mad. As he walked away, I took my hair that was neatly tucked back under my white head covering, and yanked it forward on both sides so that not a speck of my ears was left showing. This was as much a statement as any I could make, since the church constitution strictly forbade combing hair more than halfway down the ear.

While completely acceptable in the culture, these forms of discipline were disrespectful, abusive, and counterproductive, making it impossible to respect those in leadership over us. In fairness to Brother Elmer, we were probably the most hurting and bratty bunch of children any teacher had ever contended with at Lakeshore. My attention span was just a tad shy of a goldfish on a good day, and combined with my love for mischief—though I meant no harm—it worked against me, and exasperated more than one teacher. And I was not the only such student.

Even Brother Tom, who was also the church deacon, when he substituted took to yelling at Wil and me in the middle of class one day. Being a man of small stature, with a fine build and soft voice, the explosion was doubly shocking. His massive hands collided in a startling smack, followed by him yelling at the top of his lungs—which, at loudest volume was fairly quiet, albeit shockingly intense.

"This. Is. Not. A. Game. Of. Cat. And. Mouse!!!!" he shouted, emphasising each word.

It was all I could do to keep from laughing, if only because my graphic imagination immediately had a *Tom & Jerry* cartoon going on. That was the problem. My mind always pictured things and experienced life in such bizarre ways, and I didn't know what to do with it. I really, truly didn't want to be bad…

And, lest my teachers should feel as though they accomplished nothing, I did learn from them. On one of the days when Brother Tom substituted, his devotions were on Isaiah 28, "Line upon line, precept upon, precept… Here a little, there a little…" He taught us the importance of knowing God's Word and reinforcing truths through repetition—a life-altering truth I carry with me still, and use in working with sexual abuse victims.

Brother Elmer was, in many ways and even most of the time, an engaging teacher; a brilliant mathematician, with quick and entertaining wit. Had his time teaching at Lakeshore not been clouded over with abusive moments, it would all have been different. And, had teachers been trained to spot and reach out to troubled and abused children, we would have responded differently. All we wanted was to be understood, cared for, and loved in a godly way. But we didn't know it then, and they didn't either.

Grade eight was a much better year. Brother Mark Wayne was much like Brother Paul in that he never treated students with disrespect. He had one weakness, and it made him even more endearing. He had a sense of humour, making it easy to disarm him, and even when scolding us, a twinkle often played in his eyes. When the twinkle was gone—and I only saw that a few times—he was truly cross. Still, he remained self-controlled and kind. It was impossible to disrespect him.

One day Wil, at fifteen, was upset with Phil Martin, a student in grade six, and in frustration said, "You are so stupid!"

Brother Mark Wayne overheard this and called Wil out on it, and led him to the classroom for a scolding. When he finished, Wil emerged, to apologize to Phil, as he had been instructed.

From where I stood, I could see Brother Mark Wayne by the open window, just above where Phil stood, making sure Wil followed through. Wil walked to Phil, looked him in the eye, and said, "Phil, I'm sorry you're so stupid!"

Up in the classroom, Brother Mark Wayne burst out laughing, completely taken off guard by Wil's nonsense. Needless to say he reappeared, having composed himself, and sternly ordered Wil back into the school.

For a short time I loved life, and hope stirred in my heart. But it would soon be snuffed out again...

****

Bruce, a young man not quite two years older than I, started paying attention to me at school, mostly during recess. It began with innocent teasing and playful attention, the kind that made me feel like I was no longer overlooked.

My older brother had married into Bruce's "freinschaft" in September, at the beginning of the school year, and that is when it started. I assumed this created, for Bruce, a sense of connection to me personally and give him the right to tease me like my brothers did.

At the wedding his older brother, Owen, who had been excommunicated from the Mennonite church, had asked Bruce who the "cute little blonde girl" was, and Bruce told me. I was flattered.

At recess, Bruce occasionally referred to me, in a teasing way, as "the cute little blonde girl," something I pretended to mind, though I really didn't. I had always thought of myself as "plain" and not as pretty as other girls. For someone to think I was cute—that there was nothing wrong with me—made me feel special. I had no idea that it was "flirting," and maybe it wasn't, at first. The innocent teasing continued, off and on, until one day, when I walked into the two-room school to get a Kleenex, and everything changed.

91

Bruce's desk was near the front, like mine, and as I approached, he stood to his feet and walked toward me. He stopped beside my desk and stood, with arms spread out, as if blocking me. I walked slowly. Uncertain.

"I need to get to my desk... I need a Kleenex," I said, pausing. He shifted, leaving a bit more room for me to reach the front of my desk. His eyes fixed intensely on me.

"Are you winning the football game?" he asked, engaging in awkward small talk. His voice had a raspy softness.

And then, in an instant, I was in his arms. My heart melted. I had never been held by a male, and seldom hugged by anyone. In that closeness I felt something I craved. He released me almost immediately, without any further advances.

The next time he put his arms around me, something was different. The smell of Wild Country aftershave tingled my senses. Intoxicating. I closed my eyes and breathed deep, as if willing the scent to leave a "forever imprint" in my memory. And it did.

He kissed me then, a little peck on my cheek. It shocked me. I had never been kissed by a boy, or even appropriately hugged or kissed by family. The only kisses I knew previously were through the sweet affection of my friend Christa, and Grandma Steckle.

In that moment with Bruce, a deeper desire awakened in me. The innocence of childhood crushes replaced by a desire for relationship and commitment. Still, the sexual nature of it escaped me. A moment later he kissed me again, but this kiss was different. It was intrusive, repulsive, and felt violating, as he pushed his tongue in my mouth. I cringed. He pressed his body close. Much too close. I turned my face away, looking down. Ashamed. This wasn't what I had imagined it would be like, to have a boy like me.

In the days and weeks that followed, Bruce continued making random advances on me, grabbing me as I walked past him on the stairway, or pressing his body against me aggressively, when he had the opportunity. I desperately wanted affection, but not these strange behaviours.

Having never been taught about male anatomy, I had no concept of what was happening to his body, or any awareness that the end goal might be intercourse and penetration. I was oblivious to these facts of life, having only witnessed and experienced molestation in other forms.

Being a friend of my brother gave him access, not only at school, but on one occasion, also in our home. The Sunday Bruce was at our home, we went on a walk in the woods at the back of our property, as a group of youth and children, as we did with most company.

"Why don't we go see the animals in the barn?" Bruce said when we returned from the walk, looking at me. Wil jumped in and said we would do it together.

The smell of animals, hay, and straw, greeted us, accompanied by their various sounds, as we entered the barn. My comfort zone. How I loved the barn, smells and all! We only had two cows, a few calves, and various fowl. I showed him my favourite, a red and white calf that was mentally retarded since birth.

"Wil, why don't you go in and change, and get ready for chores?" Bruce suggested. "Trudy can finish showing me around, and I'll help you when you get back." Wil insisted on staying, but eventually gave in, leaving me alone with Bruce.

Bruce walked back to the red and white calf and asked a few questions. As I answered, he moved closer. He took my hand, tugged at his belt, and tried to get me to reach in his pants. My heart stopped. I pulled back. Whatever he wanted, I wasn't interested. Too afraid to look in his eyes, I simply shook my head, looking down in shame. I wanted to run but I was trapped by fear, frozen. I clutched my hands firmly, close to my body.

"Are you going to be a good girl?" he asked, mocking.

My voice caught in my throat. The words refused to form. I nodded. Of course I wanted to be a good girl. I could feel the lump growing...

I pulled away. My mind felt numb as his hands wandered over my body, fondling me in ways and places he had never done before. I felt unexplainable fear as he fondled my breasts and disregarded that I had just said no. Then, abruptly, he picked me up and started walking. Where was he taking me? What did he want? Everything felt wrong.

"How heavy is she?" Wil's voice startled Bruce. He dropped me.

"About three hundred pounds."

The instant my feet hit the floor, I fled. Shaken to the core, I didn't stop until I was in my bedroom, where I wouldn't have to see anyone, talk to anyone, or be with anyone. I wanted to be alone.

I don't know how long I sat there, my heart racing, fear surging through my body with every heartbeat. What if dad found out? He would beat me to a bloody pulp. And mom too. Somehow this had to be my secret. Mine and Wil's.

The door to my bedroom opened. My heart pounding, I braced myself for the worst and was relieved when Anna, not dad, walked in. She sat on the edge of my bed. *Wil must have told her.* I groaned inwardly.

Anna began asking questions… far too many questions. What did he do? Did he kiss my cheeks or my lips? The questions seemed to go on and on.

I answered reluctantly, but honestly, offering no information she didn't directly ask for. I really didn't want anyone to know where or how he had touched me or what he had tried to do. I wanted the memories to go away.

It felt too much like the shame of those early years—the days when I felt dirty all the time. Only now it was worse because now my body responded in ways it had not responded then—responses I didn't understand, having been awakened, but not explained. Now the violation produced pleasant physical responses that contradicted the psychological trauma that tormented my mind. It made me angry to feel so vulnerable. Why did my feelings betray me? I hated my body. I hated him. And yet, I had bonded, in a way, and discovered the desire for physical relationship. It was all so strange, and part of me wanted more hugs, more closeness, but without the "yucky" stuff.

A year or two earlier I had suggested to a girl, about six months younger than I, that we put our bodies together. Though I had no understanding of sexuality and the inappropriateness of that act, I immediately felt guilty. I wrote her a note, soon after, asking her to forgive me. I didn't really understand why, but I knew it made God sad, I wrote, and I was truly sorry.

Even without any teaching, my conscience had told me it was wrong, and I had vowed I would never suggest such a thing again, or have any part in it. By the time Bruce molested me, I had blocked that memory completely, as well as all memories of childhood molestation. Each event, in this way, became a new trauma, linked only subconsciously to previous abuses and experience.

I learned years later that I was not Bruce's only victim. Several young men had reportedly been victimized by him, including my brother. While Bruce denied allegations of victimizing my brother, he did acknowledge that they were sexually involved, but said it was mutual. This argument might have worked, had a witness not come to me more than twenty years later, to tell me the location and exactly what happened.

But there was more to the story. A man in his thirties, who dressed like the Mennonites, travelled from church to church, community to community, and took advantage of young men and boys, sexually. How many victims he had, no one but God will ever know for sure. But Bruce was one of his victims, and the same man attempted to violate at least one of my brothers.

Just when I thought life couldn't get any worse, the rumours started. The youth in other churches heard the gossip: Trudy is a second-hand girl... Bruce and Trudy kissed... Trudy is wild.... Trudy is boy crazy...

My already-devastated self-image took a hard hit. I hated that people knew about it, and felt further victimized by their "knowing," and the awareness that I was different from any other Mennonite girl. They were pure, I had been touched. Used. Perverted.

I was unclean.

This emotional, sexual, and spiritual confusion overlapped with the traditional "Instruction Classes," a requirement in preparation for church membership. I was too young the previous year, they said, when Wil, Floyd, Bruce, and David—Viola's son—were baptized, and was asked to wait until I was a bit older.

I accepted the delay graciously. But the year that ensued robbed me of innocence and, in some ways, moved my heart further from God, and deeper into performance and survival. In the same way that I had hoped making a commitment to Christ would "fix" me and make me "good," I now hoped that baptism and church membership would do so.

We learned, in Instruction Class, about many of the core values and beliefs of the church, and Mennonite doctrine and ordinances. The part about Baptism that said we are "made new creatures in Christ" gave me hope. I would be buried with Jesus, through baptism, and would emerge on the other side of that experience, a completely different person.

I enjoyed Instruction Classes, for the most part. In these sessions the leaders shone. Really and truly they showed grace and God's kind heart in ways that I longed for desperately. Peter Steckle, who maintained a warm place in my heart in all my time at Lakeshore, offered his quiet strength. Never did I see him riled or lacking in kindness. Morton spoke with fatherliness, smiling warmly at us, and leaning forward, hands pressed earnestly together on his lap—often with his Bible squeezed between—as if wanting to connect at a heart level.

In ways, I adored these leaders, and found myself wanting desperately a place in their hearts and in their church. And that was the hardest part; even when they did things that seemed so wrong, they were kind about it, as if it were the most Christ-like thing to do. From time to time they "blew it," but mostly they maintained an image of perfection and "goodness," making us sinners feel helplessly guilty.

This was the case when an anonymously concerned individual went to these same leaders with an accusation against my one sister for a certain "sin" or inappropriate behaviour. This anonymous reporting—running to leaders about another member—we called "shooting from behind the preachers" or "shooting from behind the pulpit." Not only was it a most cowardly act of self-preservation—all in the name of love and concern—it also disregarded biblical instruction, in Matthew 18, for believers to go, first, directly to the person with whom the offence lies, and go to leaders only if the individual is unrepentant. Somehow anonymous concerns had become the acceptable way of dealing with problems, and the ministry catered to it.

Upon presenting my sister with the accusations against her, she said she knew nothing of the offence. But they insisted on her guilt because their information had come from a reliable source. Still, she maintained her innocence. At length one leader lost his patience and blurted out, "You are just like your father."

Backed into a corner, facing either discipline or confessing to a sin she did not commit, my sister chose the latter and made a public confession. These were the types of things that made even the most solid of teaching, along with their kindness, bewildering.

That aside, much of what we learned in that class was Basic Christianity and Discipleship 101 and, at its core, biblically accurate. Though there was cultural interpretation intertwined with the teaching, I gained valuable truths that would empower me in my walk with God. Truths that I would eventually strip naked of cultural ties and beliefs, and continue to embrace for life—the simple, naked truth.

When we had completed the Instruction for Believers book, we spent some time studying the Constitution, and learning the rules of the church that we would be expected to follow. Having been carefully taught on all aspects of church doctrine, beliefs, and practices, if we were willing to commit to the church, and if the leaders deemed us ready, we moved ahead with baptism.

On May 22, 1983, at age thirteen, I knelt beside a few friends at the front of Lakeshore church, while Morton, along with one of the other leaders, walked by us, pausing before each candidate with a pitcher of water. Morton cupped his hands on our hands, while the other minister poured water into them, and onto our heads. This pouring, rather than immersing, was symbolic of the Holy Spirit poured onto God's people, in the New Testament.

When each candidate was baptized, the leaders made their rounds again and the bishop reached out his hand to each one, saying, "In the name of Jesus Christ, I give you my hand. Arise! And just as Christ was raised from the dead, so thou shalt also walk in newness of life. And as long as thou are faithful, keeping the commandments of Christ and the church, thou shalt be a member of the body of Christ, and a sister (or brother) in this church..." or something to that effect.

Following a hearty handshake from the ministry team, each "sister" would be greeted for the first time with the Holy Kiss by the bishop's wife, and possibly a minister's wife, who would have joined him by this time. The bishop and minister would greet the new "brothers" warmly, welcoming them into fellowship as well.

After the service candidates remained at the front while the congregation filed by, also welcoming, encouraging, and admonishing the new members. To say it was overwhelming at that young age would be a serious understatement. But, at the same time, there was a part of it that felt warm and filled with blessing.

The following day an older brother and his wife took me and my best friend and classmate, Carolyn Roth, to Blue Mountain, in Collingwood, Ontario. The mountains rose majestically before us as we drew closer. A once-familiar thrill rose in my chest...

We chose a trail and set out to climb the mountain, stopping to read the markers with interesting facts, and finding humour in "Fat Man's Misery"—a particularly narrow place in the rocks—and other creative names throughout. Following a quick lunch at Georgian Bay, we walked the shores for a while, basking in the sunshine and captivated by the wonder of creation. Cool breezes, coming from the water, teased our warm skin, reminding us it was still spring. The day couldn't have been more beautiful. But the most special part of the day was having an older sibling celebrate my life this way. The whole church membership thing was off to a good start. Maybe there was hope for me after all.

This same brother and his wife invited me for holidays a few times, allowing me to stay in their home for several days at a time. They had no idea the gift they gave me in these special moments, and the meaning they brought into my life. I felt hope, again.

The best part was that they rented a house from Maurice and Kathryn Good, Charlotte's parents, and lived on the same property. This meant Charlotte and I could spend time together. And sometimes in the evening, with only a few feet between houses, we would open windows upstairs and talk to each other. Boys being boys, her brothers, Stuart, Roland, and Ross, carried on in the background, showing off and horsing around, trying to distract and interrupt our conversations. No matter, we were together, and I felt alive.

But the summer after my baptism, as word spread of Bruce kissing me, hope slipped through my fingers again, leaving me with nothing to hold on to. Wil and I were out in the cucumber field, hoeing around the young plants, when he brought it up. "One of the boys at church said he heard about you and Bruce." He paused. "He said he would never date you... he doesn't want a second-hand girl."

Steeling myself against the piercing pain of the judgement, I laughed it off, as though it was a most humorous thing to say, but it cut deep. And with each judgement the pain shot deeper, and my heart grew harder. Anger covered the pain, forcing even the shame to go below the surface. Had I only known that I was one of countless boys and girls across our Conservative Mennonite Churches of Ontario fellowship whose innocence was compromised, it may not have felt as overwhelming. As it was, I believed I was the only "second-hand" girl, and I was doomed.

I hated church, hated religion and all the injustices I felt because of it. I had not asked for what Bruce did to me, yet I was the one blamed, shamed, and marked for life. I was the one who would end up an old spinster, alone and unloved, because the culture blamed women for anything any man ever did against them. I could hear their accusing voices. Look at the way she acts. It's no wonder it happened. She's too worldly, always pushing the boundaries. She's a flirt....

Well, I wouldn't stand by and watch my life go down the drain. There was another world, another life, waiting to be discovered, and I would find it. Maybe that world would welcome me, and I would finally fit in.

I started dreaming of cutting my hair and wearing jeans. When no one was around I went into Wil's room and slipped into his clothes to see if maybe, just maybe, they would work. They did, sort of, but not quite. Still, it was enough to help me decide if I liked them or not. And I did.

I would bide my time, but the minute I could, I would disappear from the Mennonite community. I was no longer one of them, and I would not be forever held in bondage. I would be free, one day.

Chapter Twelve

A highlight in our home was Christmas. It was the one time of year when we spent a lot of time as siblings, laughing and playing games together. Our home was always filled with harmless pranks between siblings, and even more so at Christmas, because of the combined energy of so many people in one house, each on a sugar rush.

The Christmas after I turned fourteen was my last good Christmas at home, and one of the last I would ever spend with my family. By the following year my life was unravelling all around. It started off like any normal Christmas season, but Boxing Day evening mom approached.

"Trutje," she said, calling me in German. She asked me to come with her, away from my siblings. We stepped into the hall.

"You must be very careful," she said, in German. "Dad said if you get in trouble with church, he will kill you."

Just like that, out of the clear blue sky, at age fifteen, a death threat landed on me, for no particular reason at all. I was oblivious to the trigger. I had not had any trouble with the church, other than normal criticisms over clothing details and concerns over my interest in boys.

I slipped out of the house that cold December and walked into the black night, when no one was around. I crawled into our little Datsun pickup truck, curled up on the seat, and cried.

It was ironic that I should escape to this truck, where, on another night—a much warmer night—a brother had taken me off guard completely, when he groped my breasts one Wednesday night after church. Now, in a moment of distress, it was a solace, a place to escape, where no one would think to look for me. It was a place where I could grieve alone, without letting anyone into my heart.

I stayed there for hours, alone in the bitter cold, wishing I would die. Just slip away into an eternal sleep, never again to feel anything. Not the cold in my toes, or my trembling body, nor the cold in my heart and soul. I just wanted it to end forever. Eventually I snuck back into the house and escaped to my room.

Dad's threat was one of the final nails in the proverbial coffin for me, relationally, with home and church. One final abusive event at school reinforced the vow that I would finish grade nine, and then leave. Rumours trickled out that Brother Mark Wayne had been too lenient a teacher, and Brother Elmer was back to "restore order" at Lakeshore school. If the rumours were true, I presumed it was why he showed little grace of any kind.

The bell rang, one morning after first recess, and students lined up at the fountain. Brother Elmer had strict rules about whispering after the bell, including in the fountain line, and to do so was to be sent to your desk without a drink, or worse. That morning was worse.

My brother David and his friend Wendell, both nine years old, stood in line with us. Whether in defiance or a forgetful moment, Wendell whispered to David just as Brother Elmer walked by.

Without so much as a word, Brother Elmer formed a fist and swung, hitting Wendell in the temple. Veins bulged. His face turned red in rage, and he sent Wendell to his desk.

I watched in horror as this played out, furious that this kind of violence would take place in a Christian classroom. At home I had witnessed my share of violence and had often felt helpless, but here I would not stand by and do nothing. I turned, without a word, and walked to my desk, foregoing my drink.

During science class, when I would normally have been an active participant, I sat indifferently, disregarding the teacher, and contributing nothing to class discussion, not even answering Brother Elmer's questions.

At noon Brother Elmer announced that Kathy, Carolyn, and I would be kept in from recess, after eating our lunches. This did not surprise me. He kept us each in turn, lecturing us about respect. I met Kathy downstairs after her lecture.

"He's such a jerk," Kathy said under her breath, then walked away.

When my turn came, Brother Elmer pulled out a ruler and began striking my left hand. I was determined not to break, if it took all day. He had not apologized for punching Wendell, and I would not apologize for defending Wendell. Nearly thirty stripes later, the tears started. Steaming, hot, angry tears.

Brother Elmer explained that I was the only one who had been strapped because I was the only one who had maintained a bad attitude. Kathy and Carolyn had been repentant. What he didn't know, and I wasn't about to tell him—not willing to rat on my friends—was that both of the other girls emerged angry and calling him names. Besides, he wouldn't have strapped them, regardless. They were from another Mennonite church, and a church leader's family. Their dad had influence. We had none, making me the perfect candidate for a good thrashing. And that was how the chips landed, in a setting like that.

My father was not a happy man when he heard what had happened. He gained a bit of trust from me, in that he could see through the injustice. But the church leaders stood by Brother Elmer, and said I deserved it. No one ever asked for the other side of the story. No one ever challenged his violence.

That day the religion of my childhood lost the last little sliver of my heart. I was a church member. I had stood against injustice and violence, and as a result I had been struck almost thirty times and the church leaders had justified it without bothering with the truth. In the "real world," Brother Elmer had committed not one crime, but two, by striking Wendell and me. And the church stood by and applauded him.

The imbalance of rejection, fear, and trauma overtook me in spite of the good in my culture, and in spite of the love I felt from some. I believed that I was a failure in God's eyes, and a shameful disappointment to my church and family, and I was more determined than ever to leave my home and culture. I didn't fit. And I never would.

****

Our native classmate, Elton, who lived with Bruce's family—one of my best friends and someone who had always treated me with respect—

suddenly began acting out, sexually. Rumour had it that he had also been victimized, sexually, during his time at Lakeshore. No doubt, coming from a reserve into a religious environment that was supposed to help him, and then being surrounded by sexual perversion, did him a great disservice.

Whatever all influenced it, to the horror of our community, Elton attempted to rape Bruce's sister, at knife point, one Sunday after singing. Shock rippled through the church and school in the ensuing days, all while other crimes—including rape—remained carefully hidden. Morton and Elda moved Elton out of their home immediately, but the church allowed him to continue attending school a few days while making arrangements to send him back to northern Ontario.

At the end of the day, on one of his last days at school before leaving our community, Elton threatened to rape one of my classmates. During the last twenty minutes of school, students were assigned various cleaning jobs, on a rotating basis. My classmate had the task of cleaning the girls' bathroom and was downstairs, all alone.

Elton and I were walking together when he whispered something about having failed with one girl, but he would get what he wanted downstairs. Immediately I realized he was heading to the girls' bathroom, where the two of them would be alone.

I flew down the stairs, a step ahead, and arrived at the bathroom, panting and breathless, just ahead of him.

"Close the door! Lock it! Lock it!" I gasped, as I blocked his path and pushed and wrestled him away from the door. Startled, it took my classmate a moment to respond, but after what seemed an eternity of wrestling, though mere seconds had passed, she slammed the door and locked it. I stood guard at the door until she had finished her task, and walked her upstairs.

I never told any adults, because I had no confidence that they would do the right thing, and I certainly was not willing to tell on Elton and get him in more trouble. My friend and I never talked about it again and I have no idea if she understood what Elton intended to do with her. No matter his fall, in the end, I missed Elton terribly when he returned to the reserves, and remember him with fondness still.

****

The one redemption in 1985 that might almost have convinced me there was hope for Lakeshore, and that I might have a place there, was a minister's ordination. So much in church life depends on the quality of leadership. As John C. Maxwell, a world-renowned leader who started off as a pastor of a small church, said, "Everything rises and falls on leadership."

My confidence in leadership was destroyed beyond repair when they endorsed the teacher who strapped me, especially Morton. And the thought that he might be "the Lord's anointed" scared me. I saw right through the religious façade, devoid of justice and truth, and, yet, if he was the Lord's anointed, then to speak out against him would be met with God's judgement. I saw him as a slippery fellow, more hungry for power and control than leading any soul to the heart of God for redemption. And he seemed always to be looking where he shouldn't and noticing things on women's clothing that "pointed to certain places on the body," and that sort of thing. And he mentioned it too, as if his mind was hard-pressed to pull itself out of the gutter.

At his daughter's wedding, while offering a lengthy dissertation on modesty, he told a story about a woman on a jet, during one of his mission trips to India, and how she had flirted and pursued him on that flight. I was embarrassed for his daughter, and ashamed for having had to listen to it, especially on her wedding day. What did being hit on during a flight have to do with his daughter's marriage, or modesty, for that matter? With this man carrying the bulk of power, I could not trust leadership, but, being young and inexperienced, I also couldn't put these feelings into words, and had no one to talk to had I wanted to try.

When it was announced that there would be an ordination, and Brother Paul Zehr was in the lot, I felt a tiny niggling of hope. As always the process was a solemn one... reverent... a sacred moment in the life of a man I respected. The burden of leadership seemed an exceptionally heavy presence in the ceremony, because Paul was a single man, and the lot fell on him.

In the end, as much as I liked Brother Paul, the wounds in my heart ran too deep, and the scars were too permanent—both at home and at church. For me to stay was impossible. Besides, I was not willing to commit to strict adherence to their man-made rules. I couldn't accept things like dictating the width of the band on a head veiling, and every fine detail on a dress, including how a collar was made—if one was allowed at all—the length of sleeves and the policing of colours, print size, and various other things that had no scriptural grounds whatsoever..

I had taught myself to sew, and had started making my dresses with a bit more flair than what the rule book allowed and I wasn't ready to give that up; not for a culture into which I would never fit, and without biblical authority behind the legalistic expectations. I couldn't embrace it. I could respect people who lived by it, but it wasn't for me.

****

The months leading up to my sixteenth birthday I schemed and planned. To run away, I feared, would be to risk being hunted and killed by my father. There had to be a safe way out... a safe place to go... some way to take care of myself without adding further risk and trauma. I determined that I would find that way. And then it occurred to me.

I did my homework and devised a plan. It wasn't much of an income, but it would help. I approached dad and presented it. In Wellesley, Ontario, I had found a place with room and board at low cost, in the home of a Beachy Amish –or "car Amish"—widow, Katie Steckly. I would help Viola's daughter, Florence, with her cleaning jobs. And, since Florence also boarded with Katie, I would send money home with her on weekends, or come with her and bring the money myself. I outlined how much money I would make, what rent would cost, and what personal expenses would be, and approximately how much I would have left each week. I walked dad through the details of my plan, step by step. He was hesitant, worried that I was too young. I reminded him that, although it wasn't much, the income would help with the financial burdens of raising a family, and reiterated that I would send money via Florence, and even come home with her for occasional weekends. These selling features were important enough to bear repeating.

Even so, dad was worried about the distance between us, worried about me being away from family, but the financial help was a drawing card. Reluctantly he agreed to let me go. I finalized plans with Florence and set

106

them in motion. It was my first step into freedom from fear; a wobbly baby step, but it was a step.

Freedom would come... but with a price tag bigger than I could have imagined, or would have been willing to pay, had I known what lay ahead.

PART TWO

Chapter Thirteen

Anticipation and mild anxiety wrestled inside of me—with the former overpowering the latter—as I lugged my few belongings to the front door of the pinkish-beige bungalow. Florence opened the door that led to my new world. Inside, I took in my surroundings without even a fleeting thought of the world I had left behind, or what my absence would mean to my siblings. It never occurred to me that I would be missed, that anyone cared. It was survival of the fittest for me.

Had I given it any thought, I would have known that it would be an adjustment at home. Whenever I returned after being away, for sleepovers, dad let me know things were not 'normal' at home, while I was away. He playfully told me that the house had been quiet even with eight or more other siblings still home, and the energy level and chatter had died down with my absence. "If you had wooden lips," he would say, "there would be a constant tapping." He always said it with a twinkle in his eye that told me he had missed me.

As a family we never discussed that I was leaving. I didn't tell younger siblings, or prepare them in any way for the change. I just disappeared abruptly out of their lives, and walked into a world unknown.

My new home was modest, but more extravagant than anything I had previously experienced. To the right of the entry, the living room boasted furniture that actually matched. It looked comfortable. Inviting.

Katie, a grandma in her late sixties, welcomed me into her home and her life. She pointed me to a room on my left. "That will be your room. You can put your bags in there."

It was more of a sitting room than a bedroom, with a large bay window, she told me apologetically, but she had converted it, for my sake, so that she would have a place for me. I loved it immediately and assured her it was perfect, bay window and all.

The room was light in colour, and perfectly organized, with white furniture; a dream bedroom. The bed was neatly made, with the top corner folded down and back on an angle, as if welcoming me to rest. The little details spoke volumes. More than I recognized or could express at the time, and more than Katie would ever know.

My new home was a safe place, and Katie took great care of her boarders. Everything she did, she did with gentleness, and she seemed to delight in me—the person I was—without any sense that I was a "bad" child. She giggled at my antics, chatted with genuine interest, and gave me permission to raid her freezer for treats. She did my laundry, cleaned my room, and cooked amazing food. I couldn't ask for more.

Sadly, the bliss was short-lived. A few months later my world crashed. At age sixteen I found myself surrounded by a fistful of preachers and a bishop, my sins about to be addressed and my rejection notice served. I had failed to live up to the expectations of the church, and its written and unwritten rules.

I wasn't trying to rebel against God. Not deliberately. I simply wasn't living by the rules of the system in which I was raised, and wasn't pursuing Him in the ways the church thought I should. I had visited random churches in the town of Wellesley and the surrounding area, rather than returning home regularly and attending Lakeshore, or at least attending another sister church. I especially enjoyed Mapleview Mennonite Church and my friends there, and the Wellesley Holiness Church, and tried to stay in touch with God, but not by committing to a particular group or set of rules. In fact, sometimes my only "church service" was me and my ghetto blaster, listening to Gospel Echoes in the back yard or lost in the rich baritone of Charley Pride's gospel songs. When Charley sang "Be Grateful," a song that told simple stories of the blind, the crippled, and the mute, I was reminded how much there was to celebrate in life.

I was happy in those moments, just me and Jesus and a boom box, lying on nature's carpet, the grass tickling my toes. There, Hope whispered in the wind... the sunlight offered heaven's sweet kisses... the songs a soothing balm for deep soul anguish. As my tears spilled, Heaven knelt beside me, catching each teardrop in a bottle. Never forgotten by God, I was more

112

valued and more precious than I could possibly imagine, and more alive in spirit than I had ever been in church.

I found "fellowship" in visiting the elderly in our town. They loved my company, served me cookies, and invited me to watch TV with them. Most of them were Christians and some even had Mennonite background, or were "worldly" Mennonites who understood me and my religious background. But, as the love and acceptance of these new and somewhat unusual friendships carried me through a difficult season of life, a storm brewed on another front. That is what happens when a warm front and a cold front collide.

Florence had policed my activities, and reported my delinquencies to the leaders, and told them that I was watching TV, and whatever 'sins' she was aware of. Whether she offered the information so that I would be 'dealt with', or if they asked and she felt compelled to answer, I don't know. But that is how it came about that I found myself sitting in a classroom at the Cornerstone Christian School, on the outskirts of Wellesley, Ontario, surrounded by the preachers, a bishop and one preacher's wife.

Following a time of prayer, the preachers, seated in a semi-circle around me, presented the 'sins' and charges against me. They were kind enough—I can't fault them for coming off as if their intent was to destroy me. Particularly Elmer Grove, the bishop who had supported our family through numerous occasions of dad's violence. He took the lead and spoke with a kind, fatherly tone, but the words and the tone didn't match, creating a battle in my spirit.

There I was, surrounded by adults in spiritual leadership, and not one with the ability to pursue my heart and go below the surface. It was all superficial fluff, focusing only on rules, with no awareness of my crushed spirit. Still, I wanted to believe Elmer genuinely cared for me—I needed that thread of hope—yet that very desire left me feeling betrayed as he presented my list of offences.

Was it true that I listened to Gospel Echoes cassettes, and did I have other instrumental music? Was it true that I watched TV? Why did I not attend "our" church? And then the final charges—they had observed how much darker my hair looked and wondered if I had used hair dye to darken it.

113

I was guilty as charged on the first two counts, and answered honestly. I didn't want to go home because of abuse and violence, but I couldn't say that. The last question, however, about my hair, humoured me, if only because of the irony.

I, too, had observed the change in my hair. And it was a big deal. Coming from a family of sixteen children—eight boys and eight girls—I was the only one with blue eyes and, of all the siblings with light hair, mine was the blondest. One older brother had grey-blue eyes, and the rest had brown, hazel, or green. To have the distinction of being the only 'true blonde' with sky-blue eyes in a family so large was not something I wanted to lose. As my hair gradually turned a dark, mousy blonde with reddish hints, I felt as though I was losing my distinctive identity.

I knew that dyeing my hair was sin, and going to a hairdresser would cost me church membership, so that was not an option. Instead, I decided to take matters into my own hands. Several weeks before that fateful meeting, while Grandma Katie was away, I attempted fixing the colour.

I remembered how my mother poured bleach on clothes to turn them white again, and it occurred to me that maybe, just maybe, it would have the same effect on hair. I scoped out the laundry room, and sure enough, Katie had the necessary product.

Grabbing towels and a bottle of bleach, I set up my work station and made sure warm water was running, ready to rinse my hair. Tipping my head far enough over the tub to not spill bleach on my face or clothes, I began to pour. Instantly my hair clumped together and felt like it was melting. I had watched when my mother made lye soap and lye splashed on cloth, eating a hole into it. I panicked, certain this was happening to my hair.

I set to work rinsing, shampooing, rinsing, shampooing, and rinsing again, until I was confident that all residue was washed out. To my disappointment, my hair colour remained a mousy blonde with reddish hints, but to my relief I still had hair. Reluctantly, I resigned myself to this loss of identity.

When I told the preachers that I had noticed my hair growing darker, and that I wished it was more blonde, they doubted me. In a condescending, chiding voice—one that might be appropriate for a parent speaking to a young child caught sneaking a cookie—one of them asked, "Now, Trudy, are you *sure* you did not dye your hair?"

I had never been anything less than forthright and honest with them. I had lied once in school, and on my own initiative returned to the teacher to confess. Why would I lie now? I wanted to let them in on my little secret, but that would have cost me for sure, so I said again that I did not dye my hair. They asked another time or two before finally concluding that, while they struggled to believe me, they would leave it between me and God. I was good with that. My little escapade would be God's and my little secret. I wondered what He really thought... of my little experiment... of the preachers and their accusations... of me... Did any of it make any difference to Him at all?

Having decided to leave the question of whether my hair was dyed or not between me and God, the preachers moved on. The meeting dragged on, and on. I was numb. In the end they said that I was not living in victory. As a defeated Christian, who had defied the church constitution regarding musical instruments and watching TV, and because I was not making an effort to attend "our" church, I would need to be excommunicated and treated as an unbeliever and a heathen.

While I was still welcome to attend church, I would be "marked." They would make an announcement to the church and, without them saying so, I was aware that the announcement would likely be made throughout sister churches as well, so all would know not to greet me with the Holy Kiss, if I showed up at church.

Simultaneously I felt a sense of relief and terror. Being freed from the burden of countless man-made rules and religious agenda was like breathing pure air for the first time in years. But with no family, no church, and no connections to anyone or anything, I was truly alone in the world. The freedom was... well, freeing. But with no "truth" to counteract the lies of experience I was vulnerable and fearful, creating conflicting emotions. If ever I felt spiritually bipolar, it was in that moment.

Adding to my fear were Bible verses about "whatever we loose in earth is loosed in heaven and whatever is bound on earth is bound in heaven," found in Matthew 16:19, and Matthew 18:18. Taught completely out of context, I believed that excommunication had the power to sentence me to hell. Little did I realize that these verses had nothing to do with making up rules not grounded on Scripture, and then judging people as though they were vile sinners breaking God's law if they didn't abide by those rules.

I didn't know the verses where Jesus condemned Pharisaical religion, speaking more harshly than He spoke to anyone else, going so far as to call them "sons of hell," in Matthew 23:16, who make their converts "twice the sons of hell" that they are. I had only enough information to mess with my head, not enough to bring any sense of balance to the beliefs and teachings, so I left that meeting more confused than I had ever been.

At Grandma Katie's later that night, I crept quietly into her basement, where an unused, moist-smelling family room with an old couch became my haven. I needed time alone. Curled up on the old couch, the dark sludge of religious indoctrination gurgled, like a violent volcano, threatening to explode and swallow my spirit in its death. Scattered thoughts tormented. Did God hate me? What if the preachers were right? Would I go to hell for not being "one of them"? Had I rejected the ultimate truth? Would the devil now slowly invade me? Overtake me? Destroy me? My body shook with a blend of terror and uncertainty.

The tears started, as if attempting to wash the tar from within and free me from its poison. Were they good tears? Bad tears? It didn't matter, really, their flooding came unbidden and offered no explanation. They poured so violently from a place of inner hell that my body shook and trembled uncontrollably.

Then, as abruptly as the sobbing had started, it ended. I sensed something in the room. A powerful force... a Presence. I looked around, saw no one, and fled to my room. It would be many years before that memory would return and, with it, an understanding of what took place in that moment, as my heart cried out to God... what happened to my heart... what I felt... what lies I believed because of it... And, as I worked through the memory of being excommunicated, the scene in that basement returned, and I saw myself huddled on that couch. I was alone. Abandoned. Rejected. Hated by God. Crushed at the core of my being. That is what I had believed.

The memory of the moist-smelling couch returned, and me sobbing, interrupted by the sudden awareness of a Presence. I recalled the fear I felt, wondering if Satan really was coming to claim me. I didn't even ask God where He was. The instant that moment returned, God gave me a vision of Jesus in the room with me, watching over me, as if standing guard. Nothing had changed in the Heavenly realm, based on that moment with a handful of preachers. I was still loved. Accepted. Understood. I was His.

But as a sixteen-year-old struggling through life, with no experience to fall back on to convince me of God's faithfulness, being excommunicated left me hopeless and empty. It was no comfort that I was one of about eleven members to be excommunicated for offences such as watching TV, not attending church regularly, and owning instrumental music; Southern and Country Gospel—even if produced by other Mennonites. It was evil, all of it. There was no telling where the rhythm would take you. Why, next thing you know, you'd be dancing, like King David in the streets, and lose all dignity!

Knowing the culture, and understanding how important preserving traditions is, I understand, intellectually, why they did what they did. The only way to maintain a system is to define laws that protect that system by any means necessary. But what the system didn't account for is what happens to the hearts of youth, and even adults, who are struggling, but who genuinely long to know the heart of God. That is where the system falls short and offers no life at all

But where man's systems fail, and leave the vulnerable to fall, God's grace has made a way. That way is Love, His name is Jesus. Unfortunately, many who fall, fall harder and farther than they ever would have if man's systems had never replaced His grace in the first place.

That night felt like the first official step in my fall from grace.

Chapter Fourteen

From the moment I moved into Grandma Katie's, I felt safe. More than that, I *was* safe. There were no strange noises at night. No shadows in the dark that made me hold my breath. No creaking stairs that made my heart freeze, leaving me to wonder if my father was coming for me. Would he have a knife? A gun? Some other weapon or evil intent…?

Here, with this sweet Amish grandma, my world had become more than I ever dreamed it could be. More than I knew existed. What little hope had not been destroyed and numbed through sheer terror of childhood slowly came to life. It was as if the trauma had squeezed hope from my heart, like water from a sponge, and left it dry and hard. But in Katie's care, as I absorbed her love and care, my heart filled up again, and softened.

Each morning Grandma Katie set the table for the three of us with meticulous perfection. As if measured for precision, each place setting looked picture perfect, consisting of a small glass filled with orange juice, a glass for milk or water, a bowl or plate, and silverware. Always served with a smile and a cheerful, though characteristically subdued, "Good morning Trudy," as though she looked forward to my arrival.

I wouldn't have needed this, or felt less loved had she not gone to such fuss. I would have grabbed a bowl of cereal, alone, and left for work just as contentedly. As I look back, I see that her love and care were the heart and hands of God, whispering, "I love you." The way she laughed, her eyes twinkling with delight, at my quick wit and humour, thrilled me. She delighted in me, and I knew it.

But that safe place was ripped out of my life in one instant, when the preachers came and paid that visit. After the meeting and being excommunicated, Katie spoke to me before our first meal together. With tears in her eyes, and wringing her hands, she informed me that her church would excommunicate her if she ate with me. She was required to shun me; I would need to sit at the island in the kitchen, alone, to eat my meals. She wished she didn't have to do it, but she had no choice.

How quickly the life can be squeezed back out of a fragile heart. I steeled myself against the pain. I wanted to cry. Instead, with a cold, hard heart, I told her that it would not be necessary to set a place for me at the island. I would not be eating any sit-down meals until I found a new place to live. I told her I understood, and in some ways I did, but something in me died.

The pain in her eyes, the tears that glistened, the grief that haunted her features... I knew she loved me. She said as much, without saying the words. And I never doubted that. She explained that she could not afford to pay the price, should she be excommunicated for eating with me. I don't know how many times she said she was sorry. I could see that loss was not only mine. She lost a bright spot in her life, just as I lost a bright spot in mine.

Hope. What was it anyway? An illusion? A lie? A mockery?

I withdrew from Grandma Katie from that day forward, and spent little time in her home. I didn't know what else to do, how to survive. A sixteen-year-old who had only known rejection up until this stage, this wasn't new. But I had tasted hope. I had tasted acceptance. And love. How was I to pretend that nothing was different, and return again to hard-hearted survival, as if that rejection meant nothing?

Each morning I grabbed some food item before work. I ate lunch at work, alone in the girls' change room, sometimes choking down swallows between tears, and in the evening I nibbled on bits of food, or raided Grandma Katie's freezer for baking she had done, as she had given me permission to do. I had vowed I would simply stop eating, other than lunch, but when I was hungry enough, I gave in.

In the evening I was always careful to show up when I was certain dinner was over. If I was too hungry, and had enough money, I stopped at the grocery store to pick up chips, or a pre-made sandwich and a drink.

I survived that way for a short time, while looking for a new place to live. It was a dark and lonely time. I could not pray, or connect with God in any way. Whoever He was, or wherever He was, or if He even was... And if He was "one of them," then I didn't stand a chance, and wasn't interested.

****

120

Some months before being excommunicated, I had started working at a machine shop—running lathes, drills, and presses—making gun parts. When I picked up the application, they said I would need to provide parental consent before hiring me. This meant contacting my parents, and having them join me on a tour.

In childhood dad taught me how to run some of the machines, and what he didn't show me, instinct made up for. I was confident that I would do well and dad agreed. But he was, again, concerned about my environment, and whether it was best for me to be the only female in a machine shop. I had told him I would eat lunch alone, and work by myself most of the time. There was really nothing to worry about.

Furthermore, I said, it paid better than cleaning, if only because of more consistent hours. Reluctantly he gave in, granting permission to start a new job and leave my cleaning job behind.

Now, with my church membership removed, and with needing to find a new place to live, I was relieved to not have to work with someone from the church. I wanted to leave that world behind and never look back. I would find a new church, new friends, new home, and start a whole new life.

As if fate had read my mind, it happened. I was downtown one Saturday afternoon and met a friend from my former church, a young man several years older than I, who was passing through town. He was also excommunicated, along with his two sisters, and they quickly became my party friends.

Whether I was oblivious to their real feelings, or if my friends really accepted me, I can't be certain, but it felt like they did. I loved to party with them, and be crazy, without feeling ashamed of my personality, or pretending to be more subdued than I was by nature. I wasn't overly responsible in some of my partying, but at the same time I had standards, lines I would not cross.

The discovery that I was lovable was freeing and empowering. Had the church and religious people in my life communicated this to me, and to the other youth, it would have had a deep impact on my perception of God. Instead, I concluded that to be accepted and loved "just as I am," I had to separate myself from church and from God. This made a mockery of the age old hymn, "Just as I am…" that was sung frequently at church and especially in revival meetings. In my mind that mockery justified the path I chose.

Our first outing was to Godfather's Pizza in Stratford, Ontario, where I was introduced to liquor for the first time in my life. I met new friends, all of whom were either ex-Mennonite, or liberal Mennonite, who understood and accepted me. The girls in the group, myself included, still wore white head coverings and skirts or dresses of some sort, but that didn't prevent us from partying and drinking. Being under-aged, I was not legally able to order alcohol, so my friends ordered and gave it to me.

After dinner we continued the party at an apartment, playing cards and drinking beer, though I didn't do much drinking. Darren, one of my new friends, offered me a cigarette, daring me to try it. I wasn't sure about it but eventually gave in and smoked one, inhaling deeply, just the way he coached me to.

The room started spinning and I felt as though I was going to pass out. I stood to my feet, staggered toward the door of the balcony, and stepped outside for air. I tripped and stumbled, laughing. So this was what it felt like. A guy beside me blew smoke rings. I imitated him. I would master this thing. And I did, eventually toughening up to the effects of nicotine, and smoking a pack a day.

I spent a lot of time with Darren who, for the most part, treated me with respect. He never really asked me to be his girlfriend; we hung out together by default. Since he had a car and a motorbike, and lived near Katie's house, he offered me rides to parties. This led to "sort of" dating, but never really talking about it, even landing me at one of his extended family gatherings.

We went on many motorbike rides and spent time at Darren's sister's home, an apartment above a small country restaurant. His sister and her husband were always welcoming and fun to spend time with, playing cards and watching TV, and just hanging out. One Sunday evening, Darren reached over and groped my breasts. He apologized later, and I forgave him, I said, but I felt betrayed, my trust badly shaken.

That evening another man at the party, Warren, offered to drive me home to Wellesley. It was less out of the way for him, he said. Normally I would have opted to travel with Darren, but being hurt and angered by his unexpected advances, I accepted Warren's offer.

Warren was engaged to be married, and it never occurred to me that he was not trustworthy. Furthermore, he was in his mid-twenties and I had only just turned sixteen. In my mind he was way older than I, and I didn't suspect that maybe he had ulterior motives for offering me a ride.

It was a rainy night and the ride uneventful, filled with casual conversation. That is, until we turned onto a back road leading to Wellesley. In a heavily wooded area, he veered suddenly to the side of the road and stopped. Before I knew what was happening, he popped open a button on my royal blue cotton shirt and reached inside my bra, grabbing my breast.

Stunned, I grabbed his wrist and pulled his hand out. "What are you doing?" I asked.

"One last fling before I get married," he said.

I pushed him away and buttoned my shirt. "Take me home please," I said.

An act much less invasive had triggered anger with Darren earlier that day. If my "almost boyfriend" wasn't allowed to touch me, who did this guy think he was? What was with men? What made every male feel as though he had the right to grab women? Or was it just me—was there something wrong with me? Was I the only one treated this way?

Warren took me home without further incident. But the next time I hung out with these friends, there was a noticeable tension. I finally asked one of the girls what was up. Reluctantly she told me she knew what had happened that rainy night on the back road, how I had thrown myself at Warren and tried to get him to have sex with me. That was the story he told. If wishes could kill people, Warren would have dropped dead at that moment. I had felt violated by what Bruce had done to me in the barn, but that didn't compare to being molested by a man almost ten years older than I, and then him spreading the rumour that I wanted to have sex with him and he had to

123

fight me off while driving. It was one thing to be molested, another to be blamed for it, and lied about. At least Bruce had eventually apologized.

I told her what had really happened, but couldn't tell if she believed me. I didn't ask. I never saw Warren again. But the unjust shame and accompanying bitterness lingered long after he was out of my life.

I told Darren that I didn't want to hang out anymore. The "boyfriend thing" wasn't for me, was the excuse I offered. I never told him what happened. I didn't know how to explain. It was easier just to walk away.

Chapter Fifteen

During my time at Grandma Katie's I frequented the local library, reading several books a week. For the really captivating ones, I managed one a night, sometimes two, especially the nights I didn't visit the elderly people in town. I liked mystery best. That is, until the librarian started to offer me other books.

The librarian was in her sixties, a grandma-type who invited me to her home, from time to time, to watch TV and have a snack. Through my visits to the library, she had become my friend. We watched *The Wizard of Oz, Alice in Wonderland*, and *Anne of Green Gables* together—fun and innocent shows.

When she started to encourage me to read a broader variety of books, I thought nothing of it. Soon I was into Harlequin Romance books, reading as many as two or three a night. They were sketchy and shallow, but nothing too shocking for a while.

When one of the books she recommended went beyond "sketchy" to graphic, and described blatant sexual activity, I became uncomfortable. Parts of the book remain etched on my memory, all these years later, as if I just read it today. I wanted to believe that she didn't do this intentionally, and gave me the book innocently, unaware of the explicit content, but in hindsight, I recognize that I was naïve and didn't see the signs, and how carefully she had planned it.

One evening when I arrived at the library, she said she picked out a book for me, and had it under the front counter. I asked her about it and her answers were vague but she insisted I would like it. She told me to get any other books I wanted, and she would add that one when checking out. When I placed my other books on the counter, she told me I wouldn't need to sign that one out—it was under her name. I took the book and read it first, curious as to why she thought I would love it so much.

The first chapter described an explicit sex act, using a word I didn't know the meaning of, so I kept on reading. Within the next few chapters I learned about condoms, diaphragms, explicit details of extramarital affairs, spermicidal gels, open marriages, and various shocking and overt sex acts. I stopped reading and pulled out a dictionary to look up the words I didn't understand, starting with masturbation—the word in the first chapter. When I realized the full extent of what I had read, I felt violated and ashamed. The story had drawn me in, and made it hard for me to stop reading, but the graphic information had raped my mind and taken what innocence I had left.

Embarrassed and angry, I dropped the book in the return slot and stopped frequenting the library and visiting the librarian's home. Whatever she wanted from me, I wanted nothing to do with it.

It is ironic how the source of confusion is sometimes the link to God's plan and provision. The librarian had an apartment in her basement that she rented out to a gentleman named Danny. I met Danny a few times, and heard that his brother needed a nanny to help with his children, because his wife had left him for an affair. I contacted Murray and set up a time to meet, and he offered me the position. I moved in not long after.

I liked Murray immediately. He was kind and gentlemanly and, at a time when his life was devastated, his only concern, from what I could tell, was the well-being of his children. I hoped I would do well. I desperately wanted to.

The master bedroom was nicely done, complete with an air conditioner—something that was lacking in the rest of the house—and Murray gave it up so that I could have the nicest room. He was away a lot, he said, and didn't need it.

I had not told my parents about the move, so they didn't know where I was. I was finally beyond their reach. Or so I thought.

It was mid-afternoon, one day not too many weeks after my move, when there was a knock at the front door. I opened it and, to my horror, my parents had found me. Fear threatened... the kind that debilitates the body and freezes the mind. I could not let them in. It would overtake me.

I stood there, in front of the door, opening it only far enough for them to talk to me, but not far enough for them to step inside. I asked what they wanted. Dad said he wanted the money I had made since I last sent him my pay cheques. Instead of giving in and accommodating his demands, I told them to leave or I would call the police, and said that I didn't want to see them anymore. For a short time I had known life without fear, and I wasn't going back. My world was better without them.

Dad didn't go into a fit of rage; instead, he looked shocked and distraught. Mom, pale and frightened, spoke in German, "Peter, let's just leave." And with that my parents turned and walked out of my life.

I closed the door and stood there momentarily, recovering from the shock, my heart pounding violently as it registered what I had done. I had stood up to him, to them. I had boundaries, and had enforced them... *for me.* In the past I had stood up on behalf of siblings and stared dad down in his rage, but I had never before stood up for myself. Once again, and maybe more than ever, my world was safe.

****

Though Murray was gone a lot with work as a trucker, when he was home, he was kind and gentle with his children, and treated me with dignity and respect. I had never known a man like this before. Though completely vulnerable, circumstantially—a young teenager with no accountability, living in the home of a man separated from his wife—I was unquestionably safe.

One Saturday night Murray and I had a heart-to-heart talk about God and religion, and I shared how being excommunicated had impacted me. He listened with compassion, and spoke to me of God's love and grace. I sat at his table, my head resting on my arms, and wept. I wanted to believe in that God, but I couldn't imagine any other than the one with the big stick, ready to pounce on a straying child and damning every sinner to hell, with not so much as a niggling of sorrow or care over their condition or fate.

Murray asked if he could pray for me and, when I said yes, he gently placed his hand on my shoulder and began to talk with God, as if He was right there in the room with us. I had never been cared for or mentored and as he spoke to God, my heart softened. If what he said had even a ring of truth to it, then maybe God was okay...

I attended Wilmot Centre Missionary Church with Murray and his girls the next morning, and enjoyed the service. There was something refreshing about looking around and seeing diversity, and yet feeling acceptance. No one seemed to scrutinize me, or anyone else, for that matter. The pastor

127

greeted me warmly at the end of the service, and invited me back. Once again, hope filled my heart...

But about the time life seemed to come together, and I felt safe, my world again started to cave in. Rumours circulated in the Mennonite church. "Trudy is living common law with a man almost twice her age... He is divorced.... Trudy has cut her hair and wears jeans... Trudy is no longer a virgin..."

Oh, the power of gossip to destroy the fragile heart! It was a crushing blow. I was devastated. Murray had provided me with a safe home, with not even a hint of indecency or innuendo. Never. The other rumours were, as of yet, ungrounded, but most would not be for long. Almost immediately I cut my hair and abandoned any ties to the cultural expectations of my background.

Overlapping with these rumours in the Mennonite church, lies made their rounds in the community where I lived; lies with not even a shred of truth, that I was a prostitute in Toronto on weekends.

I was in the back yard, tanning, when I heard footsteps. The children were in school, and Murray was away, and I had no one else with whom I kept in touch. I opened my eyes to see a young man in his twenties, standing about five feet away from me.

"Hi, I'm Michael," he said, introducing himself. "Are you Trudy?"

"Umm.... Yes...."

Besides feeling quite awkward in my bikini, with a perfect stranger, I felt intruded upon. He apologized for that, and asked if I had a few minutes. I wanted to say no, to tell him to leave and never come back, but I had never learned the art of saying no. Michael explained that he was the son of a local politician, and had seen me walking and biking around town. The purpose of his visit was to tell me of the rumours he had heard.

"Do you know Perry Benson?" he asked, after some small talk.

"No... I've never heard of him—should I know him?" I asked, puzzled.

His brow furrowed. "That's odd, because Perry is telling people you work the streets of Toronto on weekends, and your nickname is 'Mary the Nympho Mennonite.' Claims he's seen you there himself."

"I don't even know what nympho means," I said. A knot formed in my stomach, the kind that comes from knowing something is very wrong and being helpless to make it right. I wasn't sure I wanted to know the meaning. It didn't sound good, whatever it was. And I had no idea what "working the streets" meant.

Michael turned his face away, not able to look into my eyes. He spoke with apologetic compassion as he explained prostitution, and then defined "nympho" for me.

"I've never been to Toronto," I scoffed, covering the hurt, but inside my heart sank. "And besides, I'm a virgin." My mind raced. *Why would anyone say things like that? What had I done to deserve it?*

"You don't have to convince me, Trudy. I didn't believe a word Perry said. I'm only telling you so you know to be careful," Michael said, and I believed him. In conversation he asked about me having been Mennonite, and why I left, and said he was also Catholic Christian, and wondered if I might consider going on a date with him sometime.

I was flattered, and tempted to accept. He seemed sincere, and so kind, but the memory of recent male relationships made me think twice. Besides, if Mennonites were the kindest, truest, and best Christians on earth, and they treated me disrespectfully, what would I endure with a non-Mennonite? Particularly a Catholic? I had been taught that Catholics can't be Christians, making his statement seem like an oxymoron, and stories of their violence against our ancestors, in a moment like that, had powerful influence.

Michael said he understood, thanked me for my time, and wished me well. A twinge of regret tugged at my heart as he walked away. I felt bad for him. What if he was all that he seemed to be, and would treat me with respect?

I was still recovering from the confusion of what Michael had told me, and Warren's recent sexual advances, when three young men, absolute strangers, showed up at my door one Sunday night. When I answered, they told me that by the end of summer I would no longer be a virgin, and then left.

Fear wrapped its tentacles around my heart... reaching around my throat, choking, suffocating... and penetrating my mind.... Fear that what they said would become reality. Fear that I would be ruined. Fear that I would be raped. Fear that I would go to hell.

Fear. Constant. Agonizing. All consuming.

Added to this fear was a visit from an older brother, who reminded me of my inevitable eternal destiny, should I die in a state of rebellion. I was clearly on the wrong path, he said, pointing out that things like nail polish and jeans—which he had observed I was wearing—were carnal, worldly, and condemned by God and the church. If I didn't get a grip of myself, only God could tell how far I would wander.

My brother was kind, even gentle, and genuinely concerned, but completely missed the heart issue. Nail polish and jeans were the least of my worries.

Certain that I was "doomed and damned" after being excommunicated, I had given up on God. Soon after ending my friendship with Darren, and after the rumours circulated, I abandoned all cultural beliefs and practices, to adopt a "normal" lifestyle. I purchased jeans and other "normal" clothes, and started cutting my hair.

Religion had lost its hold on me, for a time, even if only because I locked up my heart. If life itself was hell, how much worse could eternal hell be? I had been condemned in church, and was never able to make the grade, even after accepting Jesus, and I stood condemned, still. It seemed to be a "damned if you do, damned if you don't" scenario. If I was going to go to hell anyway, I'd party on my way down.

Chapter Sixteen

While I still lived with Murray, processing the rumours of my supposed affair with him, another man in his twenties asked me out. Daniel was Mennonite, so I gave him a chance, having not yet learned that religion, or a specific culture, don't make men good, or safe.

Soon after we started dating, as more and more rumours made their way back to me, and after several people from my former church dropped by unannounced, I knew I had to move on. I wanted no contact, or family and people from my former church to know my whereabouts. I gave Murray two weeks' notice, after which I moved in with an elderly couple in New Hamburg, Ontario, and became their caretaker.

The elderly couple, Clare and Vera Maier, needed someone to cook, clean, and do laundry. The interview was nothing more than a brief phone conversation with Mr. Maier, who asked a few questions, and then said I could start any time.

Days were quiet at the Maier home. Three people don't create a lot of mess, when all they do is cook, eat, sleep, watch TV, and do daily chores. I enjoyed reading, and on sunny days, I slipped into the back yard with a book, to sun myself.

On one such day, I lathered my body in baby oil and made myself comfortable on a towel. On the "baby oil" days it was all about the sunshine; I didn't do any reading and usually lasted only a short while before the heat made me restless. Mr. Maier had given me permission to have a beer now and then, so I ran in and grabbed one. Nothing like a nice cold one on a hot summer day. I returned, lit a cigarette, laid back, and closed my eyes.

The crunch of footsteps interrupted my reverie. I opened my eyes, propped myself on my elbows, and squinted against the sunshine to see who my guest might be. When I saw who it was, I felt a bit like Adam and Eve in the Garden of Eden, and wished for a bush to hide behind... my "fig leaves" left me feeling quite naked.

"Hi, Pastor Reaney," I said, keenly aware of my bikini, and body lathered in baby oil. If ever I wished for a large woollen blanket on a hot day, it was then.

I had visited the Holiness church in Wellesley a few times, where Lloyd and Doris Reaney pastored. They had invited me into their home a time or two, and seemed genuinely to care, but this wasn't exactly how I had imagined meeting him again.

"Hi, Trudy," he greeted me cheerfully. "I was in town and thought I'd pop by to see how you're doing."

"Kind of obvious, isn't it?" I said, raising my hands carelessly, a beer in one, and cigarette in the other.

"No, I came to see how *you* are," he said. He looked me in the eyes, as if missing the little details of my near-nakedness, and the items in my hands. It was as if he looked past my body, into my soul.

We spoke only for a moment, but in that brief encounter, I felt as though I experienced a kinder God. No one had ever looked beyond my exterior before, to see the need of my soul. That God would look on us, and see beyond our sin, never made sense until that moment.

Pastor Lloyd walked away, but his visit left an indelible mark on my soul.

****

Life with the Maiers soon grew boring. The day-to-day routine of caring for the house didn't give me enough to do to pass the time. Mr. Maier and I agreed that I could find work to help supplement my income, and as long as I could keep up with my household duties and prepare the evening meals, he would continue to pay the rate we had originally agreed on.

I found a job in a small furniture factory, working on a production line. This opened up a whole new world—a much less innocent one than I had known. I kept to myself, for the most part, but saw things I had not previously experienced. It was no secret that numerous coworkers dabbled in drugs, and two young women made their competitions with each other quite public, of seeing who could sleep with the most men on any given weekend. I stayed as far away from them as possible.

I continued dating Daniel, and several months after moving to New Hamburg, I gave up my virginity to him. I wanted to belong, to be loved and accepted, and he wanted what I believed all men wanted. Maybe it was the way it had to be. A fair trade. An exchange, of sorts. But instead of creating a bond, and offering a place for my heart to belong, it had a negative impact on our relationship. Starting the moment it happened, I withdrew.

Immediately after letting him use my body, I said to Daniel, "You're not a virgin anymore, but I still am, because I felt nothing."

"What do you mean, you 'felt nothing'?" he asked.

"I don't know how to explain it, but I felt nothing," I said, trying to explain that I had closed my mind to what was happening. I knew, consciously, that it had happened, that I had agreed to it, but I had shut my conscious awareness off at that point, for him to do as he wished. I would learn years later that it was called disassociation, something I had most likely learned during childhood abuse, allowing me to "escape" trauma.

From that day forward, I resented Daniel, and was repulsed by him. His clothes bugged me. His hair. His mustache. Things that had never bothered me before, I suddenly hated. I dreaded his visits, and became melancholy and depressed whenever I was with him. Daniel noticed the change too; it was impossible to miss it. The carefree, happy-go-lucky party girl no longer made him happy.

"When you're like this," he said one night, "my body doesn't respond the way it used to." I knew what he was talking about. He had told me how he had leaned against the car every time he saw me, to avoid embarrassment with his buddies. His not-so-subtle way of saying "you're not sexy anymore," as though the sole purpose of a woman was to arouse a man, further infuriated me and affirmed my beliefs about men. Unable to express what I felt, I pushed down the anger in silence, and let it fester.

Daniel and I never fought before becoming sexually involved, but that all changed. The emotional aftermath constantly forced us to deal with my depression, while always skirting the real issues. One particularly brutal night, we stayed up until it was only three hours before I needed to get up for work. Worried I wouldn't be able to stay awake, he offered me a little "miracle" tablet.

"What is it?" I asked.

"It's an upper… it'll keep you awake tomorrow," he said. He explained that truckers use them all the time, and I should set my alarm an hour early, pop the pill and reset the alarm, and then go back to sleep. "That way you'll have no problem getting up."

I did as he said, and within an hour of arriving at work, a co-worker studied my face closely and commented, "What are you on, girl? Cocaine?"

"I don't do drugs," I said. "I never have."

"You act like you're on cocaine! You're not normal today," she said, looking at me skeptically. "You're sure you didn't take something?"

"Yeah, I took *something*, but not drugs. My boyfriend gave me a pill to help me stay awake, but not 'drugs' like that. He said truckers use them all the time," I said.

"What kind of *pill*?" she asked.

"I don't know. An upper is what he called it. He said it's nothing," I said.

"Girl, you can't go taking stuff when you don't know what it is! He could give you anything," she said.

"He wouldn't do that to me, and get me high," I replied. Little did I realize that he wouldn't likely think twice. Within weeks he would prove that, though not with drugs.

When the cycle of depression escalated to suicidal tendencies and ideations, I broke off the relationship. I didn't want to see him anymore; he was a constant reminder of what I had lost. A week after the breakup, Daniel and I were to attend a wedding together. Instead, he took a friend of mine, and I went with a friend of his. An odd arrangement, but it worked. And his friend turned out to be the perfect gentleman. Well, almost…

It was a liberal Mennonite wedding, with many conservative Mennonite guests, but not a dry wedding. Our table was a loud party group, who could put away a lot of booze. That is, everyone except me. Prior to that night, I had only had a few drinks with friends, and never enough to get drunk, or even create more than a light buzz, at worst.

My date offered to get me an orange vodka, and I accepted. When my ex-boyfriend brought me a second orange vodka, I should have been suspicious. What I didn't realize was that he served me a double, and recruited my date to do the same. They had one goal, to see if they could get me drunk.

A bar at that wedding did not bode well for our table, even apart from that conspiracy against me. We were not the quietest group to start with, and as the night progressed, we grew increasingly more boisterous. Especially me. After a certain point, I grew bolder with every sip, and less selective about what I ingested. By the end of the night, I was drinking everything within reach, anything anyone offered.

Drunk out of my mind, I stumbled out the door of the Wellesley hall, laughing hysterically, as my date, and my ex and his date, escorted me from the reception. The room swirled around me, and the people blurred together. I made it to the car before I passed out, and woke up only once to pull over because of nausea. And that's the last I remember about that night.

I woke up the next morning still wearing a royal blue dress, nylons, and makeup. The only thing missing were my shoes. They were neatly set at the foot end of the bed. And the only thing extra was a hangover, complete with a killer headache.

At nine a.m. the phone rang. It was my ex, calling to wish me a good day, and to ask if I had enjoyed my evening at his friend's wedding. He admitted then that they had conspired together to serve me doubles, and see how far they could take it.

I thanked him for the hangover, and asked how I got onto my bed. He explained how the three of them had carried me in, limp as a rag, trying not to wake up Clare and Vera with their ruckus and laughter.

It was a lesson well learned, not to trust friends to serve drinks, or accept everything they offer. But I was still quite naïve when it came to the world of drugs. About a week later, several co-workers at the factory asked me to go out with them on a Friday night. They were all within months of my age, something I was not accustomed to. Everyone with whom I typically associated was at least three years older than me, so to go out with peers was odd, but I agreed to go.

The plan was to go to McDonald's on Highland Road in Kitchener, hang out, and then come home again. Dorvan and Craig picked me up before driving to Wellesley to pick up Jorge, and then head to Kitchener. Jorge jumped in the back seat and handed a grocery bag to Dorvan.

"Hey, Trudy, would you hold this for me," Dorvan asked. "Put it under your shirt, just in case we get pulled over by a cop. You'll look pregnant and they won't ask any questions."

"What is it?" I asked.

"Don't worry about it. Just pop it under your shirt," he said.

Having never learned to say no, I did as he asked, even though I wasn't comfortable with it. I knew it couldn't be good, if it had to be hidden, but I lacked backbone to resist. Besides, I was out in the country, stuck with these "friends," with no way home. The best thing would be to comply.

We arrived at McDonald's, but rather than going in to eat, we parked the car. They had my attention when they started rolling their own cigarettes. I had been captivated, in childhood, when one of dad's friends rolled cigarettes. I had not seen it since and to watch my peers do it impressed me. They pulled the "stuff" from the bag, placed it carefully on the rolling paper, then added something from a small container before rolling it back up. They took turns passing the joint around, and then offered it to me. I took one drag and gave it back, not comfortable with whatever they were doing. Something didn't feel right.

When they had all they wanted, they handed me the bag and asked me to put it under my sweater again. Big loose-fitting sweaters were in style, so it wasn't hard to hide.

The ride home was a ride from hell. Fortunately not the other way around. We left McDonald's and traveled back to Wellesley, to take Jorge home. By the time we reached the back road leading into Wellesley from Lobsinger Line, they were all high, and clearly not thinking straight. I sat in the back seat, praying fervently as we flew over the hills at speeds even I, who loved adventure and risk, was not comfortable with.

When Dorvan climbed out the sunroof, while steering with his feet, and Jorge controlled the gas and brakes, I almost stopped breathing. It was the most terrifying thing I had ever experienced, even more so than my father's death threats. With him I stood a chance at getting away; if this car crashed, I was dead. There was no doubt in my mind about that.

We made it home safely, somehow, after dropping off Jorge and his bag of stuff, and I determined I would never again agree to go driving with a bunch of kids without knowing a bit more about them! I had more than enough excitement to last me a long time, and was quite happy to return home, away from irresponsible teenagers.

****

At first Clare and Vera's home seemed to be a safe place. I knew little about caring for the elderly, but they seemed relatively healthy, for being in their eighties, so I watched for signs indicating they were unwell. From the start there were things that didn't seem right. Had I known what I know now, I would have contacted the family.

Soon after I arrived Clare told me that Vera spent most of her time in her room and I would seldom see her. She emerged to eat breakfast, then vanished again. If I was there for lunch, the same routine took place. And again for dinner. The rest of the time she remained completely reclusive.

After a few weeks, she started with outbursts of rage that were quite frightening, while staring at me with vacant eyes. Again Clare explained that "she gets like this," and I did nothing. I had grown up in much worse and wasn't overly alarmed. But, as this behavioural change took place, so did Clare's behaviour. He started to act possessive of me in a way that seemed innocent and caring, at first. I was seventeen with no parents in my life, and wrote it off as that.

He asked far too many questions, including wanting to know if I was a virgin and if my ex-boyfriend and I had been sexually involved, and admitted that he had tried to keep an eye on us. He told me he only had one testicle—just what every sixteen-year-old wants to know about an old man— and added that it was a miracle they had been able to have any children at all, given that fact. I wrote it off as a "miracle story" with no ulterior motives.

137

Little by little things digressed. He told me how this condition had affected their marriage. He was quite certain Vera got pregnant with their first baby through affairs, and wondered about some of the others. What were the odds that he could have produced so many pregnancies?

As the information tumbled out, my guard went up. I didn't want to hear about his body, or their marriage, but I didn't have the courage to say anything. He was a man, and elderly at that, and must be treated with respect. So I smiled and nodded and acted as normal as possible even when I wanted to vomit.

In hindsight it is easy to see, but at the time I didn't understand why Vera's outbursts became more aggressive, even directed at me. The time her husband spent with me, talking and interacting, should have been spent with his wife, even if she was slipping mentally. She was jealous, and rightfully so. But at the time I thought she was simply going mental. Her ability to speak coherently was long gone so, in her rage, she yelled unintelligable words, shaking her fist in my face.

****

Clare announced, one day, that he was setting a curfew for me. He wanted me home by eleven and if I arrived even a minute late, he said, the outer door would be locked—one to which I did not have a key—and I would need to fend for myself outside. I saw no need for a curfew. I did my duties in the house, and had a key for the main door. I always entered quietly, and was usually home before midnight. Still, I needed a place to live and had no choice but to give in to his controls.

I returned minutes after eleven, one evening soon after he set the curfew, only to discover I was, indeed, locked out. Necessity breeds innovation; it had in childhood, and it would again. I tried every window and door I could reach, before discovering one small sliding window, under the large kitchen window, was open. Unfortunately a screen covered it and would not be easily removed. I worked at it until the screen came out and, thankful for my slender frame, crawled in. Once inside I replaced the screen and closed the window. I then walked to the front door and unlocked it, leaving both doors unlocked for the night.

The following morning I greeted Clare cheerfully for breakfast. He seemed friendly, if not a bit bewildered. After a few minutes he burst out laughing. "You know, I thought I had locked you out last night!" he said. "But I got up this morning and saw your bedroom door was closed, so I checked the front door and here I left it unlocked all night!"

I laughed heartily. It was funny indeed! And he never locked me out again, regardless what time I showed up.

Clare and Vera both went to bed quite early, leaving me to have some alone time at around nine p.m. I didn't go out often, so evenings were spent watching whatever comedy or sitcom might be playing. Clare always stuck his head in the living room door to say goodnight before turning in, but one night he walked toward me with his cane. I assumed he had left something on the coffee table and was coming for it, but instead, he turned and hovered over me. My instincts said, get up, push past him and run, but I couldn't move. He leaned over and kissed me smack on the lips and mumbled some affectionate good night.

Taken by surprise, I lay there, wiping my lips over and over, screaming inwardly. The smell of his garlic lingered. I wanted to get up, walk over to him, and beat him up. Instead, I made a mental note and avoided evenings in the living room. If I saw him coming, I cleared out, staying as far from him as possible.

As his obsessions grew, Clare admitted to rummaging through my personal belongings in search of birth control. The thought of it repulsed and angered me. I would need to find a new home, yet again.

Chapter Seventeen

It was a cool and rainy fall night when the depression took me to the lowest point of all time. I had struggled, from time to time as a child, with suicidal thoughts, even going so far as tying a large bandana around my neck, at about age eleven, and tightening it to see if I would have the courage to follow through. Aside from that, it had always been thoughts and ideations without plans.

But that night, in October 1986, was different. The only thing preventing me from popping the bottle of pills I had spilled into my hands was the fear of hell. What if... just what if it was a real place, and I would end up there, burning forever, in endless torment. But the torment of living consumed me, and the battle raged.

At length I picked up the phone and called a woman I had met in the summer. Marlene Herford-Martin had Amish background, like Grandma Katie, but she and her husband had left the church, and eventually divorced, making her an outcast in her culture. Yet, from the moment Marlene met me, she loved me. A virtual stranger, she talked to me about everything from God, to boyfriends, to day-to-day life stuff. She listened to me when I was hurting, and offered motherly advice. In my moment of despair, she was the only person I could think of to call.

I dialled her number. She answered. I told her I was tired of life, and I couldn't think of any reason to live. I played with the pills in my hand and, past tears, told her about them. The empty bottle lay on its side, on my nightstand. I pictured someone finding it... finding me.

"Trudy, I'm going to come over. Don't you do anything before I get there!" Marlene said. She didn't want to find a body. "Promise me you won't take them, and you'll stay right where you are. I am on my way."

I promised her I wouldn't do anything, and with that I hung up the phone. Hot tears spilled down my cheeks, as hopelessness washed over my empty spirit.

I slipped into my coat and shoes. I couldn't stay there, in my room. The pills. The thoughts. The hopelessness. It was all overwhelming. I stumbled down the walking path that led across the river and made my way to the bridge. It was cold outside. So cold. Just like my heart. I stood there a long while, looking over the rail, imagining the headlines in the *New Hamburg Independent*: "Teen girl's body found in Nith River." I pictured my parents and the church reading the story.

I wanted my pain to end, and theirs to start. I wanted my death to haunt everyone I had ever known, and punish them for the abuse, the violence, the trauma... the neglect... the shredding of my spirit.

Tears splashed into the swollen waters, swallowed up by the waves, but making no impact. I wondered if my family and the church would even miss me. Would they even grieve? Or would I disappear in their memories, the way my tears disappeared in the river? Did my life have any meaning at all? Did God even notice, or care? My thoughts rambled.

I thought about Marlene, who would be well on her way to see me. I had to get back to the house so she wouldn't be afraid that I had done anything foolish. That wouldn't be fair to her. I turned and retraced my footsteps, arriving at the house just moments before Marlene.

Like other conversations with Marlene, nothing was off bounds. We talked about anything I wanted to get off my chest—even having lost my virginity. She reassured me that my life had purpose, that God wasn't finished with me yet, and nothing I had done was beyond His redemption.

But nothing she said meant as much as her presence. She was there. For me. No judgement. No new and great revelation. Just present, without any personal mission or agenda. It didn't solve all my problems, but it got me through a hopeless night. And, while I didn't let God into my life immediately, there was that glimmer of hope again, that maybe He still loved me.

When she offered, I agreed to visit Marlene's church, the Good Samaritan Community Church in Kitchener, from time to time, starting that next Sunday. She and her husband would pick me up, she said. It was something. A place to start finding my way back.

At church I met a young woman in her early twenties, Cheri, who invited me to join her and her friend Annette a few weeks later, on Friday night,

October 31, to what I thought was a Halloween dance. Though I found it a bit odd that a church would have a Halloween dance, I was excited to go.

When the day arrived, I spent hours preparing. Assuming I was to be in costume, I settled on black slacks and a yellow sweater, with my face painted like a tiger. I had never done face painting before, but the kit gave step by step instructions, and with a little creativity, it was easy enough. I curled and back-combed my hair into a big frizzy do, and carefully applied the paint, then stepped back and studied the end result. *Not bad!*

At the Kitchener bus depot on Charles Street, I looked for Cheri and Annette, who had agreed to meet me and walk with me to the event. I spotted them and observed that they were not yet in costume. They didn't recognize me, so I waved and walked toward them.

Both girls stood there for a moment, staring with peculiar expressions. After a moment they asked why I had painted my face.

"Aren't we going to a Halloween dance?" I asked.

There was an awkward pause. "No. We're going to a church service."

"Oh," I said, taking in the new information. "Now what?"

"Well, you're going to have to go like that. We're already late." With that we made our way to the school gym, where church was already in progress. We snuck in as quietly as possible, trying to be as inconspicuous as one can be, looking like a tiger in church.

The speaker, Howard Ellis, was addressing the children, speaking to them about Noah's ark and the animals. "And, as it turns out," he said, turning his attention toward me, "it looks like we have a giant cat with us tonight." The children turned to look at me, some giggling, others looking unsure.

I giggled, a bit sheepishly, and said I thought I was attending a Halloween dance, not a church service. This was met with a ripple of laughter from the adults.

After the service a small group congregated at a small hole in the wall café across from the bus station, where we chatted and laughed for a while before heading to my new friends' apartment. The night wasn't what I had expected, or even hoped for, but it was a good night. And the interaction with Cheri and Annette led to another life change soon after.

****

The following week Marlene took me to Fairway Mall in Kitchener, where I applied for jobs in every retail store that looked at all interesting. Within days I was hired as a cashier, working for Sears.

I moved in with Cheri and Annette, just minutes from work, in November 1986. It was my fourth residence in just over a year since leaving home. Too much had happened during that time, but I was determined to pull myself together and make a good life for myself.

Things went well for a few weeks. I didn't give up my smoking habit, but I stopped drinking, and spent my time either at work, at home, or at church. Away from the party scene, and party friends, I made better choices, and felt pretty good about life.

And then one day, as I was leaving Fairview Mall, I met Rick, a young man with whom I had worked in the factory in New Hamburg. Rick was a heartthrob. Incredibly tall, with shoulder-length, medium-toned auburn hair, a chiseled jaw, and gorgeous eyes. He was a wild rocker who played in a start-up band, and had a reputation as quite a womanizer.

When we worked together, we never paid attention to each other more than a passing hi. But that day at the mall, as he walked across the parking lot with a twenty-four-pack on his shoulder, he stopped and chatted. I still had no self-esteem to speak of and for him to initiate a conversation with me was huge validation. He flirted a little, but I told myself I was misreading him. He wouldn't pay attention to someone like me.

As we spoke, my confidence grew, and I kidded him about the case of beer and his plans for it. He said he was having a party that Friday night, and wondered if I'd want to join in. Two girls from our former job would also be there. "You remember Jan and Victoria?"

My heart sank. It was the two girls who spent weekends competing with each other, to see who could sleep with the most men. I didn't really want to party with them, but I didn't want to say no to Rick, so I agreed to go.

144

I took the bus to his house that Friday night, for the big party. We played "bottle caps" a while, a game I wasn't good at, and with each "fail," the loser had to take a swig of beer. My skill didn't improve as I drank.

After a few drinks, Rick started making advances at me. I had the presence of mind to know what was happening, but without the sense of reason to say no, or even to want to say no. He took me to another room....

But then, in a moment of unexpected grace, Rick lifted his hands off of me and looked me right in the eyes. "You don't want to do this," he said.

"Yes, I do," I argued.

Rick shook his head. "No, you don't. You're not that kind of girl. I can't do this to you." And with that he took me back to the game. We kept playing until I was so drunk I fell asleep. But just before I faded, I crawled over to a corner in the family room, onto an air mattresses spread out across the room. This was intended to be an all-nighter, and I was the first one down.

At three a.m. I awakened, the alcohol having worn off enough to end the deep sleep. What greeted me when I opened my eyes was shocking. Never since early childhood had I been exposed to such vile sexual perversion. All around me, naked bodies shamelessly engaged in sexual intercourse. My halo wasn't polished and shiny so that I could judge them, but that scene repulsed me.

I fumbled in the dark for my coat and purse, before stumbling through the maze of bodies, out into the cold November night. I had no idea where I was or where I was going, but I couldn't stay. I staggered down several streets and found a pay phone at the back of a building. Beside it, through blurred vision, I saw a taxi phone. I had never used one before, but took my chances that it would get me what I needed. I picked up the phone, and immediately it rang at the other end of the line.

"United Taxi," the voice greeted.

With slurred speech I explained that I was drunk—as if that wasn't obvious—that I didn't know where I was, but needed a ride home. The gentleman asked me to look around and describe my surroundings. I squinted past blurred vision, and managed to read a few signs, including a Laundromat.

"Stay where you are," the gentleman said, "I know your location. I'll have a taxi to you in a few minutes."

A taxi pulled up moments later, presenting me with the next dilemma. Having just moved in with Cheri and Annette, I couldn't remember my address. I told the driver to take me to Fairway Road, and from there I would recognize my way.

As we drove the gentleman spoke gently, telling me of his faith in Jesus, and how much God loves me. It was almost as if I was stuck with an angel in the middle of the night. A stark contrast to the horror I had left behind, only minutes earlier.

I told him that I, too, had once believed, but I had left home at fifteen, and had lost my way. I really wanted to believe, and wanted to know God, but I couldn't seem to get on track. He assured me that God was with me.

As we neared the apartment, I realized I had no cash with me. It was supposed to be an all-nighter, after which I planned to take the bus home, and bus fare was pocket change, unlike a taxi ride. Apologetically I explained this to the driver, but promised that if he would tell me where and when I could meet him on his next shift, I would pay. He would pop by the next evening, at seven p.m., at my apartment, he said, and, with that, we parted ways.

Like clockwork, the next evening, the taxi pulled up. I thanked him for his kindness, paid him, and never saw him again. But one day, in Heaven, I will know him by what he did in my life, and I will thank him.

Chapter Eighteen

My home with Cheri and Annette, as we had agreed, was a temporary landing place while I searched for something more permanent. Marlene had done some investigating and soon let me know she had found a place. She didn't know Kyle and Amy personally, but she knew Amy's parents and if that was any indication, it would be a good place.

And so it was that only weeks after I moved in with Cheri and Annette, I moved out again and settled into my new home with Kyle and Amy. We had arranged one quick meeting for me to check out the bedroom and agree on rent, and it was a done deal.

I arrived at their door with my belongings and was greeted by a large black dog, barking furiously. Dogs are wonderful pets, when they like you, and you are familiar with them. Large, strange black dogs, who bark like you're their lunch, are not so nice for pets.

Fido was gated in the kitchen, so that he could not come to my room, but every day I had to step over that gate, dodge through the kitchen, jump over the other gate, and go downstairs to shower before work.

I refused to admit it, but that dog terrified me. "No, no, I'm fine," I said, when Kyle or Amy asked, but every time I faced that dog when they were gone, my heart first stopped when the dog barked or growled at me, then restarted with furious energy as I braved the kitchen.

For several weeks I silently endured that dragon-sized beast. Daily I imagined my remains on the floor, for Kyle and Amy to clean up when they returned home. But each day I survived the mad dash, and landed on the other side of the gate laughing from the adrenaline rush.

Needless to say I didn't eat much when Kyle and Amy were away, as I never lasted long enough in the kitchen to scrounge together a meal. Gradually I accepted these inconveniences as part of my new environment, and stored food in my room.

Then, suddenly everything changed. Kyle and Amy decided they wanted to parent me. They set a curfew. I would need to tell them who I was with, where I was going, and how long I planned to be gone. And any other detail they would like to know, I would be required to tell them. I had been on my own for a year, with no one demanding those things, and I was not about to play that role in a tenant relationship. I came and went as I pleased. I was responsible for my own meals and groceries, except the occasional dinner in the evening, so there was no need for them to know my plans. I was renting a room. Nothing more.

One evening a male friend dropped by and we sat in the car for a while, parked in the driveway, until we noticed that Kyle and Amy took turns standing by the window, watching us. That's when we decided to go for a drive. When I returned, Kyle and Amy were waiting for me, looking for answers. I told them it was a friend, not a boyfriend, and nothing had happened. But they were not satisfied with that.

About that time I met up with my past party friends again. In conversation I told them about my living conditions—the dog, the "babysitting" and curfew—and they offered me a room in their apartment. I accepted immediately.

We drove to Kyle and Amy's to collect some basic items, and I informed them of my decision to move out. I made arrangements to return for the rest of my belongings the next day. But by the time we returned, they had changed the locks and refused to let me in, or release my belongings. In the end we called the police, who told Kyle and Amy they had to let me get my belongings.

So began the adventures, in early December 1986, of living with my party friends. They were "responsible" party friends, and great roommates. Other than normal minor relational stresses, my time with Elayna and Fran, and my relationship with them, was good. Granted, I was young and immature, and probably more of a burden on them than I realized, but they seldom let on.

I worked several part-time jobs, and my roommates both worked full time, but that didn't prevent us from finding time to party. I was the only one who smoked, and wasn't allowed to do so in the apartment. We all did our share of drinking, but I was careful not to get stone drunk again. I hated the complete loss of control and being at the mercy of other people like that.

Thursday nights tended to be girls' night out drinking and dancing, and Friday and Saturday we spent with other friends, clubbing. Saturday nights we frequented a country bar, the Stampede Corral, where we met up with our Mennonite guy friends and partied with them. The thing about being male in the Mennonite culture, if you intended to break the rules, was that you were not as easily identified as Mennonite, with just one glance. They could get by with a lot of rule breaking without ever having the church find out. For the most part these particular friends were safe and respectful, and most never made any attempts to cross any boundaries. In fact, when hit on by girls in the bar, they mostly disregarded them, with only a few exceptions.

It wasn't much of a life, really, working and partying, but it kept reality at bay, and prevented me from facing memories of home and childhood. And it effectively drowned out the voice of God, so that I didn't need to contend with Him, or the reality of my sin and rebellion. Most of the time…

Every now and then, when I watched *100 Huntley Street,* and listened to the testimonies and stories of Jesus, or when I was alone at night, and sober, His voice would whisper, and I would find myself contemplating God, and my eternal destiny. When friends or roommates were present, I boldly cursed Him, even dropping the "f-bomb" when we stumbled upon Christian TV programs. But in the absence of company, I listened and wept. On one occasion, I even called in for prayer, after listening to Reverend Donald Mainse, and a sweet Grandma prayed for me and encourage me. Still, had someone asked me, I would have said God didn't exist, that I didn't believe in Him and, at best, I was an agnostic. Probably atheist. There was no way, in my mind, that a loving God could exist, given the life I had known up until that time, and with my experiences in church. But in those moments, alone, when I heard His voice, and felt Him move deep in my fragmented spirit, I was compelled to believe.

What was more, in those moments He was not condemning or harsh. When that Grandma, in her shaky, aged voice, told me of God's love and prayer for me, it was as if God Himself reached down. And the voice I heard in the stillness, alone in my room, was one of love and invitation. Standing at my window, looking up into the night sky, I felt as though my chest might burst and the tears would fall, unashamedly, as my heart cried out to this

Being, whoever He was. And, if just for a moment, my spirit would come alive, and life would breathe into my soul. And then the moment would pass, and life, with all its harshness, returned.

On the harsher days, when God was far away, I scoffed and mocked the very God who breathed that life into me. On one such day, walking down King Street just outside King Centre Shopping Plaza, a group of Beachy Amish Mennonites congregated, handing out religious tracts.

I resented my cultural background and wanted to be rude, but I recognized the man reaching out his hand with the tract. Elroy Wagler. He didn't recognize me, but my older sister had worked for him and his wife, Dianne, and I had visited their home and played with their children, Anita, Loretta, Nathanial, and Timothy. Suddenly it was personal and I didn't have the heart to decline or be rude. I didn't identify myself, but I smiled and graciously accepted the pamphlet.

As I walked away I shredded the pamphlet and tossed it in the garbage can on the sidewalk. *Why did the people seem so nice when, in my reality, so much of the culture had been harsh? Were they all pretending? Was any of it real?*

In spite of what I had seen and experienced, and the corruption that lay shrouded in secrecy, there were those who genuinely loved God, and represented Him well. It would have been easier to disregard Him altogether if the whole lot of them were corrupt, and no kindness remained. Then I could have justified my hatred and turned my back on Him—even believe that He was not real. But always, it seemed, the fluke—that one person who had represented God well in my life—would bring me face to face with a Living God.

I was forced to see good and evil, so that I could not simply write religion off as a curse or a fantasy. And always I would find some chaos, drama, or party to push that reality far away, and leave God lost in the shadows of the past, the shadows of religion and time.

Had I known how to look past both—good and evil—to see only God's pure love, and His desire for relationship, then I might have believed and been transformed.

Chapter Nineteen

By Christmas 1986, I was nicely settled into my new home, and the weekly party routine. I had started dating Larry almost two weeks earlier, my first steady boyfriend since breaking up with Daniel in early October.

The relationship cycle that ensued with my new boyfriend ended in the same hopelessness and depression as with Daniel. But this time my heart was hardened to the pain, trauma, and loss, and that hardness prevented the suicidal tendencies, pushing me deeper into the world of alcohol, cigarettes, and bar hopping.

At age seventeen, I easily passed for someone in her mid- to late twenties, and carried myself with that level of confidence. When asked for ID, I always reached for my wallet, only to fake being flustered at not finding it.

"I'm sorry," I would say, "I must have left it in the car, or at home. I'll check my vehicle." With that, they would either say, "No worries" and let me in, or our group would walk away. Only twice did that method not work to get me into a bar.

The party scene exposed me to more and more risk and, with that risk, trauma after trauma. But I buried the trauma deep in denial, as men used me without a second thought. I had learned that this is what men do, and if you said no, they would find one way or another to seduce you, or use you. The best thing to do, I concluded, was to hope that one day the right one would come along and treat me well.

To some men I surrendered willingly, while others disregarded me when I said no. Whether it was Larry, who called after a weekend with the guys to ask permission to stop by "for a quick one" while his buddies waited in the truck, or some guy trying to seduce me, or use me against my will, the end result was the same. I was an object of lust, used and abandoned, and it all blended together into one empty existence.

I had dumped Larry over the phone the night he made that call. I was no one's prostitute. I wanted security—a place to belong—not some arrogant, self-centred man who was willing to use me like that. I had accepted that the trade-off for a place to belong was to give my body, but this crossed a line.

151

As things got worse, I ran further and faster from God, trying to escape myself and the broken life I lived. But always hard reality stared me in the face, in one traumatic event or another. And that's precisely what happened at the end of January, several weeks after I broke up with Larry. I had returned to the single life of barhopping, partying, and having fun with the guys, with no commitment or relationship, and no one using me...

One Thursday night in late January, Elayna, Fran, and I decided it was time for a girls' night out again. It had been a while. We visited one of our regular bars and had a great night, drinking a little and dancing a lot. The night was uneventful, and an early one. We all had to work the next day.

We returned to our apartment somewhere between nine and ten p.m. to find several friends waiting for us, having slipped the lock to our apartment. After lecturing them not to do that again, we played poker, had a few more drinks, and danced like fools. The party was still going strong when I excused myself to go to bed. I didn't want to be too tired for work the next morning.

****

I awoke from a deep sleep, at five a.m., to someone pulling down my panties. Suddenly Barry was on top of me. His breath reeked of alcohol. He was drunk, but not drunk enough...

"Barry, please don't..." The shock registered. Slowly. He was forcing himself on me, against my will. At six foot four, and well over two hundred pounds, he had a good eighty pounds on me, and seven inches taller. I didn't stand a chance. My body was stiff, closed up, but that didn't stop him any more than me saying no.

I closed my eyes and turned away from the nauseating stench of his breath. Tears trickled down my face. I could feel them running down my temple and into my hair. I felt weaker, more vulnerable, and more betrayed than I had ever felt, but didn't understand why. And I certainly wasn't going to let him see it.

He had the gall to look at me then and ask, "Can I do it again?"

I couldn't speak. No words would come. Something broke inside me, and my whole body shook with sobs. I pushed myself out of the water bed and stood to my feet, weak and trembling. Barry rose from the bed and stood in front of me, leaning in to see my face. I turned away.

As if registering with Barry for the first time that there was something wrong with what was happening, he stepped back. "What's wrong, Trudy? Did I hurt you?"

As I stood there sobbing and unable to speak, Barry clearly felt remorseful. "I'm sorry," he said, "What is it? Why are you crying?"

I pressed my hands against the sides of my head, as if pushing back an invisible force, and closed my eyes, as if willing myself not to see. "I don't know," I sobbed. "I don't know... You remind me of my dad..."

The colour drained from his face. "Your dad did this to you?" he asked, shocked.

"I don't know... I don't remember..."

As quickly as I had lost control, I regained it. Barry had not intended to hurt me. He was drunk. He was remorseful. I needed to let it go.

"What are you going to do now, Barry?" I asked. He wasn't sure. He needed to go home, he said.

"You can't drive. You're drunk. I'll call you a cab." I picked up the phone, called a taxi, and sent Barry on his way, then showered and got ready for work. With that, Barry disappeared out of my world. I didn't ask him never to come back. He just stopped coming around, as if his conscience wouldn't let him face what he did to me.

I blocked the events of the morning, pushed them down, as if they never happened. Especially what I had said about my dad.

****

It was Saturday night and my friends and I were at Lulu's in Cambridge. Being Valentine's Day, I wore a red dress—a colour I didn't wear often. It was a cute dress. Not too long, and not too short. Not too revealing. I was always self-conscious about anything too short or low cut. I had a thing about showing cleavage and that red dress was as close as I got, with gathered panels that criss-crossed over my chest. But to keep it in place, I used a safety pin where no one could see it. On the one hand I was conservative that way, and on the other hand I was out to party. Hard. Drown the pain. Party now, contend with hell later.

I liked to dance, after a few drinks, when inhibitions were lost in the buzz. But until those drinks took effect, I stood at the sidelines, trapped by my insecurities.

At Lulu's a low wall divided the eating area from the dance floor. I stood there alone, that February night, watching the crowd dance. The band played "Walk Like an Egyptian" and the crowd lined up, many of them, and moved almost in sync. I lacked coordination, drunk or sober, for that kind of dance, but I loved to watch.

A clean-cut man, who looked to be in his mid-twenties, came and stood beside me a few minutes, before introducing himself. "I'm Glen Khol," he said, reaching out his hand.

"I'm Trudy. Nice to meet you," I said.

"Care to dance?" he asked, when a slow song played.

"I'm not that good," I said.

He charmed me into it, and I found myself on the dance floor, not at all inebriated for a change. I lasted a dance or two before returning to the sidelines. Glen joined me. We talked about work. I had a few odd jobs. Retail. Fast food. He was an undercover cop in a big city, some distance away, he said.

"Show me your badge," I said, making sure he wasn't pulling the "handsome man in a uniform" to impress me. He pulled out his badge. "We're celebrating the sergeant's birthday," he said, as he led me to his friends and introduced me to the entire team, who were obviously having a great time. We engaged in small talk with them for a while, then returned to dancing.

"So how old are you?" Glen asked.

"You're a police officer. I can't answer that question," I said.

"Oh come on... You can tell me how old you are!" Glen persisted.

"What if I said I was underaged, then what would you say?" I asked.

"I wouldn't do anything. I'm off duty," he said.

"In that case I'm seventeen," I said. "I never get carded."

"Wow! I wouldn't have guessed you for seventeen!" he said.

We talked, indulged in a few drinks, danced again, and had a good time. "Hey, would you like to go out for a walk," he asked when I tired of dancing.

I hesitated. He was a cop, but who was to say that made him safe? I pushed my fears away and stepped into the winter night with him. I took a deep breath. The air was crisp. Clear. Beautiful. The moon was bright and round—full or almost full—as it rose in the east.

Glen walked to the white twelve-passenger van they had rented for their party. "Want to sit in here and stay warm?" he asked, opening the side door.

In spite of misgivings, I agreed. We sat in the back seat and talked. Before we went back inside, he asked if he could come back, maybe in a week or two, and take me on a date.

"I don't trust men right now, Glen," I said. So much had happened in a short time, leaving too many scars, too many betrayals. And I wasn't ready for a relationship. I told him what had happened a few weeks earlier with Barry and that I had not acknowledged what it was right away, but Glen assured me it was rape.

As an undercover officer, he said, you see everything, and proceeded to tell me about a rape scene he had been called to with his previous partner. It got ugly and someone was shot. Even for him, an officer who was trained for this work, it was pretty traumatizing, he said.

He wondered if I would consider a double date with his partner, Randy, and I could ask one of my roommates to join us. I agreed to it, and we made tentative arrangements before we parted ways. Glen gave me his undercover name and work number, so that I could call during the week to confirm the time and day.

****

Friday night, one week later, Glen arrived with his partner, Randy, right on schedule, in a sporty little black car. Before heading out, they showed us the magnetic cop light kept inside the car, ready to mount on the roof when needed. It all sounded fun, the high-speed chases, catching the bad guys, protecting victims. A noble career choice, filled with sacrifice and risk.

We went to a sketchy place on King Street that served dollar beers and had a few, before returning to the apartment. Arriving in the parking lot, Randy and Elayna went inside, but Glen made no move to get out. A moment later I understood why.

Glen reached down and unzipped his pants, then pulled my head onto his lap. The same old sense of obligation forced me to comply, and a sense of indebtedness over a stupid one-dollar beer came over me. I had told Glen what my boundaries were, what I wanted, what I didn't. I had told him what I had been through, and that I was tired of being used. I had trusted him to respect that.

Yet, here I was, offering my services. I hated it, being bought and used like that. Even prostitutes were paid better. I felt the urge to vomit, but resisted. I spit in my hand, when he wouldn't see, and slipped my hand into the pocket of my new dressy green coat, wiping the slime inside.

I opened the car door and walked to the apartment in awkward silence, but, once inside, I partied like nothing happened. As always, I buried the pain and pushed down the disappointment. This was one of the costs. Just life.

Glen and Randy left, and with that Glen walked out of my life. He had not been any different, after all. When he was the perfect gentleman that night at Lulu's, I started to believe that he was trustworthy. Maybe that was the plan. Build trust on a night when doing anything at all would have been risky, with a party of almost a dozen police officers who might show up any time. And then, when trust was established, move in for the kill.

Truth is, as much as I was hurt, repulsed, and disappointed, if he had apologized for disregarding my request for respect I would have forgiven quickly. But to take a part of me, and walk out the door as if that was the best I deserved, especially when he knew what had happened only weeks earlier... that cut deep.

The experience wasn't totally wasted. I finally started to get it that men didn't have the right to dance into my world, use me and ask for sexual favours, and then go waltzing back out. Something about a police officer, a man in authority, telling me it is wrong and then doing it, knocked some sense into me.

In about five months' time, starting with the loss of my virginity in October with Daniel, I had been used and abused, raped and violated, to varying degrees, by numerous men. But the last several were different in that they were not mutual consent, and were not men with whom I had established any relationships. It troubled me that almost any stranger could overpower me, through various methods, and use me.

I had had enough. My life was about to change.

Chapter Twenty

Geoff first crossed my radar in my late preteens when he visited his uncle, a church leader at Lakeshore Mennonite church, and his cousins, my classmates. We had spent little time together, but he visited Lakeshore school a time or two, and I thought he was nice enough. When he reappeared in my life, casually, in early 1987, we immediately connected on a friendship level.

No sparks, for either of us. It was a casual encounter with a group in a restaurant, followed by a visit to a bar and dance. He came by a few weeks later for a party, and again sometime after my night out with the police officer, for a whole weekend.

Somewhere in those times together, Geoff and I went deeper, and eventually I told him about the preceding five months of my life, what I had lost, and how devastating it was. He asked a lot of questions. Deep questions.

Geoff was a Christian. A struggling one, maybe, but with high standards and a good heart, and he wanted to honour God. I did too, I said, but it didn't mostly work out well when I tried. It definitely hadn't worked in the Mennonite church, and it wasn't any better living the messy life I had made for myself.

In conversation, Geoff encouraged me to go to the police about the rape, if for no other reason than to have it on record, in the event that other victims eventually came forward. I promised him I would do that in the coming week.

Before he left for home that Sunday night, he asked if I would be his girlfriend. He could come up on weekends to see me, and we could get to know each other, go to church, and hang out with friends. I was delighted. Finally, a man who wanted a relationship, not just a body, and a connection with God, not a girlfriend to use. And that is how our relationship started, only weeks after one of the most traumatic experiences of my teen years.

I called the Waterloo Regional Police the following week, and said I wanted to report a rape. It had been a few weeks, but a friend had recommended it, and even if they could do nothing, I wanted it on file.

Two detectives arrived at the apartment to interview me and get my side of the story in writing. They listened compassionately, as I recounted the details of that night. My body trembled, and I struggled to stay composed.

The detectives asked for Barry's contact information, including his work address. They said they would interview him, but there wasn't really anything they could do, unless he confessed. And that wasn't likely to happen. Still, they agreed it was good to have it on file. They instructed me to call immediately if he should contact me after they confronted him. They would need details of all our interactions.

It was late afternoon, soon after the officers confronted Barry, when the phone rang. I picked up. "Hello…"

Silence.

"Hello…" I said again.

"You whore."

The caller hung up. My heart started pounding. Would it end with that call, or was it a warning, a prelude to another move?

I called the detectives and told them about the phone call. I asked if there was anything else they could do to protect me. I was paranoid that he would come, and maybe do something worse. I didn't know him well, and had no idea what he was capable of. Would he rape me again? Would he threaten me? Kill me?

They said to keep reporting every little detail. Everything would be recorded, but unless he did something to harm me, there was nothing they could do.

****

My relationship with Geoff was unlike any other I had known. He treated me like a person, not an object, and valued my heart and my feelings. We had relationship boundaries, and tried to respect those boundaries. On occasion we crossed the lines, but the fact that he wanted to protect our relationship showed me that he respected me and had self-respect.

In the weeks and months that ensued, our relationship grew stronger, and the trauma of what had happened faded into the background. But occasionally the phone would ring and I would be greeted only with heavy breathing and silence, forcing my mind back into panic, fear, and anxiety.

Late May I connected with my sister-in-law Susan, married to my second-oldest brother Jacob, who lived in California. Other than occasional updates through my parents, I had not had any contact with them since I was ten. Even when their son, Bobby Jo, had drowned as a little toddler, when I was about twelve years old, none of the family had gone to the funeral. I had been sad about that, wishing desperately we could be with them. Behind our barn I had found solitude, wondering about the little boy I had never met, never known. It seemed a tragedy to lose a nephew, and never to have known him.

Susan and I chatted a while, just catching up on life stuff. I told her bits and pieces of what I had been through since leaving home, and the harassing phone calls. She was the first family member to whom I breathed a word of what life had become. At the end of the conversation she asked if I wanted live with them. She would talk to Jacob later and get back to me, if I was interested.

I told Geoff that if my brother agreed to it, I would fly to California within weeks, and stay there for the summer. Possibly longer. Geoff wasn't overly alarmed by that, but he did have one concern.

"What about us?" he asked.

"I'm not breaking up with you, Geoff," I said. "I just need to get away for a while." I was thrilled when he asked if he could fly out to see me later in the summer. Planning his visit made leaving easier. He gave me his class ring, to wear on a chain around my neck, as a symbol of our commitment to each other.

Susan called back to finalize details, and with that the plan was in motion. I would take the bus to the Buffalo Airport and fly out from there, to save money. They would buy me a one-way ticket and send it in the mail.

Geoff and I spent my last day in Canada together, and then I was off. I wore a pretty yellow sleeveless summer dress, with a cowel collar, a fitted waistline, a long flowing skirt, and a hat that complemented it. I wanted to look every part a lady, and be treated like one. If I was to travel alone, I had to look sophisticated, so that I would be taken seriously.

The outfit worked. At the Fort Erie border, the bus had to pull over, and each passenger go through customs, one at a time, answering questions, then moving through some sort of security before getting back on the bus. The officer who questioned me was a kind, fatherly man. After giving me a once-over, he asked all the necessary questions. Where was I going? How long would I be away? Who was I going to stay with? And so on. But when he asked for my ID, I didn't have any.

"I'm sorry, sir," I said, "I lost my citizenship card." The officer had already questioned the fact that it was a one-way ticket, with no commitment as to how long I was staying. This was a bigger hurdle, I feared.

"Ma'am... You expect me to let you cross this border with nothing more than a smile and your word?" He asked the question with a twinkle in his eye.

"Yes sir," I answered with a smile. If the smile was the first requirement, I'd start with it.

The officer grinned, shook his head, and picked up my bags. "Right this way please."

"Thank you, sir," I said, accepting my bags again. Not only had he let me through, he had carried my bags for me. It wasn't half the battle Susan and I had anticipated, knowing that I had no identification.

I had made it across. It was almost ten p.m. when the bus arrived at its destination near the airport. I spent my night wandering the airport, never straying far from the bench I had claimed as my personal space. Every now and then, a nighttime employee—whether a janitor, security, or some other staff—stopped to talk with me.

One tall gentleman stopped numerous times, just to chat. At about three a.m., he said he had an hour break and, if I wished, I could join him in Buffalo. He needed to slip out to grab a bite to eat.

He put my belongings in a safe place, so I wouldn't need to take them with me, and with that I rode into the night with an absolute stranger. When we returned to the airport, he tried to kiss me. I should have expected it, but I didn't.

I pulled away and shook my head. "I can't do that," I said. "I have a boyfriend—a truly good guy. I love him, and would never cheat on him." I had not intended my conversations or my ride as flirting. Clearly he had misunderstood. To my amazement, though, he respected my wishes, took me back to my bench, and returned my belongings to me.

Trusting to a fault, and a risk taker who loved adventure, I seemed always to get myself into situations that I should have seen coming, but didn't. Street smart, I wasn't. Not in any sense of the word.

If I didn't believe in God, I might have, if I had known the number of angels He kept on "Trudy duty" those years. And for all the tragedies I faced, it was nothing short of a miracle that I survived without more scars than I had. In hindsight I would be able to see that it was only the grace of God that kept me.

But that night in Buffalo, I was aware of only one thing: my flight to California, and the distance it would create between the trauma of the preceding months, and those terrifying phone calls.

Chapter Twenty-One

The airport started to buzz with activity early in the morning, waking me from my nap, having fallen asleep after my little excursion. I collected my belongings and prepared to check in for my flight. A few more hours, and I would be reunited with my older brother.

What I remembered most about Jacob was his love for children, but I had limited memories of him. He was a good-natured man with a gentle heart, and a bit of a temper, but not a quick one. I could only think of one incident when I had been on the receiving end of it, during one of our first years in Canada. He had played a prank on John, who was only ten months younger than him, and was hiding.

I knew where Jacob was and whispered it in John's ear, hoping to stir up the action between the two. Jacob had heard me whispering, and rather than fighting with John, walked over to me and smacked me across the face. But that was water long gone under the bridge.

It had happened at the red wood house, the one we called the old bee hive, where we lived when we first landed in Canada. Jacob had come for a visit, to spend a few days with his family. It was on that same visit that a dispute took place between him and my mother and I stepped around the corner of the house to see her walking toward him with a rolling pin raised over her shoulder, ready to strike him. Sadness overtook me, as if squeezing the lifeblood right out of my heart. I didn't want to see her that way, or know that she, too, was this violent.

In another scenario, Jacob had collected beer bottles that he planned to return for cash. He had enough to get quite a handsome sum, but not enough to reach his target. He had stored them in the warehouse section of our home in Corinth, to wait until he had enough to purchase some special item or another.

John had known about them, and that awareness gave him an idea. Jacob had a birthday coming up... If he returned all those bottles for a refund, he would have enough money to buy Jacob something special. And that was precisely what he did.

When Jacob received the birthday surprise, he was impressed. His brother had thought of him, and bought him some nice tools. But that thrill quickly faded, resulting in a tussle between the two, when Jacob discovered that his bottles had been returned to foot the bill for that gift.

Jacob always had a great sense of humour and loved to laugh. I looked forward to getting to know him as a husband to Susan, and a daddy to his three beautiful children. I looked forward to having children in my life again. It had been a while. I tried to imagine what it would be like, to be with a family again and function within that kind of structure. It wouldn't be long...

Boarding my flight, all went well. For never having done anything like it before, things went more smoothly than I had anticipated. Being a teenager with serious attention deficit, and in many ways lacking attention to detail, I learned that when push came to shove, my mind could be forced to focus and observe. But I didn't really think about those things other than to breathe a sigh of relief at every step conquered.

With the time difference between New York and California, we were set to land at nine a.m., and by the time we landed, I had slept a good portion of the six-hour fight and it felt like evening, when, in reality, it was breakfast time. Having landed, I scanned the crowd for Jacob and Susan. I spotted them. When they last saw me, I was a slight, ten-year-old girl with braids, and I didn't expect them to recognize me, so I walked over, introduced myself, and hugged them.

"Wow!" Jacob said, laughing. His eyes twinkled, like they always did. "I didn't know who to expect. All I could picture was your reddish blonde hair, when we visited Ontario last. You're tall!"

Susan, who was only about ten years older than I, exclaimed enthusiastically with Jacob how tall I had grown and how much my looks had changed. She welcomed me with open arms and great affection.

I quickly observed that they were madly in love with each other. In ten years or so of marriage they had not suffered in that department, it seemed.

We stopped at Denny's for breakfast. "You'll get used to going to Denny's," Susan said. "Johnathan loves it! Every time he sees one, he will ask, 'Denny's... Denny's??' And it has to be Denny's, not some other restaurant."

The more they talked about their children, Melasi, Leona, and Johnathan, the more I looked forward to meeting them. The girls, at ages seven and six, sounded to be a handful, and Johnathan a busy little mischief at almost two years old. I would have a family again, with the noises, the laughter, and the spats of an active household. I could hardly wait! I took in the scenery as we drove through the mountains and hills. It was breathtaking. *I could get used this.*

We pulled up to a nice trailer situated on a giant ranch, where Jacob worked. I met the kids, settled into my room, and made it through the rest of that day in a blur, too tired to absorb it all. That evening we had a barbeque, where I met a number of Susan's siblings. The next thing I remember is waking up the following morning, to the pitter-patter of little footsteps running into my room, bright and early.

****

I settled into my new action-packed home with ease. The children were well behaved, and Susan had organizational skills second to none. The trailer was always spotless. Each morning, at seven a.m., it started. First she dusted everything, followed by vacuuming, and then laundry. There was never dirty laundry in the house. Not one pile, in all the time I stayed with them. If the children were muddy, which she allowed, then they had to change and clean up the minute they walked in the door and she washed their clothes. And the meals... Wow! Were they good! When it came to cooking, Susan lacked no skills.

I met more of Susan's family, who lived nearby in Fresno, and quickly formed a friendship with Lisa, who was near my age. Every chance I got, I spent time with her.

Together Lisa and I dreamed of what we would do, what we would be. Typical teenage girls, we were both interested in fashion and hair. I told her I had dreamed of being a model, but had dropped out when too much chaos happened in my life. Maybe I would go into makeup and hairdressing. She wanted to be a hairdresser too.

167

We did each other's hair, had fun with makeup, listened to music, and talked, heart to heart. We talked about what was important to us. We both believed in God, though in my estimation, she had a much better relationship with Him than I did. She had a strength and confidence that I longed for. She had strict boundaries with boyfriends, something I envied. Hearing her talk, I started to see what I had lost.

Our family dynamics were not worlds apart when it came to dysfunction and trauma. Her father had a temper, as mine did. He was suicidal, as mine was. We didn't talk about those things a lot, just enough to really "get" each other.

From time to time Lisa's dad sent us to the store to pick up beer for him. He gave us cash and a note, and that was all that was required. Lisa and I would hide out in her room if he had too much to drink, or was otherwise out of sorts. That, again, was so familiar to me.

When I was eleven, I had invited Carolyn Roth over for a sleepover. Hesitantly. I was always afraid my father might lose his temper and embarrass me or hurt my friends. Carolyn and I had shared a single bed and woke up to my dad yelling in rage about one thing or another. In an attempt to drown him out, I had started singing quite loudly.

But with Lisa I wasn't afraid, and felt no need to pretend. If she was embarrassed, I never caught on and since we had talked about it, there was nothing to hide. This added a whole new dimension of trust to our friendship, something I had never experienced with a girlfriend before.

Life, all around, was pleasant. Other than occasional contact with Geoff, I lived a quiet single life. No dates. No parties.

One day Susan asked if she could see a picture of my boyfriend. I got the picture from my wallet and showed it to her. One look and she exclaimed how "not good looking" Geoff was. I wasn't prepared for that. I tried to tell her how kind he was, what a good person he had been. She didn't doubt that, she said, but he sure was ugly!

I thought he was pretty good looking, so I took her words as personal rejection, more than rejection of my boyfriend, or even his looks. I had to do something, and stop him from visiting. The thought of making it through an awkward week with him there, worried about what she felt, was overwhelming.

I called Geoff and told him he would need to cancel his flight. It wouldn't work for him to come see me. I didn't give an explanation, just that it wouldn't work out. I didn't have the heart to tell him the truth.

Geoff asked if I was seeing someone else, or had cheated on him. I hadn't. Didn't want to. When he asked more questions, I didn't give him straight answers. How could I tell him that my sister-in-law thought he was ugly, and I didn't have the backbone to defend him, and get past that rejection?

In conversation with Geoff not long after this, I sensed that he was falling in love with another girl, whom he had met at some cabin. I couldn't tell if he was trying to make me jealous when he talked of her, or if he really had feelings for her, but with me being gone indefinitely, the relationship wasn't worth fighting for. Especially if he was in love with someone else. With that, it was over.

Geoff asked if I could get his class ring back to him somehow. I said I would, but didn't know just when or how. I promised to take good care of it, and had every intention of following through on that promise.

However, only days after making the promise, the most unlikely thing happened. I had taken the chain and ring off for my bath and left it on a countertop. When I returned for it, there was only a chain. A search and find mission produced a badly smashed class ring, lying beside a hammer and a proud Johnathan, who had done the honours. If it hadn't been so important to Geoff, it would have been funny. I felt bad about the damaged ring, but saw irony in my little nephew taking a hammer to it, so soon after the breakup, as if to send a message.

I put the ring back on the chain and kept it in a safe place, intending to return it to Geoff. Hopefully a jeweller would be able to fix it. I called Geoff and told him what happened. He sounded skeptical, as though I was stringing him a line, and it was an unlikely story, I realized, but the truth nonetheless. I promised to return it, even though it was damaged.

A promise made is a promise to be kept, at all cost, if possible.

Chapter Twenty-Two

By July, Susan told me I needed to find work, with or without my papers, and she would help me. She didn't have enough for me to do at her house and, truth be told, I needed something to keep me busy. A woman who could accomplish pretty much anything she set her mind to, it took no time at all before I had a job as a nanny, working for a cardiologist, Dr. Jerry Reid, and his wife, Maureen, a nurse, in Merced.

The Reid family had four beautiful children; Sarah, James, Brendon, and Emily, ages twelve, eight, five, and three, respectively. They were normal children, with better than average behaviour.

Sarah, going on thirteen, had a bit of attitude about the new nanny, and let me know it, but never caused any trouble. I couldn't blame her. They had loved their previous nanny, she told me. And my insecurities, having little to no experience with children, and no role models to speak of, didn't help. It was a sharp learning curve for me and a huge adjustment for them.

James, a fiery redhead, was a cute boy, going on nine, with freckles sprinkled across his nose. Though not often, he gave me the most trouble and disrespect, but naughty behaviour became infrequent after discovering the perfect consequence. Finding the right "cure" took some creativity.

One of my first attempts at behaviour modification was to pull a tin of soup from the cupboard, set it on the floor, and then tell him it was his "consequence chair." When he was naughty, he had to sit on it for a few minutes. He thought it was hilarious and sat there laughing. That method wasn't effective, unless both of us laughing hysterically was the desired end result, with no change in behaviour.

Several failed attempts later I resorted to a consequence I despised growing up. Writing out lines. He sat at the table staring at that paper, looking about as sad as if his favourite pet had just died. When he said he was not doing it, I told him he stayed until he did it. I don't remember what the lines were, but something that started with the typical, "I will not..." From that day forward, James listened much better. Brendan and Emily were both sweet little angels. Or maybe that's just how I remember them because they were so little, and "non-attitude," therefore non-threatening.

I struggled to run all the duties of the house, having never really been taught those things, having preferred the animals in the barn as a young girl. In my opinion Susan had oversold my services as a young ex-Mennonite; I was no typical Mennonite girl. Never had been. Never would be.

Maureen was kind and gracious. She left me task lists, and when she came home, we worked together on dinner. She was a wonderful mom whose children loved her, and a beautiful woman whom I admired. I imagined being like her, happily married to a good man.

Jerry was a proud dad who loved his wife and kids. At sport events he was fully engaged, cheering for them enthusiastically, and beaming with pride. He treated me with respect and care, and when I developed a skin condition, he helped me find treatment.

I loved being in their home, but with my insecurities, I felt unworthy. Everywhere I looked, I saw beauty, love, and wealth, in glaring contrast to the violence, poverty, and hate from which I had come. I felt lost, out of place. I didn't deserve a nice home, with loving people, away from the people who had brought so much fear and trauma into my life. Yet, there I was, in a spacious bedroom apartment all to myself, in a beautiful home, in upscale Merced, California.

My space became my retreat, a place to listen to music, spend time writing, reading, or calling the few friends I had made. In the safety of my giant bedroom, complete with a desk, sitting area, and bathroom, I found solace from the fears of days gone by. Only brief moments of panic tormented me—fear that some terrible thing might happen, or someone might break in and harm me—but, for the most part, I had left that life behind.

I started to think about God, faith, life, death, and eternity. The chaos and busyness of my party life in Canada had kept those thoughts at bay, pushing them constantly to the fringes of the conscious mind. It's why I had partied. With that behind me, I could no longer fight the still small voice of God. I found myself reaching, almost against my will, to know truth, to experience Him again. Truly experience Him.

But where was I to turn? Who did I have? I knew no one in my new world who would be willing to teach me, or explore with me. Not without agenda. And, while my search was genuine, soon the voices of religion and culture started to haunt me.

What if they were right, back at Lakeshore church? What if they are "the way" to heaven? Had they ever said it in so many words? Not that I could remember. And yet, in subtle ways, they had communicated it, in the judgement and condemnation of all other churches and people. It was in looking down on sister congregations and their "wild" youth. It was in mocking the man who showed up at church in cowboy boots. It was in the criticism of the visitors whose son had longer hair than the boys at Lakeshore. It was in the attitude of religious arrogance and piety that some displayed.

I began to question if I would go to hell if I didn't get myself back there to make peace with the church. Would I be cast aside by God? Discarded? Made to burn in hell for eternity, just for that, regardless of all other things I had done, even if I repented? The torment became all-consuming, especially after another "incident" with a male.

The Reid family was going on vacation to a beautiful cottage in Nevada, along with their friends, Tom and Shelly, the children's godparents. And I was invited to go along. I was excited. I had never been to a cottage before, and to have a family to spend time with, just enjoying life, was a bit surreal. I spent time on the beach with them, reading, sunning myself, and playing beach volleyball with a group of strangers. It was lovely.

Walking along the shore, several young men introduced themselves to me as marines, and asked if I would like to go boating with them. I talked with Jerry and Maureen, to see if it would be okay. They said they didn't need my help for anything, and I was free to leave.

The lake was a beautiful blue. The sky bright and clear. A perfect day, in every way. Out in the middle of the lake, the young men told me the water was a minimum of sixty feet deep. Even though I was in a life jacket, that thought made my heart skip a beat.

I couldn't swim. In early childhood my mother had instilled an ungodly fear of water in us. I never understood why all my siblings overcame that fear, to one extent or another, but I didn't. Even water in my face, in a shower or bathtub, sent me into near panic for years. And even in my teens I struggled with the feeling that I would suffocate or die if the water ran over my face. It was as if I had nearly drowned, somewhere in time, and was having a flashback, so intense was that panic.

I looked into the beautiful, deceiving water; a giant puddle waiting to swallow me alive and, yet, so heavenly and inviting.

"Do you want to go in?" Matt, one of the gentlemen, asked.

"Not really… but sort of, I do." I wanted to be able to conquer my fear and say "I did it," but that was my only driving force. Nothing else could make me abandon the boat, apart from being forced overboard against my will. They helped me into the water, then moved the boat a small distance away, playfully threatening to leave me there.

I laughed, a nervous, helpless laugh, begging them to come back. It was exhilarating and terrifying all at once. Matt turned the boat around and picked me up again, and we returned to shore. Before we parted ways, Matt asked if he could take me out for the evening. We'd grab dinner someplace nice, and then go wander the streets and casinos of Reno. Again I spoke with Jerry and Maureen, and they said I was free to go.

Matt picked me up, as promised, and we headed out. After dinner we went to several casinos. It was all quite fascinating, the nightlife in Reno. When we had our fill of wandering and watching people, Matt asked if I wanted to see their family cottage. I did, and I didn't. Something in my instincts told me to say no, but I didn't want to be rude and hurt his feelings. He had been nothing short of the perfect gentleman. I agreed to go.

Inside the small cottage everything was dark. The bit of lighting we found was dim. Very dim. We had not more than arrived when Matt started kissing me. A moment later I was on a bed, being undressed, with not even a conversation. Again, I felt as though I had no voice. Powerless.

It was all too reminiscent of another time, not so many months ago… The tears started, and my body trembled with suppressed sobs. This wasn't what

I had wanted. But I was alone, in the middle of nowhere, in a strange cottage, with a strange man. Would I ever learn?

"Trudy..." Matt spoke my name gently. "Are you crying?"

I turned away. I didn't want to talk about it. Didn't want him to know. I just wanted him to finish using me, get it over with, and take me back to Jerry and Maureen's cottage. After that I would never have to see him again.

"Trudy..." Matt paused for a moment, and then continued, gently, apologetically. "Tell me why you're crying. We don't have to do this. I'm really sorry. I shouldn't have..."

Matt let me get my clothes back on without a struggle, without using me. I thanked him, calmed myself down, and then we talked, heart to heart. He apologized several times for assuming, for undressing me, for even starting anything.

"I'm going to make this right with you, Trudy," he said. He wanted to continue the relationship when I returned to Merced, he told me, and hopefully get married one day. I assured him I wouldn't consider marriage, that I wasn't ready for any such commitment. All I had wanted was a friend, someone to spend some time with. We fell asleep, and first thing in the morning, he took me back to Jerry and Maureen's cottage and dropped me off. But not before he took my phone number and gave me his.

That experience awakened something old and painful in me, leaving me confused and emotionally raw, but with the Reid family, I pretended that I was better than ever. If Maureen suspected something had happened, she never let on, but I could tell she was concerned, not only for me, but for what it all meant for her children. I wasn't in a position to give the kind of stability and care children need; I knew it, and so did she.

Maureen took me aside a few days later to tell me that they would be looking for a new nanny. She was kind, and said she was sorry it didn't work out, but it just wasn't a good fit for the children. I understood, I told her. I didn't tell her what happened, and they knew none of my story. "I'll probably go back to Canada," I said.

Immediately after returning from the cottage, in a moment of desperation, I called my former minister's wife, Elda Brenner, to ask some hard questions. I wanted peace, but didn't know where to turn. If the church was the answer, if it was my only way out of the soul torment and life of trauma, then I would go back. I would return to wearing a white bonnet and a cape dress and commit to following their rules. The cultural expectations still made no sense, but if that was the price I had to pay for freedom, then I would do it.

Elda encouraged me to come back. Of course she did. And, for all that had happened, she sincerely seemed to believe that the key to my freedom was inside the doors of their church. I would do it, I said. I was coming home to reconcile with the church, and repent.

Soon after, the phone rang, as if to tempt me to change my mind and not follow through on my pursuit of God. Offering me the phone, Maureen told me it was "some gentleman," and then left the kitchen to give me privacy.

"Trudy, I called to ask if you will marry me," Matt said, minutes into the phone call.

"What?!" I exclaimed after a moment of shocked silence. "You can't be serious!"

"Trudy, you seem like such a wonderful girl..." Matt went on, saying he shouldn't have tried to use me like that.... and he really wanted to make things right.... I needed someone to take care of me...

The words barely registered. Was he for real? I couldn't comprehend it that a man, a perfect stranger whom I had met on a random beach and spent an evening with, would call me days later and, in all sincerity, ask me to marry him. It was all too "fiction storybook" to even absorb it.

I told Matt I was flattered, but that I couldn't do it. I wasn't ready to get married, and felt too mixed up about everything. I tried to explain that I had a lot to work through, emotionally, and even though he seemed like a gentleman, there was no way.

"I'm sorry... I can't," I said.

"Can I come see you? Could we start with dating, and go from there?" he asked.

"No. I'm sorry. Matt, I'm going back to Canada in less than two weeks."

"Can I come see you one more time, before you go?" he asked.

"No, it won't work. I'm so sorry."

I hung up the phone without leaving him any of my contact information for Canada. Not that I really could. I didn't know where I would go, other than to show up at my parental home for a little while and take it from there.

His sincerity touched me. The remorse in his voice tugged at my heart. Was it my "second chance" — another man with the character of Michael back in Wellesley, slipping through my fingers? Or was I doing the right thing?

As the final words to another chapter of my journey made their way onto the pages of my life, I was left, again, with more questions than answers, more fears, anxieties, and unknowns, than securities and sense of direction.

Yet, everything in me said, "keep walking, and don't look back." So I did. I packed my bags, took care of farewells with family and friends, squared my shoulders, and did what I had to do.

Chapter Twenty-Three

I wore my pastel, faded-look, floral cotton pants to travel home, and a solid cream-coloured top. Geoff's chain, complete with the damaged ring, hung around my neck where it would be safe. This time I wasn't wearing dresses and hats, or trying to be ladylike. I wanted to be comfortable. This trip would not take a few hours. It would be days.

Arriving early, I placed my bags near a pillar before settling in on the floor to read, using the pillar as my back rest. I pushed down all sad thoughts and focused on the book in front of me, pausing now and then to entertain myself with people watching. Several young punk teens stood out in stark contrast to the rest of the crowd.

I didn't understand it. Why they dressed like that, in ripped clothes, black leather and chains, with hair spiked up six inches tall in the middle of their heads, and dark makeup around the eyes and lips. Couldn't find the beauty in it for trying. Being an independent spirit, I understood the need for expressing oneself, and that personal identity thing, but the way they did it looked so harsh. I wondered what hurt they had suffered, to look so defensive.

Not far from them, a girl in a simple top, casual jeans, and no makeup appeared to be studying. Probably a college or university student. Each person in the crowd, lost in a personal world, carrying a story, just like me. It was a fascinating thing, to observe body language, facial expression, and eyes. You could almost know a person without ever meeting them.

The long wait finally ended and we boarded the bus, homeward bound. It was a full bus, denying the luxury of a private seat. I kept reading. I could endure anything for approximately three days. That was the anticipated travel time.

On the first night the "best laid plans of mice and of men" started to unravel. The bus engine broke down without any warning. It just stopped. So there we were, in the middle of nowhere, beside the road, waiting for a mechanic.

Almost two hours slipped by, and with the passing of time, the morale of travellers deteriorated. A few passengers started whining and complaining. Fortunately, we had enough optimists to keep the group grounded, reminding them that things happen. No one can control a bus breakdown. We should be thankful we were alive and safe; it could have been a deadly accident.

When the mechanic finally came and checked out the bus, we were informed of further delays. The bus needed to go to a shop, where we would wait, indefinitely, while the mechanics repaired it. Further grumbling ensued. We were all tired and would have given anything for a nice bed and soft pillows. Instead we scattered ourselves, here and there, to wait. It was a long night, but finally we were back on the road.

The bus driver pulled over for one quick rest stop in the morning, and everyone was asked to get off so he could lock up, and to return by an appointed time. While boarding, a tall African-American man, who looked to be in his early twenties, slipped past the driver—who had stepped around the front of the bus—and made his way onto the bus. He walked to the back, seated himself in the farthest corner, and slouched down.

We arrived in Salt Lake City, Utah, well behind schedule. Trying to navigate my way, lugging a three-piece travel set with me, was complicated. I set my bags down and stepped a few feet away to confirm my next bus. When I turned back to check my luggage, the man who had snuck on the bus had two of my suitcases in hand and was walking toward the exit.

Without skipping a beat or thinking of potential consequences, I marched over to him, grabbed the bags from behind, and yanked them out of his hands, startling him.

"Those are mine, sweetheart," I said matter-of-factly. He turned, surprise registering on his face. The thief towered over me, at about six foot four, but I just stood there, glaring at him. Off to the side, out of his line of sight, I could see what he could not.

Several police officers had been alerted and marched toward him purposefully. They threw him on the floor, handcuffed him, and then took my statement before marching him out the door and releasing me to board my next bus.

Slowly it sank in what had just happened, and the risk I had taken, without a second thought. Angels to the rescue... again.

There was a buzz of excitement on the bus when I arrived. "You just marched right up to him!" ... "Weren't you scared?"... "Did you see the look on his face when the cops threw him on the floor?"

I didn't mind being the life of the party at social events, but all eyes on me, as I recovered from the adrenaline rush, I didn't enjoy as much. I had done what I assumed anyone else would have done, if everything they owned was about to be taken away. It hadn't occurred to me to not do it, or to be afraid. I just acted.

As the hullaballoo died down, a man came over for a more personal conversation. He introduced himself as Dodi Dumey, and said he was impressed with my spunk and confidence. It was unusual.

I introduced myself and admitted it was simply a reaction, what seemed the right solution in the moment. It was nothing.

"I had my eye on that guy," he went on to say. "Did you see how he snuck on the bus when the driver wasn't looking?" I told him I had noticed, and Dodi continued. "From the moment he got on the bus, he had his eyes on you. He was in the back, talking about you, so I decided to watch him, and make sure he didn't do anything to you."

"What did he say that made you think he would do something to me?" I asked.

"I don't want to repeat it. It really wasn't good," he said, apologetically.

We compared our routes and discovered we would travel together to Chicago, before parting ways. Dodi chose a seat directly behind me, so that we could continue our conversation. He was on his way home to Fort Wayne, Indiana, from Florida, he said. He had served in the army and was retiring, settling down, and living off of the pension, set to start in a few months. With time he would find some mindless job to keep from getting bored. As if to prove it, he lifted his T-shirt, revealing a massive scar where something had gone in his chest and ricocheted out his side. His uniform was being shipped separately, he said.

When he talked about Vietnam, I became suspicious. The timing seemed off, for how old he looked. "How old are you?" I asked.

"I'm forty-two," he said, not missing a beat.

I looked at him in disbelief. "You don't look a day past twenty-five," I said.

His stories were impressive, and convincing. No wonder he was so quick to protect the vulnerable, and keep an eye on anyone questionable. It all made more sense. He had done a lot of living.

Dodi pulled out a cigarette and offered me one—the same brand I had started smoking in California. I accepted.

"Do you want to join me in my seat? That way you don't have to turn around to talk," he said.

"Sure," I agreed, "that would be more comfortable."

He cleared the seat for me as I slipped back. We talked well into the night, eventually dozing off for a few hours.

By the time we arrived in Chicago, I was convinced that he was a man most capable of caring for me, and protecting me. With nothing to gain, he had taken that responsibility, and had continued to be there for me to ensure I was cared for the rest of the trip. When he invited me to come live with him in Fort Wayne, Indiana, with the intent of marrying me, I agreed. What more could a man prove, than what he had already proved to me?

He said he would pick up his Firebird in Fort Wayne and take a trip to Ontario to pick me up, the first weekend he had available. He had a few things to sort out, and couldn't say for sure which weekend it would be. With that agreement in place, we parted ways, and I continued to Clinton, Ontario, where my family planned to pick me up.

I wasn't sure how to break the news to my family, how to tell them that I had changed my mind about staying home and going back to the Mennonite church. Even more difficult was telling them that I planned to move to Fort Wayne, Indiana, where I intended to marry a forty-two-year-old man.

I'd figure it out. Break it to them slowly and then disappear, but for the time being I couldn't worry about it. I still had a good day's travel ahead of me, and the drama wasn't quite over.

It was the home stretch, from Chicago to Clinton. As much as I dreaded dealing with whatever reality waited for me there, I couldn't wait to get off the bus. A real bed, solid footing, and normal food all looked like luxuries, not to mention real bathrooms. I slipped into the bus bathroom one last time to touch up my makeup. Three days with no shower was too much. I felt disgusting, my hair greasy and skin oily. The least I could do was try to keep my makeup looking fresh.

I leaned over the toilet to do my mascara, when it happened... The gold chain around my neck snapped. I tried to grab the ring as it slipped off my neck, but missed and watched, in horror and disbelief, as it flew into the toilet, swallowed up by human waste

Any other toilet, even a public one, I would have found a way to retrieve it, scrub it up, and return it without ever uttering a word. But the bus bathroom wasn't an option. I felt sick. Somehow I would have to explain it to Geoff.

If the story of my nephew taking a hammer to the ring seemed far-fetched, this was more so, and I couldn't imagine trying to convince him... *"Yeah... Geoff... I don't know how to tell you this, but your ring—you know, the one that my nephew took a hammer to right after we broke up—well... it fell in the bus toilet and got swallowed up by human waste. Sorry."* Even to me, who had seen it, it sounded unbelievable when I thought about telling it. It seemed an unlikely coincidence that he was my ex-boyfriend, and his prized ring had all these bad things happen to it, and it wasn't cashed in at some pawn shop. But it was the reality, and the only story I could tell honestly, so I would do it.

With all the delays and disruptions, I was relieved to set foot on solid ground in Clinton, four days after leaving California. Immediately I picked up the phone and called my family to come get me. When I went to retrieve my luggage, I learned it was lost in transit. I would have to make do with what I had in my small carryon until the rest arrived. I was too exhausted to care. I just wanted to go home.

Chapter Twenty-Four

It felt strange being at home again. There was a tension in the air that was almost unbearable, especially when dad was around. My fears were less intense than they had been years earlier, but they were not completely absent. Meal times were especially awkward. Dad ate his meals with little to no conversation, which I interpreted to mean he was displeased with my presence or perhaps the life I had chosen. I did my best to keep a safe distance, always sitting at the far end of the table, away from him.

He took me off guard when he paused at the door one day before heading out to the shop, when I was alone in the kitchen. His head was slightly bowed, and his shoulders, I noticed, were not the proud, strong, square shoulders I remembered. There was a sadness I had seldom seen. He just stood there for a moment, as if contemplating what to say. Then I saw the tears and realized he was choking back emotion. When he finally spoke, the words were gentle, and filled with grief.

"I just want you to know that I have prayed for you every day," he said. With tears running down his cheeks, he turned and walked away. It touched my heart deeper than I let on. There was confusion about all that he had been, and done, and what I saw in him at that moment, but I knew sincerity when I saw it.

I had seen it in him before. When I was a young teen struggling with anger, he had sat down with me one day to tell me a story of when I was a little girl. I had heard the story before, but not from him. He spoke with deep emotion, as he told how badly I was burned when I was a little girl, and the agony I suffered. He spoke with pride when he told of my resilience, and how I joined Pastor Levi Dueck singing, *"Oh Mein Jesus du Bist Wert"* a song I had since learned to love in English; "Worthy Art Thou Lord Divine." He choked up as he described the sweetness of childlike trust, singing praise to God, in the middle of pain and trauma. How he longed for me to return to that childlike trust in God, he said. But because of who he had been, and what he had done, my heart was hardened, unable to receive what he said, unable to trust that God.

I had closed my spirit and refused to be moved. He had betrayed me, so he could suffer and grieve for the rest of his life, for all I cared. I had acted

185

bored and disinterested as he spoke, but deep down inside a longing had stirred. A desire to know him, and be known. To love him, and be loved by him. That desire stirred again when he walked away from the house that day. I knew that he had missed me, but I couldn't find it in my heart to be vulnerable. Too much had happened to trust him again.

I told mom I would be leaving again, and that Dodi planned to come in just over a week to pick me up. She asked questions, trying to get as much information as possible, but I kept my answers vague. It had been a long time since they had known where I was, and what I was doing with my life. That was not going to change.

The time passed quickly, and before I knew it, the weekend arrived when Dodi would pick me up. But days before he was to arrive, he called. Dad picked up in the shop and talked to him awhile. I never heard much about the conversation from dad, but Dodi told me about it later.

Apparently dad wasn't too happy with him, and let him know it. No forty-two-year-old would get his blessing to date or marry his daughter. Dodi told dad, then, that he was really only twenty-five. And that is the only thing dad told me about the conversation, that Dodi was a liar, claiming to be twenty-five, simply to try to get his approval. Well, he wasn't going to fall for that, and he told Dodi that I had already told the family that he was forty-two. It was too late to pull the wool over his eyes.

On the weekend, when Dodi was to pick me up, there was a problem with his car. Just a minor problem, he said, but he would have to get it fixed before he could come. He was apologetic and said he would try again the next weekend.

Why my mother sent me to Peter and Rita Steckle's home, to have Dodi pick me up there, I'm not certain. Possibly to keep dad from doing something rash. However it came to be, I was at the Steckles' the second time Dodi was to arrive.

The night before my scheduled departure, the phone rang at the Steckles' house. It was my brother Wil, wanting to talk to me before I left. The irony was that he, a rebel himself, called to challenge my lifestyle choices. His evangelism was a bit unconventional, if only because he didn't believe in God. He ranted about the path I was on, the terrible choices I was making, then he cut to the chase. "Trudy, if you keep on this path, you're going to go to hell."

"Whoa! Wait a second! Me? I'm going to hell? You're one to talk! It's not like you're such a saint! You're going to hell as much as I am!" I said. I couldn't believe he had played the "go to hell" card!

"Trudy, do you think I don't know that? I know I'm going to hell! I think about that! But I don't want you to go there!" There was a short pause before we simultaneously erupted in laughter. Such absurdity! We were running parallel, headed for the same end, and he was preaching!

Still, he tried to reason with me and tell me how foolish I was to go to Indiana, to be with some guy I hardly knew. He didn't like it. Not at all. I refused to debate it. I loved my brother, but this was none of his business. If Dodi was half of what he said, then my family was all wrong about him. With time, they would get used to it.

In the wee hours of that Sunday morning, I got up and started to prepare for my day. I showered, washed my hair, and packed up my bags. Dodi was scheduled to arrive early in the morning, and I wanted to be ready.

The phone rang, and it was Dodi, apologizing that the car had issues again. He would not be able to come. He was very sorry. I began to question then if I was a fool. Was he pulling my leg? Had he ever intended to come? Or was I being pranked repeatedly? But Dodi quickly put my mind at ease. He would mail a ticket, and I could take the bus. That would remove the car dilemma. He would meet me at the station in Fort Wayne, and take me back to the apartment he shared with his sister, Marcee, and her boyfriend, Stephon. We would all be one big happy family.

True to his word, the bus ticket arrived, via Express Post, several days later, and I found myself, yet again, boarding a bus and heading for the USA.

I lived life so fast that I lost track of time. There are strange details that I cannot recall. Little things like how I got to the bus station. Who took me there? Did I tell my family or simply disappear again? Even when, exactly, I went... It must have been late August or early to mid-September...

All around the trip was uneventful. Nothing exciting or catastrophic happened. A simple bus ride that lasted almost eight hours and landed me in Fort Wayne by early evening. Dodi was there waiting for me, just as promised. We collected my items—the same bags that had disappeared on the way home from California and reappeared just in time for this trip.

The nice red Firebird Dodi had described was waiting for us, in the form of an old beat-up clunker of a rust bucket. I overlooked it. So he had exaggerated a little. Maybe he really loved his car and was blind to the discrepancy between his description and the reality.

On the way to the apartment he gave me some basic instructions. The apartment was Marcee's and he was just crashing there until he could find something better. We would need to do our best to give Marcee and her boyfriend space.

We stepped inside the apartment, and the guidelines continued. The large L-shaped room was our common sitting area, and I was welcome to use it. I looked around. A chair, a small coffee table, and a futon-type seat occupied the room. An old leather bar stood awkwardly off to the side. On top of it sat a ghetto blaster and a few cassette tapes.

The kitchen, in the other corner, was ours to use, but with restrictions. We would only use what he provided, except dinner. The evening meal would be a shared with Stephon and Marcee.

He took me down the hall and showed me into a small bedroom, directly across from the bathroom. I put my bags in the corner. There was no dresser, or furniture of any kind. Not even a bed. Only an old double mattress on the floor, immediately to the left of the door. At the end of the bed was a tiny black-and-white TV, one of the smallest I had ever seen. The doors to a small closet were broken, and Dodi's clothes lay on a heap inside, spilling out onto the floor. The bar where clothes should have hung was missing.

This would be my living quarters until his pension cheques started, or he had a job and found another place. It was more than I had as a child in Mexico. I could survive anywhere, under any conditions.

Clearly defined expectations and "house rules" created the illusion of healthy family relationships, but I quickly learned that all things are not as they appear, not only on that front, but in every way, starting with Dodi's stories and history. Dodi's car, aside from the fact that it was an old, beat-up thing, not the car he had described, had another catch. It wasn't really his car. He had borrowed Marcee's car to come pick me up, and didn't actually own one. Every time he needed something, he had to ask to use her car.

The Friday night after my arrival, we decided to have pizza and rent a movie. We wandered to the small video rental store. Scanning the walls for something of interest, I saw the title *Jaws*. I had been completely captivated by the story, in spite of the horror, in *Reader's Digest* as a teenager, so I asked if we could watch it. Dodi looked surprised, and warned me it was quite horrific, but I wasn't swayed. We took the movie to the checkout and handed it to the cashier.

"ID please," the young man said.

Dodi reached for his wallet and pulled out his driver licence, but before the young man could take it, I snatched it out of his hand and ran across the room, giggling. The cashier looked startled. Dodi knew what I was up to and followed, in hot pursuit, but I kept the licence in front of me, scanning it for his date of birth. I found what I needed—proof that he was born in 1963—and handed him the licence. Quick math gave me his age.

"You're not even twenty-five," I said, as we left the store. "I knew it! So... why did you lie to me about your age?"

"I did it to protect you," he said. He made up some story about why he needed me to think he was older. Another little detail not worth fighting over, but it did create other discrepancies in his story, and meant that his service in Vietnam couldn't be real, since the war was over by the time he was twelve. When I questioned it, he convinced me I had the dates wrong and he had, in fact, served in the war as a very young man, having lied about his age. In the end I concluded it wasn't worth the fight, and let it go. Besides, what good would it do? I was in too deep, stuck, with no money and no way out.

****

I had noticed the tattoo on his arm the first day in Indiana, but I didn't have the courage to ask him about her. Now, with the rest of his story unravelling, I needed to know. Who was she? Why did he have her name tattooed on his arm? He had told me he was never married before, but that tattoo.... Why would anyone tattoo a name on their body, unless it was a committed relationship?

It took a bit to work up the courage to ask, and I did so, over a backrub. "Who is Maria?" I asked casually, running my hand over the tattoo on his arm.

"Oh... Maria... she was a high school sweetheart. The tattoo was a terrible mistake," he said.

He offered no more information, and didn't seem stressed by the question. Either he was the best liar I had ever met, or she really was nothing more than he claimed she was.

****

With time Dodi told me he had received word that his uniform was lost in transit. They were trying to locate it, but it could be some time before it arrived, if they ever found it at all. It all seemed too coincidental that everything he told me was coming apart at the seams, but with each unravelling there was a story to explain the situation. Stories that I couldn't prove or disprove. There were just enough hints of truth to make some stories believable, and just enough lies to make me doubt everything. Even the fact that he had been a soldier was convincing, in spite of the discrepancies and the tales he spun when facts didn't quite match. Not only did he have scars to prove it, there were times that his reactions corroborated his story.

Late one night, while watching TV, there was a loud explosion outside not far from our apartment. I was startled and let out a scream, but Dodi instinctively dove for cover in the corner of the room, away from line of vision, and huddled down, terrified. Because of my childhood, I had my own fears, but the reaction seemed exaggerated, without some terrifying past experience.

When I asked him about it, he immediately said it was a flashback to war. I had no reason to doubt that he was telling the truth. It was evident that his terror was real. It never entered my mind that any number of experiences other than war could have triggered a flashback so extreme. I took him at his word, but with time, the truth would all be revealed.

Chapter Twenty-Five

The week after I arrived in Indiana, Dodi spent most of his time job searching. He applied numerous places before landing a job at a local blood donor lab. The good news was that he had a job. The bad news was that, other than a few hours in the evening, I would spend all my time alone, with nothing to do.

Before starting his job, Dodi took me on a walk by the river not far from the apartment. He warned me never to leave the apartment alone. As we strolled beside the water, he told horror stories about what happened in Fort Wayne, and how countless bodies were pulled from the water every spring. No one really knew how they got there, or why. Unsolved murder mysteries, suicides, or accidents. Even though he had never given me any indication that I should fear him, the thought occurred to me that he could push me into the river, and no one would know.

What if that is what he plans to do with me? As quickly as the thought entered my mind, I pushed it away and chided myself for having entertained it. His intent may just as well have been to instill fear in order to control me, should I ever contemplate leaving him, but that thought never occurred to me then.

Regardless of the how and why of those mysterious deaths, it was not a safe community for a young woman to go walking, he said. He gave me explicit instructions to stay indoors during his absence.

In the months that followed, never once did I risk to venture past the doors of the apartment without him. Even in the apartment, I stayed cooped up in my room for the most part, day and night. If he didn't take me out, which only happened a few times a week, at most, then the mattress was my space.

It wasn't much of a life. There was no work to do in the apartment, and I had no friends, no one to talk to. I was completely isolated, and interacted with no one outside of my small world in the apartment. Gradually my mind shut down. I settled into a meaningless existence, and lost track of time. One day blended into the next, without purpose.

I ventured out of the bedroom for food—if there was any to be had—and bathroom breaks. Most mornings I had a piece of toast, if there was bread in the kitchen. Some days there was, some days there wasn't. Either way there was never much food, so I lived on one full meal a day for the most part.

My entertainment was limited to one small TV, and my badly neglected "Dear Jesus" diary—the one Geoff's mother gave me before I left for California, saying, "You might need it someday." I didn't use it a lot, but in these lonely times I occasionally put my thoughts on paper in the form of a letter to Jesus, if any words would form at all. With my Bible lost in the bottom of my suitcase, that diary remained my one link to God.

Sometimes, just looking at it brought me fleeting comfort, and stirred an awareness in my spirit that there must be more to life. Something deeper. Something real. And that awareness fed a deep soul craving.

What I didn't realize was that God was in intense pursuit of my heart, and a spiritual conflict was in play, all around me. In a matter of weeks my world would be rocked and my sanity tested, as the demonic and the divine collided in battle.

****

Dodi walked in the door mid-afternoon, hours before he should have been home from the lab. And before I could ask any questions, he offered the explanation.

"I've been fired," he said. One look at him and I knew there was a story behind it.

"What happened?" I asked.

"I got in a fight with some black dude, and punched his lights out," he said.

"What did you do that for?" I asked.

"He was rude, and wanted to pick a fight, so I beat the crap out of him. He asked for it," Dodi said.

"You can't just go beating people up like that!" I said, stating the obvious.

"I know. But it was his fault. He tried to pick a fight, and I lost my temper. It turned into a fist fight and they called the cops. I got arrested and my dad had to bail me out." He paused, and then, as if proud of the moment, added, "I got him good. Flattened him right out and he was huge—at least four inches taller than me."

"I wouldn't be proud of that!" I said, frustrated. The flood of information had my mind spinning. I had wondered what he would do if his buttons were pushed hard enough. Confronted with his violence, I was forced to ask some hard questions. What was to prevent him from doing the same thing to me, one day, if I crossed that line, intentionally or unintentionally? What if I became a threat?

I realized, suddenly, how little I knew about the man in front of me, and how much of his world didn't add up to him being the protective gentleman I had met on the bus. Something was wrong with this picture. Who was he really? I pushed the thoughts away. We had issues that needed to be dealt with, not the least of which was the loss of his job. Without that income, we would be on the streets, if his sister decided to kick us out.

This was no time for questioning who he was, or what he could do to me. That would need to wait for another day.

****

Dodi started the hunt for a new job the following week. Everything from fast food restaurants to trucking was fair game. Any job would do. I went with him on one excursion, wandering from place to place, watching him fill out applications. He almost convinced me to lie about my identity, to see if I could get by with it and work at a fast food joint. But the more I thought about it, the more I feared the consequences, should I get caught, whatever the consequences might be.

Late one afternoon, when Dodi was out, Marcee and I met in the sitting room and got to talking. She said something to me then, about his history as a drug dealer, and mentioned the massive scars on his chest and side. She went on to say how he acquired them in a drug deal gone bad. He had almost lost his life, and if she hadn't been there, he probably would have.

193

I tried to engage in the conversation without letting her see the shock. I didn't know her well enough to trust her, but she seemed sincere and it did explain why his stories never added up. Dodi had seemed sincere too, when he became my protector. What if she was trying to get back at him for something by lying to me?

The conversation soon changed direction, and Marcee asked me about my family. How many siblings did I have? Where did they live? What were they like? After I told her I had grown up as a Mennonite, she asked a lot of questions about our way of life.

"Why don't you like being Mennonite?" she asked.

I told her a bit about my childhood, and shared the "other side" of what it was like in a Mennonite home and church, and that it wasn't all it appeared to be from the outside. Much of it was an illusion, though some of the cultural traditions were good. But it wasn't for me, I told her.

Marcee asked if I missed my family, or if I ever called them just to talk, and to let them know I was okay. I told her I had closed that door, and felt no need to go there.

I answered her questions honestly, thinking that she was just trying to get to know me. I sensed a hint of concern, that maybe she didn't think Dodi was right for me, and I'd have a better life back home. Little did she know what it had really been like, and little did I know she had a bigger plan in play.

Unbeknownst to me at that time, Marcee took the information she gleaned from our conversation to track down my family. When she found them, she called my mother to tell her I was okay, but more than that, she told her it wasn't a good place for me, and there were things I didn't know. My life with Dodi wasn't what it appeared to be, or what I believed it was. If there was anything at all that they could do to influence me to leave, they should do it, even if it meant driving to Fort Wayne and taking me home, against my will.

****

Whatever stirred it up, whether it was all that talk about church, religion, family and Mennonites, or some other random thing, the spiritual battle never seemed to stay away long enough. Just about the time I thought I had

194

closed that door, it would swing wide open in the form of dreams, flashbacks, or some other torment.

It all happened in a matter of seconds, one night, as I fell asleep. Seconds that would stay with me for a lifetime, and evoke deep emotion for many years to come. I was caught in that state between wakefulness and sleep, when I saw his face. Evil. Dark. The kind of blackness that can only come from deception and lies. It was as if I was nose to nose with him. His eyes could only be described as dark light, staring directly into my soul.

His voice, wicked and hopeless, spoke, "I've got you now... You've lost your last chance...."

Angst, so deep that it squeezed the life out of me, gripped my spirit. I sat up, terror-stricken, gasping for air. Waves of nausea overcame me. I jumped up and stumbled over Dodi, who had fallen asleep on the mattress beside me. I stepped on him again as I fled to the bathroom.

I vomited and heaved, my whole body shaking violently. At length I composed myself and stood at the sink, half panting, half gasping, and still trembling. I cleaned myself up and returned to the bedroom.

Dodi had turned on a light to see what was wrong. "What the...?" He stopped short, staring at me, eyes wide. "You look like hell! You're white as a ghost! What was that...?!"

I lit a cigarette, too shaken to speak. I lit a second. And a third.

Finally I regained my voice. "Dodi, I saw the devil. It was awful." I tried to explain what happened, what I had seen, what I felt, but it all sounded too weird, like I was going completely mental. I lit a fourth cigarette. My body gradually stopped trembling, and I lay back down.

It was a long time before I settled down enough to sleep, but at long last I faded. The nightmare, or whatever it was, finally over.

But for the rest of my life, regardless of where or how—whether overhearing children in a game of tag, or when playing a game of checkers, or any other context—if I would hear the words "I've got you now," they would trigger flashbacks to that moment of sheer terror.

Chapter Twenty-Six

Whether Marcee told Dodi that she had called my family, and he worried that they would come for me, or if she was sick of her brother mooching off of her and asked him to leave, or some other sibling rivalry took place... whatever it was, something sparked another abrupt move.

Dodi announced one day that we would be leaving the apartment. Our long-term plans were uncertain, but for the short-term we would move in with his dad. It wasn't a discussion, or even a visit to his dad's house to meet him, and go from there. It was an announcement.

I packed my bags, which didn't take much, since I had lived out of my suitcases during my entire stay, having never unpacked them other than the clothes I wore. To pack I only had to collect my dirty laundry, zip up my bags, and leave. It was that uncomplicated.

Dodi grabbed some clothing and personal items, and with that we were off. Just like that, another world opened up in front of me. A world that exposed me to things I had never seen or imagined. Depths of spiritual darkness that my mind could hardly grasp even when confronted with them firsthand. Dodi gave me fair warning...

"Dad's girlfriend is a bit strange," he said. "She's into some weird stuff... pretty creepy, actually. Krissy's last name was Hallermann, and she had a legal name change to 'Hellerman.' She says she's the 'daughter of the devil.'"

"How did your dad get mixed up with her?" I asked.

"Dad used to run a local strip joint, but got shut down when things got out of hand... you know, with illegal activities of some sort. I don't know the details," Dodi said. "He picked her up there a few years back, and they stayed together." He paused, as if contemplating whether he should say more. At length he continued. "She's been pregnant a few times but always loses the babies to miscarriage, early on. Probably from all the screwing around, drinking, drugs, and God knows what all she does to make it happen. Dad found her on the floor a few months ago, not dressed properly, drunk out of her mind, and with the dog cleaning blood off the floor, after her miscarriage. It's not the first time. She lets the dog eat the fetus."

He paused again. I tried to absorb what I had just heard. Was all of this for real? Or did he make this stuff up as he went along? I tried to reconcile that this would be my new home. But I had no choice. I would have to make the best of it.

Dodi continued. "Dad caught her in a group orgy with eight men a while back. So if she asks you to go out with her, it's probably best to say you're not interested." Based on what he had told me, I didn't think declining an invitation would be a problem.

We arrived at his father's house in mid-November. No one was home, so we let ourselves in. What met my eyes cannot be fully described with words. Words don't begin to do justice. Dodi apologized for the sight that greeted us. I said it didn't matter. How could it matter? There was no other place to go. This was home now.

Having grown up in a home with as many as twelve children in it at one time, I knew chaos and mess. We had created it. But even with so many of us, and no sense of order some of the time, we had never had chaos that held a candle to what I saw in that house. The walking path that weaved between boxes was littered several inches deep with newspapers, dirt, various scraps and random items. Boxes filled with stuff were stacked up to the ceiling in some places, and several layers high in others.

Kitchen counters were piled up to a foot high, or higher, with dirty dishes, with hardly a square inch of space unused. Pots, pans, and roast pans. Everything sat, helter-skelter, as if ready to topple at the smallest disturbance, and might have if not glued together with food matter. Some looked to have sat there for years. The table was littered even higher.

Past the kitchen would have been a nice little sitting room if everything hadn't been cluttered with yet more boxes. Stuff everywhere; it was too much for the mind to absorb. One recliner sat empty, carefully situated in front of the TV. I would have bet money it was Dodi's father's chair.

To the left of the small, overcrowded sitting room, a set of stairs curved up to the bedroom levels. A hallway—which had become more of a cow-path between more boxes—led to two separate bedrooms, and a bathroom. Dodi led the way into the first bedroom. It was littered also. The bunk beds that we would use were covered. We set our bags out in the hall, on top of the boxes outside of the bedroom. There was no other space for our belongings.

For the next ten days of my life, memories are unusually blurred. I don't know what I ate, or if I ate. I stayed clear of Dodi's dad, Ray, other than one quick introduction. He gave me the willies and reminded me way too much of my own father. I rarely saw his girlfriend, Krissy, who worked full time at a fast food restaurant, and part time evenings as a stripper.

I watched TV while everyone was away—a nice, big colour-screen TV— and I certainly never set foot outside the front door when Dodi wasn't there. If it was dangerous where we had lived, it was nothing compared to this community. To say it was a rough neighbourhood would be a gross understatement.

****

Being alone, day after day, was difficult. I vacillated between lecturing myself about forgiving Dodi for all his lies and the insecurity he had brought into my life, and hating him with such a vengeance that thoughts of murder toyed in my mind. Given the opportunity, I feared I would actually do it. It was no small wonder that my mental health started slipping. I had been cooped up, with little human interaction and nothing to do, for almost three months, with my life in a constant state of drama and trauma. And the never-ending lies were making me crazy; there was no way to trust Dodi, and no way out.

To occupy my mind, I set about cleaning the kitchen one day, but after hours of work, and hardly a noticeable change, I gave up. It was an impossible task. Even so, when Krissy arrived home that evening, she immediately noticed and thanked me. To my surprise, I had started to enjoy her company. In spite of everything I knew about her—the stripping and orgies—I liked her as a person. If anything, it saddened me. She was young to be living with a man in his forties, and Ray wasn't kind to her. Not only did he treat her with general disrespect, he beat her and threatened to kill her.

I wondered how she had lost her way so badly, to be willing to settle for this life, and the abuse. Then again, how had I? Life, it seemed, just happened, leaving some of us lost and victimized. Maybe she and I were not so different after all. I comforted myself with the fact that Dodi had never threatened me or harmed me. At least not yet.

When he took me to Krissy's work for lunch, to celebrate being hired by an international transport company, there was an incident that again warned of potential danger. Everything was fine until she introduced me to her boss, her co-workers, and her manager, Paul, a male in his twenties. He paid too much attention to me for Dodi's liking. I didn't play into it, but Dodi rushed me out of there and took me home in a huff.

He said little on the way home, but was clearly irate. Nothing more was said until Krissy returned home from work later that afternoon. The three of us stood in the kitchen, talking, when she brought it up again.

"My manager thought you were pretty cute," Krissy teased. "He asked a lot of questions after you left."

I laughed it off. "You told him I'm with Dodi, right?"

The back door slammed violently, and I realized then that Dodi was no longer there. I followed him, opened the door, and asked him where he was going. He ignored me, but his body language screamed rage. He returned an hour later, still angry.

"Don't ever walk out on me like that again and treat me like garbage," I said. "If we have something to fight about, we'll get it out in the open, and talk. Not crap like that, walking out on me. Got it?"

"I walked away so that I wouldn't do something stupid and hurt you," he said.

"Why? What did I do? I didn't even flirt with him, or pay any attention to him!"

"You didn't do anything. I was just jealous. And Krissy knew it. I know it's not right, but I had to walk away and cool down," he said.

At least he had the common sense to do what he had to do and not hit me, but that didn't erase the fact that he was obviously capable of violence, and over things I had no control over. What if he didn't have that self-control next time?

When I accompanied him on a truck run to Chicago, the side of Dodi that frightened me and reminded me of my father came through again. On a busy freeway he asked me to navigate and watch for vehicles on the right, to prevent collisions or cutting off other drivers. When I missed a vehicle in my blind spot, and he started to pull right without checking the mirror, he flew into a rage, cussing. "Watch what you're doing! You could have caused a terrible accident and killed someone!"

I sat in silence. How could I control what I could not see? I wasn't the driver, and certainly not accustomed to semi-trucks and city traffic. I had never even had a license. It was all too reminiscent of how everything in my father's world that ever went wrong was always someone else's fault.

With each incident, my trust took another blow. How I wished for a way out! Who was he really? It seemed the longer I was with him, the less I knew him, and the more that question haunted me.

Chapter Twenty-Seven

The beginning of the end started on the American Thanksgiving Day, Thursday, November 26, 1987. And that end would result in a whole new beginning. But first there are some other things I must tell you.

Less than two weeks after we moved in with Ray and Krissy was my eighteenth birthday. To celebrate, the four of us went out for a bite to eat, and then went five-pin bowling. We partied hard, laughed a lot, and made fools of ourselves. Before leaving, Dodi dared me to find something to steal. Anything. It wasn't the first time—he had dared me once before. I had never been one for shoplifting, but the day he dared me, I did it, just to prove I could get away with it. It was a small convenience store, with only one cashier. I moved away from Dodi and wandered to the cigarettes. When the cashier looked over at Dodi, who was an experienced shoplifter and looked the part, I slipped a pack of cigarettes into my pocket.

When we returned to the vehicle, I proudly produced my prize. I knew I could do it. But I had never wanted to. Having proved my point, I had no intentions of doing it again. Furthermore, there wasn't much to steal at a bowling alley, but I finally found something, just before we left. Once inside his dad's van, I opened up my oversized winter coat to reveal several rolls of bathroom tissue. It wasn't much, but I had met the challenge.

If someone gave me a dare, competitiveness had a way of overriding all sense and reason. I had done more than one foolish thing, just to prove that I could. Shoplifting, to prove something, directed all my focus and adrenaline into conquering the challenge, distracting my mind from the moral issues.

Having conquered the challenge, I was the proud owner of bowling alley–quality bathroom tissue. Not Cottonelle, but, hey, it was free.

That was the end of the excitement of my eighteenth birthday.

****

Back home, in Ontario, I had not been forgotten, nor had my birthday. But I had no way of knowing it then, nor would I have cared had I known. If anything, I would have mocked it.

Someone had organized a prayer watch for me, I was told later. Who signed up to pray, or what they prayed, I don't know. I never asked, and no one ever told me. But in the days that followed, my world completely unravelled.

****

The bowling night created a sense of kinship between Krissy and me, and I found myself even liking Ray a little bit. He had another side to him than the harsh, evil monster he had been made out to be. Granted, even his "angel side" was pretty rough around the edges, but it gave a glimpse of a man who, like my father, had the capacity for kindness, but had too many demons to contend with to do day-to-day-life well.

With a bit of relationship established, we had decided to spend Thanksgiving Day together, and get to know each other better. With it being a holiday, Ray was home for the day, but he was out of the house at the crack of dawn, working on his oversized van. He had purchased a large white van, ripped out some seats, and turned the back into a bunker. If not slightly redneck, it was creative, and relatively well done. But the motor had serious issues.

Dodi went out to help his dad, leaving Krissy and me to do a Thanksgiving turkey dinner. I had never done that kind of a meal, and Krissy didn't seem to know much more about it than I, so we guessed at it.

While the turkey cooked on low, Krissy and I bonded over wardrobe decisions, makeup, and hair. Dinner wasn't scheduled until early evening, so we planned to slip out to a local bar for drinks shortly after noon, and maybe a quick bite, to tide us over.

Late morning Krissy asked me to do her hair and makeup. She didn't have much talent that way, she said. I obliged. I loved transforming hair and faces by bringing out natural beauty, and seeing the thrill when my art was complete.

We chose our outfits first. I wore a semi-fitted, black and silver sweater dress that reached almost to my knees, accented with a wide silver belt and black mesh pantyhose. Krissy wore fitted cotton pants and a sweater.

Eighties hair was all about the volume, something that was a challenge with someone like Krissy, who had little hair to start, and hair that lacked any body, naturally. We only had hairspray to work with, and the ten-dollar curling iron left much to be desired. A lot of back-combing and teasing later, Krissy sported the popular big hair look, giving Dolly Parton some competition. My hair took much less time. With an abundance of fine hair, and the leftover body of an old perm, I had mastered getting it to take to curls and work up the volume with my brush.

While we worked, we talked. Like everyone else, Krissy started asking about my background and my family and, like the others, she was fascinated with the Mennonite world. It seemed so peaceful, idyllic. How could I not want that?

If one more person idolized it that way, and thought I should stay, I swore I would strangle them bare-handed. Why did everyone think it was such a perfect world? I had no problem seeing the good, but it was a host of human beings trying to live by a human system. How peaceful could such a thing ever be, in a system with a measuring stick, and people assigned to police how well each individual lined up to the expectations? But trying to explain that to someone who had never been in the system, let alone in any Christian-based faith, was useless.

As I applied the finishing touches to Krissy's makeup, she looked intently into my eyes. Face to face like that made for a level of intimacy that I didn't share with too many people. I had a personal bubble that didn't allow for physical contact with many people, up close and personal. And I definitely didn't let them look into my soul.

"Trudy, there's something you need to know," she said. Her eyes shifted, as though she couldn't say it with me in her face like that. I leaned back. What could she possibly have to tell me?

"Dodi was married before. He hasn't told you, has he?" she said, sounding apologetic.

"You liar!" I spat the words as I stepped back and glared at her. I knew what she wanted. She was tired of the old man and wanted Dodi. The way she flirted with him, it was quite obvious, but before I could say more and confront her, she spoke up again.

"No, Trudy, I'm not lying. Why would I lie about that?" she asked.

"Because you want Dodi!" I said. "If you can get rid of me, you'll dump Ray and hook up with Dodi... Well, you won't get rid of me that easily!" I spoke with hate-filled determination.

"No! Trudy! ... Please! I'm risking everything to tell you this! Please, trust me," she pleaded.

"You better have proof, if you're going to throw something like that at me," I said, inserting expletives to make my point.

"I do. I can get proof," Krissy said.

"Then prove it, or I'll kill you. I don't like games, so don't mess with me," I said, adding more profanity for impact.

Krissy disappeared for a few minutes and then returned, grasping a folded paper in her hand. She handed it to me. "His divorce papers. They just arrived last week."

Having stepped inside the bedroom door, I unfolded the paper. Words jumped off the page. Divorce... Dodi Daniel Dumey... Maria Santos Dumey... And the date of the divorce.... October 23, 1987, only a month and three days earlier.

"Oh my God... Oh my God!" I cried out. I leaned hard against the bed, bracing myself. My legs felt weak, shaky. My hands trembled so that the paper shook violently.

Tears stung my eyes, rolled down my face. It was the final betrayal. The last lie. The one thing I could not... would not... forgive. For every lie, he had offered a story, an explanation, and I had turned a blind eye. What a fool I had been!

"Swear to me that you'll never tell Dodi, or Ray," she begged. "Ray threatened me if I tell you, he'll kill us both. He kept the paperwork here for Dodi, to help him hide it from you. Please swear to me. I'll help you get out of here, quietly. Safely. You deserve better. You're not one of us, Trudy. You don't belong here."

Who did these people think I was? Some God-forsaken saint who lost her way? Did they know who I was? What I was? Clearly not, or they would stop saying these things.

Rage overtook the pain and disappointment, bringing a sudden, terrifying calm into the room. "Thank you for telling me, Krissy. You did the right thing." I said it with quiet resolution, as though nothing untoward had taken place, as if it was a most ordinary day.

"Trudy, you're not going to do something stupid, are you?" Fear filled Krissy's eyes.

"Krissy, I will do what I need to do," I said.

She disappeared, running downstairs as if her life depended on it, returning moments later. "I have something for you. You need to calm down."

"I'm calm, Krissy. I don't need calming down," I said, scoffing.

"Trudy, he's a dangerous man," Krissy said. "He's been arrested countless times for threatening and attempting murder. It isn't safe..." Krissy led me downstairs, offering me a joint. I accepted.

It was the second time I smoked weed. Unlike cigarettes, marijuana offered a slightly sweet taste. I inhaled, welcoming the deceptive calm as it invaded my body, my mind. But it wasn't enough. Krissy offered me a beer. Then a second. I had only taken a few swigs of the second beer when Dodi walked in the door, shortly after one p.m.

Krissy made one final attempt, whispering in quiet desperation, "Trudy... Please..."

"I'm going to kill him," I muttered.

I felt sorry for her, in a way, but the calm rage was deeper, stronger, than any compassion or sympathy I could muster. And I appreciated her offer to help me disappear quietly, but this level of betrayal required a conversation. And how it shook out would be left to the hands of fate and a few evil men.

I would be damned, or dead, before I walked away without that confrontation.

Chapter Twenty-Eight

Dodi walked across the room almost cautiously, as if sensing something. His eyes registered the beer in front of me. Our eyes met briefly. I turned away, picked up the beer and had another swig, then set it back down. He had never seen me drink before. Oddly, having spent so much time drinking in the past, it was one of those things I didn't miss.

"What the...." He stopped momentarily, dropping the f-bomb, cussing under his breath. "Krissy! What are you doing to her? What is going on?"

I felt his hand on my elbow. Instinctively I formed a fist and spoke slowly, emphatically, matching his language and dropping the f-bomb repeatedly throughout. "Get your hands off of me, or I will kill you. Don't you ever touch me again!" I turned to face him, fist tightly clenched.

"Why did you lie to me, Dodi?" I asked stoically.

His brow furrowed. He looked pale, bewildered. "What are you talking about?" he asked.

"You know what I'm talking about, Dodi," I said. "You don't need me to spell it out. Why did you lie to me?"

Dodi looked at Krissy, as if expecting answers. She said nothing.

"I saw the divorce papers," I said. "Why did you lie about Maria?" I watched as it registered.

Dodi's eyes fell. "Because I didn't want to lose you." For once he spoke truth.

"You should have let me decide that," I said.

"I see that now," he said.

He had committed the ultimate betrayal. I had overlooked a lot, but for this I could offer no forgiveness. If he did this to his ex-wife, for me, I had no reason to believe he wouldn't do it again. When I spoke, I spoke with finality. It was over, for me.

"Let me explain," he begged.

"I don't need an explanation," I said. "I get it." The beer and the joint were kicking in. I felt peaceful, euphoric.

As if sensing a shift, Krissy and Dodi started talking about going to the pub. We would lay all this aside and party awhile. We could deal with this stuff later. I agreed.

The pub was almost empty in the middle of the afternoon, on Thanksgiving Day. We drank beer and ate French fries. I had enough of a high to take the edge off of the events of the day and I talked and laughed as though nothing had happened. But it wouldn't last. Something was going to give; there would be a blowout before the end of the day. Of that I was certain.

It was almost dinner time when we returned home. The turkey was still cooking. Whether the other menu items we had prepared that morning had ever been cooked, I didn't know, or care. I had no appetite. I disappeared upstairs, drunk enough to want to crash, yet "with it" enough to be aware of my surroundings, and what was happening.

****

I awoke some time later to the profane yelling of a man in uncontrolled rage. It had been several years, but some sounds one never forgets. My heart stopped, and it was as if I was a helpless child again. *Ray must have found out.* I was done living in fear of ignorant bullies. Courage rose up within me, and I got up to face whatever showdown was brewing. Halfway down the stairs I saw Ray and my courage threatened to give way to fear again, but I held my chin up in feigned confidence.

He looked at me with disdain, and then, as if I had been part of the entire conversation, which was more of a yelling match, he addressed me. Voice dripping with contempt, he spewed profanities, attacking my identity. "And you... you... You're a whore!" He spat the words, half wagging, half pointing his finger at me, as he continued with the derogatory name calling. The f-word decorated each sentence, as if it was the only adjective he knew.

Looking him in the eye, I spoke calmly when he finally ended his rant. "You will treat me with respect. I did nothing except discover the truth. I'm not the one lying here. So don't speak to me that way. You can apologize."

Dodi and Krissy looked shocked. The colour drained from their faces.

"Like hell! I won't apologize!" he scoffed.

210

I walked calmly past him to the door, as though nothing had happened. Hand on the doorknob I paused. "No one treats me this way. Ever."

With that I disappeared down the streets of Fort Wayne, Indiana. Even the bad parts of town are only as frightening as you let them be, and depend on what you compare them to. I reached the sidewalk, and it registered what had happened. I broke into a run, heels and all. I would run and never look back. Whatever busy street I came to first, I would dive in front of some vehicle, and that would be the end. Tonight was the night it would all end.

I ran, breathless and weak. Behind me I heard Dodi calling my name and running after me. I didn't want his help. Didn't want to see him, or talk to him, so I pushed myself to keep running.

I lost my shoes, but kept running. My silver belt popped off and landed on the grass. Even that meant nothing to me. I wouldn't need it, dead. Whether it was the blend of beer and marijuana, or complete exhaustion, eventually I collapsed beside the road, vomiting.

Dodi caught up then and stood there, helpless, as I heaved, breathless and panting.

The night air was cold. I had not realized it as I ran, but now, kneeling there, the bitter cold penetrated, mercilessly, right to the bone. I shivered as Dodi led me back toward the house. He made sure the way was clear, before going back in for warmer clothes.

I paused by the phone before going upstairs, and tried to collect call my family. Maybe, in spite of who I was, and all I had done, they would help me find my way back to God. The phone rang. And rang. And rang. But no one answered.

I slipped into jeans, a sweater, a winter coat, and running shoes. It was going to be a long night, wandering the streets. Warm clothes and comfortable shoes were not optional, they were survival. I threw a few extra items in my purse, and with that we were off.

We wandered until we came to an area with coffee shops and fast food restaurants. A few stayed open all night. We stayed just long enough in each place, drinking coffee or hot chocolate, to stay warm and not get kicked out.

At about ten p.m., before going into a restaurant, I asked Dodi for a quarter to make a call at a pay phone. I flipped through the phone book until

I found it. Goshen. I scanned the list of names, searching for Gospel Echoes. I dialled the number, but it just rang. I let it ring longer than usual. Maybe, just maybe, someone would wander through and pick up the phone.

I prayed frantically. "Please, God. I need help... Please... Please... Please, let someone be there!" But the phone just kept ringing, as if mocking my desperate prayer.

I searched the list of names for staff members whose names I knew. If I could only find them—even one of them—they would be able to help me. These people did prison ministry, and did it well. If they helped criminals, surely they could help me too.

I scanned the names... Dan Utz... Paul Kurtz... Glendon Bender... but my search came up empty. I tried the Gospel Echoes office number again. Someone out there had answers to my questions, and I needed to find whoever that was. The most authentic Christian Mennonites I had ever met were the Gospel Echoes Team. They were Christians who put feet on their Gospel. They went into prisons, to those who had nothing to give back, to the broken of humanity, and loved on them, without judgement. They sang for them and told them about Jesus. They didn't make them be Mennonite to be saved. With them it was all about Jesus, and somehow I knew He was the answer to my need, if only I could find Him. And when they told stories of people accepting Jesus, they clapped and cheered, as if they actually meant it. They were happy about what Jesus was doing. Their music had been my lifeline before, and I was so sure they would help me again.

But the phone just kept ringing....

We went into the restaurant and sat there a long while, talking, trying to sort out all that had happened in a short time. As always, Dodi had a story, a convincing way to explain why things were as they were.

Yes, he had been married, but he didn't really consider it a marriage. It hadn't even been half a year after the wedding—which wasn't a real wedding—before she had an affair. He was a trucker in South Carolina, and his run changed, so he came home a day early to surprise his bride. He surprised her all right! She was with her lover, in their bedroom, their bed, when he walked in on them.

"All I saw when I walked in that bedroom was red," he said. "I had to leave." He told me how he grabbed his stuff and walked out the door, without looking back. He was on his way to his sister's apartment following that betrayal, when our paths crossed on the bus.

Their wedding had been a quick visit to the judge, he said, with a few family members present. It had not been a celebration, just some promises made to a judge, not before God and church, he explained, and that meant he had never been married. It wasn't an ideal situation we were in, he agreed, but it was nothing that couldn't be fixed. He would call the priest and see about getting the marriage annulled. It was different than divorce. Something reserved for specific situations. He was quite sure his situation qualified.

By the time morning rolled around, I was so tired I thought I was going to collapse. Somewhere in that long night, Dodi had completely convinced me that the annulment was going to resolve everything. We returned to Ray and Krissy's house after we were sure they had left on their annual Thanksgiving road trip. They planned to be gone for a few days, making it safe to go back to the house.

We would need a place to go after that, as it was no longer safe to stay with Ray and Krissy. There was only one person to call. And as a result of that call we were back at Marcee's apartment before Ray and Krissy returned.

****

Adjusting to the constant moving around, with no say in the matter, became wearing, and the stress started getting to me. During the day, when Dodi was at work, I found my mind turning toward thoughts of murder, more than before. It had started before I knew about the last lie—the unforgivable one—but, since then, the thoughts were all-consuming at moments.

In a state of absolute boredom one afternoon, I did something completely out of character. I wasn't one to invade people's personal space and go exploring, but that day I did. I went into Stephon and Marcee's bedroom, out of curiosity. Who were these people really? And what could I learn about them?

Centered against the wall in their bedroom, directly in line of sight from the door, was what appeared to be an oversized podium. I had seen it countless times, walking by the door, and wondered what it was. On this day, I decided to satisfy my curiosity.

There wasn't much to see, to my disappointment. Whatever it was that I hoped to find, there was nothing more than an odd collection of knickknacks and things. A shaving kit. Nail clippers. Combs. Brushes. Stuff. Boring, meaningless stuff.

And then I saw it. Toward the back of the second shelf a little handgun lay partially hidden. It was a girl's gun, I decided—silver and white, not black. Probably Marcee's. She could hold her own pretty good. I could see her with it.

I picked it up. I knew I shouldn't, but I had never held a handgun before. It was so different than a rifle. Little butterflies toyed in my tummy. What if I got caught? What if I accidentally fired it? I held it in position in front of me, my hand on the trigger.

Slowly I raised it to my head, placing the barrel against my temple. I had no idea if it was loaded. I could pull the trigger, and let God and happenstance decide my fate. Life had been pretty painful. If the gun was loaded, it would end. If it wasn't, I would put it back in place, and walk away as though I had never been here.

I lowered the gun. The risk was too high. What were the odds that the gun would not be loaded, in a family like Dodi's, and a community like this? Besides, why should I be the one to die? It was Dodi who had caused all the pain with his lies. For a moment I wished he would walk in the door. I'd blow his brains out, if the gun was loaded. And if not, I'd be in big trouble.

I put the gun back in place, just as it had been, with a few items partially covering it. There was too much at stake. There had to be another way out, and I had to find it. Soon.

Chapter Twenty-Nine

The last while in Fort Wayne—before divine intervention—fears, dark thoughts, and confusion hounded me. As the desire to truly *know* God awakened, spiritual conflict, with powerful emotional and demonic manifestations, pursued me. And, if not that, then the opposite extreme, a complete loss of feelings, or thoughts. A deadness.

Always intertwining with spiritual experience, there was the niggling of religious voices, competing with the truth of Jesus, distracting my spirit. Always religious thoughts tempted me to shift my focus and draw me away from that thing my heart longed for—relationship with Jesus—and settle for a set of rules, or fight against them, as the case may be.

As if to add to the mounting confusion, I had an unexpected conversation with Stephon. It was the only time we were in the apartment together with no one else there. Both Marcee and Dodi had jealousy issues, so the fact it happened at all was surprising.

Stephon was six foot five inches tall, and well built. With strawberry-blond hair and blue eyes, and a boyish grin, he was easy on the eyes. His features were unusually youthful for his age, making him appear a good ten years younger than his thirty years. When we went out, he was the oldest, and the only one who got carded, even to buy cigarettes. At seventeen I could walk in and buy mine without any problems from the cashier. On my heels he, at thirty, had to produce ID. I found it funnier than he did.

Stephon was good-natured. The carefree type, if not somewhat irresponsible. He spent all his money on drugs and booze. Mostly drugs. If he was ever not high after work, I missed the moment, though sometimes he was less high.

We met in the hallway, and he asked about my family, and the Mennonite people. What did they believe? What did I not like? The questions went on and on. It wasn't curiosity. It was genuine interest in me, and intrigue with the culture.

"You should go back," he said.

Seriously, again? Why did they think I had to go back to the life of religion, God, and all things boring? I shook my head. "I'm done with that," I said.

"You don't belong here. You're not like us," he said. "You're... different.... And that's a good thing," he said.

Like a broken record, I replayed the tune I performed for Marcee and Krissy, thanking him for his concern but assuring him I couldn't do it. It was all an illusion, the Mennonite culture, and the "Jesus and religion stuff" didn't work. If he thought I didn't belong in their world, he clearly didn't know how lost I was in the other world.

Stephon lived on the edge. A few times when we were out with him and Marcee together, we made suspicious stops at random homes which, in hindsight, had to have been drug deals. I was too naïve to put the pieces together then. Or maybe, subconsciously, I didn't want to know the truth because I was afraid of it. I didn't totally turn a blind eye, and questioned the stops a time or two, but the answers were casual, superficial. "Just need to take care of something... Will only be a minute."

On one occasion, Dodi went in with Stephon while Marcee and I stayed in the car. I asked questions later, when Dodi and I were alone, but the answers offered nothing more. I even dared to ask him if he still did drugs. He said he didn't. Ironically, he had hallucinations later that begged an explanation, but he insisted they were a random occurrence. Something he suffered from since the war. I let it go, even though I didn't believe he had been to war. And I never did tell him that Marcee had ratted him out about drug dealing being the source of his scars.

Whatever they picked up that caused the hallucinations, it was crazy stuff. Days later Stephon ended up in the hospital, after a close scrape with death. He and some buddies were drunk and high, then went out driving. Feeling invincible, he crawled on the roof of the car to take a leak, at the speed of sixty miles an hour. It didn't end well, when he landed on the pavement face first. That he survived was nothing short of a miracle. His jaw had to be wired shut for weeks, putting him on a liquid-only diet for the duration.

216

For this man to offer me any advice at all was ironic. For someone who didn't seem to think seriously about life at all, even laughing off that accident, his advice was deep, sincere, and passionate. It struck me, each time someone told me that I didn't fit, didn't belong, that I never wondered, even for a moment, if they were rejecting me. In every case I felt as though they were trying to spare me some great tragedy or evil, without fully realizing what I had come from.

More than that, I had this sense that God was trying to tell me something. A whisper of His love, reminding me that I was His and He had not forgotten the cry of my heart.

****

After Dodi, Marcee, and Stephon left for work one morning, I turned on the ghetto blaster, rather than returning to my mattress. It was a mixed artist cassette, and REO Speedwagon, one of my favourite bands, played "Take It On the Run." I liked it because that was what my life felt like, always taking life on the run. Several songs played before "Running with the Devil," by Van Halen, came on. My blood ran cold with the chorus. A heavy presence settled in the room with the bold declaration in their words. The song invited a darker spiritual power, taunting what my life had become.

I felt suddenly lightheaded. My breath caught in my throat, my heart pounded, my body trembled. I could feel the darkness, but not see it. It was there in the room, coming for me with its claws, its blood-sucking tentacles, coming to claim my soul for the dark side. I turned off the music and fled into the bathroom, locking the door behind me, as if any dark spiritual presence could be kept out with closed and locked doors. I stayed there awhile, panting and afraid.

It was somewhat of a déjà vu. In childhood I had often feared the "dark presence," feeling it, and consciously aware of it. I could never sit in a room alone without facing the door, and even when I was with other people, I preferred to sit facing outward, never the wall. Especially when I had played the old organ, or the off-tune piano, my whole body tingled with the awareness of the dark ones there, ready to destroy me or hurt me. But I had so desperately wanted to play music, and hear those happy sounds, as I

217

discovered chords and played little tunes. So I had forced myself to ignore them. When I could bear it no longer I had fled the room, heart pounding, and not looking back until I was outside where the darkness seemed to melt in the light of the sun.

When I was alone, I sometimes had that creepy feeling of not being alone. As though there was some unseen danger, in the spirit world, that I could not defend myself against. The horror stories my parents had told me in early childhood played out this way in my mind, but more than that, the trauma of sexual abuse had opened doors to spiritual battle that I did not understand or recognize. Furthermore, my family history of dabbling in the darker realms had sensitized me to that world.

The hypersensitivity to the spiritual realm, from early childhood, never left during my rebel teen years. Always, when confronted with one evil thing or another, I felt it, and cringed. But in the area of sexuality and sexual abuse, I was oblivious to this spiritual dynamic. However, when it came to music, that sensitivity seemed to climax, with both good and evil.

Music always had a way of touching my spirit in a way that nothing else could. During the most traumatic years at home, listening to music had kept my heart soft and connected to God, when I was alone with Him. Listening to truth in that form, whether hymns or other meaningful songs, had opened my spirit to Him, and unleashed tears that otherwise remained trapped deep in my soul. To have "dark truth" sung over me sent my spirit into complete panic, bringing confusion and terror, in contrast to the peace and healing I had found in "God music" during childhood.

When I had calmed myself down and convinced myself that God would not strike me dead, and no evil thing would eat me alive for having listened to Van Halen's song, I dashed into the bedroom, closing the door securely behind me.

In that little room, I felt a certain security I couldn't explain. Maybe it was the few familiar things I had brought with me. The photo album in my suitcase. The Dear Jesus diary that lay badly neglected. My little brown Bible, even more neglected. Whatever it was, there the panic disappeared.

****

218

I dug through my suitcase, pulled out my Bible, and flipped through the pages. I knew the stories of the Old Testament better than I knew myself. The prophets, not so much. But it was the New Testament that drew me in. I had read and loved the stories of Jesus, but they collided with the god of religious experience. I couldn't reconcile them. Which one was real? Which one could I trust? What really was the truth? The gap was expansive between what I had been taught about the God with the big stick, and the gentle Jesus, who healed, loved, and brought hope. Both could not possibly be true.

I skipped over the gospels, flipped to the book of Romans, and started reading. Chapter six got my attention. "What shall we say then? Shall we continue in sin, that grace may abound? God forbid! How shall we, who are dead to sin, live any longer therein?"

I kept reading, but it was as if it was Greek. What did it really mean? Did it mean, as I had been taught, that I should follow a religious constitution, and wear cultural clothing—dresses, head veiling—and embrace that lifestyle? Did it really mean that I was to be so different from the world around me, in dress and all things external?

I tried to pray. Maybe God would speak and tell me what it was all about. I closed my eyes, tried to speak from my heart, but nothing came out. It was as if a wall had been erected between God and me. I opened my eyes. A deep ache in my heart wanted desperately to reach God. What could I do to make Him love me? What could I do to appease His anger? And what could I do to make myself be good enough? Were the Mennonite people right? Was the key to God hearing me, as a woman, for my head to be covered? I had long since discarded my yellow hat, and couldn't even try that, to see if it would work.

Finding nothing in my suitcase that resembled a hat or bonnet, I scrounged through Dodi's belongings. There had to be something I could put on my head, to see if God might hear me. At last I found it, in Dodi's closet. A baseball cap. I put it on, bowed my head and closed my eyes, and tried again to pray. Nothing. Nada. Zilch. I wasn't getting through to Him. No connection. Maybe it was their white, neatly pressed caps that did it. Whatever the case, it wasn't working, and there was no use trying.

I returned my Bible to my suitcase. Clearly God had abandoned me. It was probably too late for me. I had worn out His grace, and sinned too deeply for redemption. I was doomed to hell, without mercy.

The thought made me cringe. My heart choked up in fear and anxiety. What if hell really was my destiny? What if I had committed the unpardonable sin? I had heard preaching on it, and my sister had even told me once, when I was fourteen, that she feared I may have already committed that sin. I had been angry with her. But what if she was right? What if I was hopelessly, helplessly doomed?

In a state of panic I prayed one desperate prayer to this God who didn't seem to notice me, or care. If He was up there, somewhere, and if He was more like the Jesus I had loved, then maybe He would listen. It was nothing more than a silent whisper in my heart.

"If You will speak to me one more time, I promise I will give you the rest of my life, and never look back."

The prayer was quite simple, without any formal "Thee" or "Thou," as I had been taught to pray, but it was the most sincere prayer I had ever prayed. It put the ball in God's court, to do what He had to do to get me back.

Had I understood it then, I would have known that even that simple prayer was a response to God whispering my name. He was moving in my spirit, in my world. I just didn't recognize Him, or His moving, because it came in the form of one disappointment after another, and one desperate longing after another.

****

By Wednesday, the week after our Thanksgiving escapade, Dodi told me he had been given a truck run to Kitchener, Ontario, that Friday. We had crossed the border numerous times at Sarnia on previous runs, and never encountered any problems. I offered to go with him. Little did I know that this excursion would bring me to a crossroad, and God would toss the ball right back into my court.

"I know Kitchener, I could help you. That's where I lived before we met. What street?" I asked.

"Wellington Street," he said. But it would be an overnight run, and I would be stuck in the truck for twenty-four hours, maybe longer. That was good with me. I had lived around the corner from Wellington, in the apartment with Elayna and Fran. Even if only for one night, the thought of returning to my "home" was inviting. And so it was decided that I would leave with Dodi on Friday morning, December 4, 1987.

The week sped by. Anything was a good change from sitting at home, alone, in an apartment or house. To be out and about, even just sitting in the truck and watching the scenery go by, was so much better. And it was an added bonus that the dark forces seemed mostly to be kept at bay when I was with other people.

The trip to Kitchener was uneventful, with sporadic light snowfalls after we crossed the border. But even the snow caused no trouble other than to slow us down, ever so slightly. We arrived on schedule, and did our drop.

When we stopped at the Short Stop for snacks and a bathroom break, on the corner of Weber and Fairway, for one brief moment it occurred to me that I was "home," and I could escape and stay in Ontario. But just as quickly I realized that I had no place to go, no one to reach out to, so I returned to the truck and we headed for Sarnia, where our next load waited for pick-up on Saturday morning.

A glitch with our load put us on a tight schedule the following morning, but if nothing else went wrong, we would make it to Georgia on time. We headed to the border.

When we arrived, the border official asked us to pull over and come inside for questioning. No problem. I had done this before. I would simply charm the officer again, and all would be well. My confidence shriveled when I saw the officer. Charming wasn't going to cut it. *She* was a foot shorter than I, and what she lacked in height, she made up for in attitude and authority.

"ID please," she said.

"I'm sorry, ma'am, I lost it," I said. She looked up, eyebrows raised.

"How do you expect to cross the border?" she asked sternly.

"I've crossed without ID before, quite a few times, and it's never been a problem," I said. She sighed.

"What's your dad's name and address, with lot and concession, and phone number?"

"Peter Harder, RR 5 Clinton, Lot 28, Concession 5, 519-482-3242...." I answered, giving her the information.

She walked to the computer and punched in the details. A frown spread across her face, her eyebrows furrowed. "Give me that information again, please," she said, sighing again.

I wondered if she was always cranky or if that was special treatment for me. I repeated the information, and she typed it into the computer.

"I'm sorry," she said, speaking without emotion, "there is no such address. You are sure you have it right?"

"Yes," I said, repeating the information one more time.

"It's not here. Do your parents rent or own?" she asked.

"They own," I said.

"How long?"

"Nine years," I said.

"Then it should be in here, but nothing shows up. I'm sorry," she said. But she sure didn't look sorry.

I politely answered her questions. All of them. Even the ones that seemed irrelevant, as she shook out my purse and let the contents spill all over her counter, and demanded an explanation for each item, and each snippet of paper. One item at a time, this was going to be a long day.

When she was satisfied that there was nothing of interest, she replaced the contents and handed my purse to me. Returning to the computer, she checked the information one final time. "I'm sorry, you will need to get a deed for the property, as proof of residence, or find some kind of ID before you cross the border," she said. She almost sounded sorry.

"Excuse me, ma'am," Dodi interjected, "you can't keep her here."

"And why not?" she asked.

222

"We're getting married in February," he answered. "She is my fiancée and I can't just leave her here."

"Do you have fiancée papers?" the officer asked.

"No. I didn't know there is such a thing," he said.

"Well, you'll have to get fiancée papers and then try again. For today, she won't be crossing the border. I'm sorry, sir," she said.

Dodi tried to plead with her, but she wasn't going to budge. We had to come up with plan B. Fast. We were already half an hour behind schedule. Our options were to find a way to sneak me across the border and risk getting caught, or I could stay and try to cross later with a stranger and hitchhike to Fort Wayne, or I could call my family for a ride home. There were no good options, just three bad options, with only one being reasonable. I had no choice but to call my family for a ride, and Dodi had no choice but to leave for Georgia without me, or risk losing his job.

"Don't worry about me," I said. "I'll be fine." With that we parted ways.

Earlier that morning I had whispered a prayer. It wasn't formal, just a cry from deep in my heart, in a moment of loneliness. Curled up in the bunker, while Dodi drove, it had formed, more as a longing than actual words. A desire to be free. More a statement than a request. The words never made it past my lips, but those fleeting thoughts were shared in intimacy with God.

I don't want to go back... I want to stay in Canada.

A tear had threatened. I knew what waited for me in Indiana. Having whispered that prayer, I had immediately returned to my reality, with a resolve to make it work, to make the best of it. I had no choice. Fort Wayne was my new home, no matter how messed up it had become. Maybe with time it would get better.

Standing there at the border, watching Dodi drive away, I had long since forgotten that desperate cry. But God had heard it. He had a plan, a purpose. Redemption was on its way.

Chapter Thirty

I found a pay phone and dialled my parents' number. It rang... and rang.... and rang. I waited a while and tried again. It was early afternoon before I got through.

"Hello." I recognized my youngest sister's voice.

"Hi, Martha, it's Trudy." I paused, letting it sink in, before I explained my situation, then ended with my request. "I wondered if anyone would be willing to come pick me up. I have no place to go."

"I'll talk to the family. Call back in about an hour and I'll try to have an answer," Martha said.

Time passed slowly as I paced in the cold. I wandered back to the office where the "small but mighty" officer worked. She was still on duty. I warmed myself and then returned to the docks and lit another cigarette. It was my only pastime, and it seemed to calm my mind and occupy my hands. Finally the hour passed. I called home again. Martha answered. Yes, they would come and pick me up, she said, as long as I promised to keep some basic rules. I was not to wear jeans or slacks at home, only dresses. Swearing was forbidden. And no smoking or alcohol.

I agreed to the rules, as long as the dresses didn't have to be "Mennonite," but I would have to come home in jeans. It was all I had. With that agreement in place, we arranged a specific time and location where I would expect to meet my brother and his wife, some hours later.

I thanked her, hung up, and returned to wandering aimlessly on the dock, in the cold. At least I wouldn't have to spend the night on the street. The time passed quickly and soon I was in the back seat of my brother's car, engaging in awkward conversation. I had abandoned my family for more than two years, with almost no contact. My pride had taken a hard hit when I had to call home for help. Their lives appeared "religiously perfect" and mine was a mess. To keep them a safe distance from my heart, I told them I would be returning to Indiana at my earliest convenience and said that I had gotten married while I was away. In my mind I wasn't lying.

Dodi and I had held a private ceremony at the apartment and said our vows to each other, but with no witnesses, no judge, and no pastor. Just a candlelight pre-wedding promise that he had said made us married and gave us "rights," so that I would not feel guilty about our living arrangement. The mind is a strange thing, and so easily deceived. The ceremony had removed my guilt, for the most part. I couldn't tell if my brother and his wife bought my story or not. And I didn't care. As long as they left me alone, I had accomplished what I needed for the purpose of the ride home.

Mom, when I saw her, was a step ahead of the game. She had received a phone call from Dodi's sister Marcee, she said, telling her I was not in a good place, and my family should try to get me home. Dodi wasn't who I perceived him to be, she told mom, and had divorced his wife while we were together. She believed I had no idea that he was a free-loading mooch who used Marcee, borrowed from her, and never repaid what he took. She was tired of taking care of him, and didn't want to provide a home for me, but didn't have the heart to kick me out with him.

Either Marcee had lied to mom, or things were not as I had been led to believe. The latter was far more likely. Still, I resented that mom knew, or thought she knew, things she had no right knowing, things that were none of her business. Things she could not change, or even influence. I brushed off the conversation and made a point of keeping it superficial.

****

Back at home life was relatively peaceful. For the most part I kept the ground rules. Keeping "the law" of those rules meant I could go for walks and break the rules off site. Two inches off the property meant I wasn't "at home," so by walking toward the back of our property and stepping onto the neighbour's field I could have a smoke behind the shed. And by leaving home in a dress or skirt, and changing into jeans in the car, I kept the letter of the law, but still did as I pleased.

I mocked their religious beliefs and practices, not so much to be antagonistic as to create a barrier against any religious indoctrination from siblings. By putting them on the defence, I made it almost impossible for them to preach at me. It surprised me when they didn't react to my taunting. And it surprised me even more when no one tried to convert me, judge me, or preach at me.

For several weeks I lived relatively peacefully with my family, leaving home only occasionally to party with my brother and friends.

Dodi's truck runs took him to the southern states, making it impossible for him to pick me up, but he called me several times each week, promising to come for me as soon as he could get a truck run to Ontario, or had a weekend with enough consecutive days off work to come to Ontario and pick me up. It wasn't an option to send me bus tickets. Things were too volatile with his family.

Krissy and Ray were still fighting over the whole ordeal, and Ray had pushed Krissy down the steps and threatened to kill her. She had fled and locked herself in the bathroom, screaming for her life, later calling the police, and then dropping all charges when they arrested Ray. It was all part of relationship for them, and they each took their turn being the villain. When the tables had turned, it was Ray running for his life when she had pulled a knife on him.

Dodi didn't want me caught in the middle of that, he said. It was best if I stayed in Ontario for the time being, and hopefully he could pick me up before Christmas. But, as the holidays drew near, it became more and more obvious that I would be home for Christmas. And, truth be told, the longer I was in Ontario, the more I wanted to stay.

Away from Dodi and the dark life of Indiana, the dark beings never came. Only a gentle whisper of Love, now and then, reminded me that Someone had His eyes on me, inviting me into divine romance. It was as if two lovers vied for my heart. Both jealous for me. Both making promises. But one breaking his promises, deceiving me and crushing my heart. The other simply loving with compassion, never faltering in His promises.

More and more, my heart longed for the One... The One whose name I had whispered with my first breath—Yahweh. The One whom I had loved first, as a little girl in Mexico, when His Spirit had bathed me in the wind. The One who had kissed me with sunlight and invited me close to Him, on top of that mountain... The One whose angels I had believed danced in the puddles when it rained...

But I was used.... and sinful. And He was so holy... I was unworthy... so unworthy...

Chapter Thirty-One

Christmas Day that year was as if it didn't happen. Apart from being a day on the calendar, I have no conscious memory of it. But the next day, December 26, 1987, is a day I will never forget.

My parents were gone to visit Grandma and Grandpa Wall, and some of mom's siblings. How times had changed. For many years it was all twelve uncles and aunts, their spouses, and all their little children, if they were in the area. Dozens of us crammed into one small house, with people everywhere. No one spoke of it, but too much abuse had happened, and lay buried; one by one, around age thirteen, my siblings and I stopped going. Eventually, the cousins drifted apart, and we seldom saw our relatives. Not even Grandma and Grandpa.

When we were younger, a day without parents, doing our own thing, cooking our own food, and developing our independence, was a real treat. Mealtimes were the best. Accustomed to the formality of rigid silence before dinner, and a time of silent prayer, we took that leadership and had fun with it. With mock reverence someone would clear their throat, and in all seriousness ask a sibling to "please lead us in silent prayer," at which everyone erupted in laughter. At length we managed a prayer of some sort, distracted from time to time by the ongoing ripple of laughter or suppressed giggles from those of us who lacked the self-control to remain silent.

That Boxing Day, with older siblings at home, the nonsense was lacking, and the formality to which I had been accustomed was kept. A chicken dinner, prepared by older sisters, cooked in the oven, and the house was clean and welcoming.

An unusual buzz of excitement filled the air that day. Anna's boyfriend, Leonard Hursh, from Mount Joy, Pennsylvania, was in for a visit. Leonard was not quite two years older than I, making him six years younger than Anna. We had fun teasing her about robbing the cradle, but the moment I met him, I thought he was just the kind of person she needed. He seemed gentlemanly, and had a sense of humour. The former was important in relationship, the latter critical to survive in our family with our warped "Harder humour."

Mid-morning, my siblings suggested we sing while dinner finished cooking. Our family has strong voices and, since childhood, spent many hours singing in beautiful harmony. Still, when asked to join in, I declined. I wasn't interested in their religious hymns and songs. I was into Bon Jovi, Chicago, Genesis, Peter Gabriel, Eurythmics, U2, REO Speedwagon, and a variety of other rock artists.

"It's just Christmas carols," a sibling insisted. I obliged. What harm could it do? I remained disengaged, as we sang song after song, paying no attention to the religious message. The songs were festive, and I enjoyed singing with my siblings. We worked our way through the carols in the Christian Hymnary, taking turns choosing songs, staying in the "safe" zone.

"Can we sing number 915?" my youngest brother, Abe, asked.

That's no Christmas carol, I thought to myself. They start at around page 110 and end around page 117. I flipped to the song, looked at the title, and groaned. "By a Crowd of Worshippers." It brought back memories of school days when slow songs made me feel faint, as though I might fall asleep standing up, or simply pass out. We had sung it countless times, and it bored me to death every time, dragging on forever. But that day, as we sang, the story unfolded in the words and came to life in my heart. Had anyone else chosen the song, my guard would have been up and I would have been suspicious that they were trying to evangelize me through manipulation. But my little brother didn't have it in him. All my guards were down.

The song, based on the story in John 8, tells of a woman who is caught in adultery, "in the very act" and is brought to Jesus for judgement. It is the religious leaders, who hold themselves in fairly high regard, who bring her to Jesus to see if He will stand by the law of Moses, and order her to be stoned.

But Jesus disregards them and starts writing on the ground. When they persist, He acknowledges them, and gives them permission to stone her, on one condition. "Let the one among you who is without sin cast the first stone," He urges, and then continues writing on the ground. As He writes, they begin to walk away, in order of age, starting with the oldest one, down to the youngest. We don't know what He wrote, but whatever it was, it brought conviction to the men present, influencing their exit.

In the end, abandoned by her accusers and waiting to be sentenced, the woman is left standing in front of Jesus, with a crowd gathered around her. Jesus simply asks her, "Woman, where are your accusers? Is there no one left to condemn you?"

The woman answers, "No one, my Lord."

Jesus looks at her and says, "Neither do I condemn you! Go, and sin no more!"

Suddenly, I saw myself—not the woman caught in adultery—standing there in front of Jesus. I was waiting to be sentenced for my sins. But, rather than hearing judgement and condemnation, He looked up at me and spoke those words, filled with grace and mercy, "Neither do I condemn you! Go, and sin no more!"

In an instant, my life of sin collided with undeniable love and grace. If that story was true... if Jesus truly offered that kind of pardon for the guilty... if He looked beyond the life that woman lived, and beyond the life I had lived, to the deeper need of the heart, then I had spent my entire life misunderstanding God.

As that thought registered, deep emotion welled up in my chest. It took every ounce of self-control to push it down and maintain my pride. There was no way my family was allowed to see this! I walked slowly from the room, as if going for a bathroom break. But the instant I rounded the corner, I fled upstairs to what had been my room for many years, and where I stayed when I was home. There I wept.

Overwhelmed by who I had become, all that I had done, the life I had lived, grief flooded my spirit. As reality settled in, of the magnitude of my brokenness and all I had lost, a wave of nausea washed over me. There was no undoing it. No going back. Like the woman in the song, I felt ashamed, broken, and beyond redemption. I didn't deserve freedom. But I longed for it with my whole being.

Having left home in a desperate attempt to be free, I had run hard and fast, only to be overtaken by the very darkness I tried to escape. Two long years, which felt more like twenty, had left me, not only with the burden of sins committed against me in childhood and youth, but with the burden of my own sinful choices.

If the Jesus in that song was real, and everything that story said about Him was true, it would change everything. Then I had spent my life running from a god who did not exist, while the love and acceptance of the true God pursued me, always within reach; a gentle invitation of grace. If this God was real, then there was hope for me. I wanted desperately to believe that He was real, and that I could commit to leaving the broken path I was on, and follow through with a life of faith. But I faltered...

Dodi... The thought of him tugged at my heart. I felt sorry for him. And, in my dysfunctional way, I loved him in spite of all the lies. I had given myself to him emotionally and the thought of life without him felt lonely. Could I turn my back on him, break off the engagement, and return again to live as a Christian among the Mennonites?

I sat there awhile in front of the old dresser, cluttered with a variety of knickknacks, hair care items, and hairspray, contemplating. I had made a vow to God, back in Fort Wayne, that if He would speak to me one more time, I would give Him the rest of my life. I had to be certain that this was Him speaking, and just as certain that I was ready to take that step, and keep that vow.

My heart pounded violently inside my chest, heaving from the torrent of tears that spilled from the blackest place in my soul, until I could hardly breathe. *My God! What have I done? What have I done? Are You really enough for the mess I've made of my life? Will you really forgive me? Release me from this dreadful curse?*

The party life had grown tired, yet held a bit of appeal. The darkness of my sin haunted me.

I stood again before Jesus, and saw Him writing in the sand. He looked again into my eyes, a deep and tender look. A dam burst. The tears started again. My heart pounded more violently inside my chest, causing a hot rush to flood my whole body. I felt nothing but love; pure, unadulterated, sacred love, flowing from the Divine, into my scarred soul.

I fell to my knees, still sobbing. There was no fancy sinner's prayer. No saying the right words, or making promises. Only the deep, silent unburdening of a soul, tired of running. And five simple words, "God, have mercy on me."

I stayed a long while on my knees, weeping. Unable to form words of confession or commitment, I could only give Him my heart, raw and bleeding, to hold in His hands and clutch against His own chest, as if teaching my heart to beat in time with Him.

Yahweh. It was as if He breathed real life into my spirit for the first time. Eternal life. I rose to my feet, keenly aware that I would never be the same. I could not be the same. Eighteen years of longing for my father's love, in search of my identity, and running from a terrifying illusion, had climaxed in one moment of love and acceptance by my Heavenly Father.

In the dresser I found items I needed to wrap my hair up in the traditional manner—in a bun at the back of my head, tucked inside a hairnet. I wrestled with my short hair, but won out. With enough bobby pins and hairspray I tucked it in place. In my sister's closet I found one of her traditional cape dresses and slipped into it.

With one final glance in the mirror at the "new me," I turned my back on all that had grown familiar, and returned to life with my people.

Epilogue

December 26, 1987, it was as if I was walking due west, and suddenly started walking due east. The lines would never cross.

I remembered my promise to God, that I would give Him the rest of my life if He called my name one more time. And that day in December, He called and I answered. In Him I found what I had been looking for—peace, identity, acceptance, grace, and salvation.

The teachings of my culture—some of which were good, others not so much—had tormented my mind through the rebel years. The confusion of sorting out God's truth—salvation through Jesus—from cultural interpretation of religious practices, along with the trauma of abuse and violence in a religious home, had made it nearly impossible for me to get close to God. But that morning it was as if I saw Him for the first time, in the love and grace Jesus showed to the woman in adultery. It was as if God Himself looked into my eyes, and I understood Emmanuel; God with us.

Knowing God as Jesus—a God of grace and forgiveness—changed everything. As a young pre-teen I had responded at revival meetings out of terror that I would go to hell but my fear was never dealt with. No one taught me to look into God's eyes, to see love, and to see my reflection in that love. So my fears grew stronger with that experience, rather than bringing me peace, because I never could and never would measure up.

I needed to know that God loved me, that it was not my goodness that saved me, but the blood of Jesus Christ, and His blood alone. I needed to know that any goodness I might bring Him was merely a gift of thankfulness for what He has done. Instead, I had become a slave to effort.

By age eighteen I knew my goodness wasn't much of a gift to offer God. I had discovered evil in my heart and, if pushed into a dark enough place, even murder was not beyond me. By the time I turned my heart to God I understood that even the invitation to do so came from Jesus. It wasn't anything I did. But that "knowing" didn't erase the questions about faith, religion, and culture, and how they intertwine. What I knew in my head had not yet made its way to my heart—that the secret to salvation does not lie buried in any culture or attaining, and I didn't need to go back to the Mennonite church to be a Christian. Those demons haunted.

Niggling what-if's played at the fringes of my mind. What if God did expect me to be Mennonite, for me to be saved? What if it was the way to "live out my salvation, with fear and trembling"? And what if rejecting it meant that I was rejecting God? What if they were right?

I returned to the Mennonite culture to sort through the confusion, but made it clear to myself and my friends that my salvation was in Jesus, alone. In the Mennonite culture I had abandoned God and my Christian faith. I would return, live for Him there, and let Him lead me in His time, His way. Wherever He wished to take me. This time I would not run.

A few months after becoming a Christian, I paid a visit to Doris and Pastor Lloyd Reaney—the pastor who first showed me "the true Jesus" when he paid me a visit that day in the back yard in New Hamburg.

I was in Wellesley for meetings with some friends. When we drove past the little church they pastored I saw that the lights were on. I sat through the service, but the whole time I couldn't stop thinking about Pastor Lloyd and Doris, hoping they were there.

Immediately after the service I made my way down the street. I stepped inside the little white church. The auditorium was dark, but the basement was lit up, and voices carried upstairs. I made my way down the steps. There, ahead of me, sat Lloyd and Doris. They looked confused, as if trying to place me.

I introduced myself. It took a moment for everything to register. It was always interesting, if not a bit awkward, meeting up with people who had never known me as a Mennonite. I learned to break the ice by addressing the change light-heartedly.

"I've changed a bit since we last met," I said, as if they might not have observed the white bonnet and cape dress. They laughed good-naturedly and agreed, but got to the heart of the matter right away, and wanted to hear how it all came about.

I didn't have time to tell the whole story, so I gave the short version and wrapped up my testimony with the following statement: "I'm not sure why, but I know I'm supposed to be in the Mennonite church right now. I feel that God wants me to live out my faith where I abandoned Him. One day I will leave the Mennonite church again." I thanked them for caring, and especially thanked Lloyd for that day in the back yard, and for showing me who God really is. It had left an everlasting impact.

****

When I returned to the Mennonite church, I invested myself whole-heartedly in their faith and practices.... Well, most of them. I never quite managed to master all the rules, but I tried not to live with one foot in the church, and one foot out.

Little did I realize that the reason I thought God had me back there—to pick up my faith where I had abandoned it—though likely true, was not complete. There were much bigger plans in play, one of which I couldn't possibly fathom at the time—that He would heal me there—and another I would not have believed, had someone told me... a plan that would impact hundreds, even thousands of people, in the long term.

In His infinite wisdom, God brought a Mennonite couple—Howard and Alice Horst—into my life, in 1989, to help me acknowledge, for the first time, the story in the pages of this book... a story that had been buried deep in my subconscious. They pursued me, listened to my heart, and even took me into their home as one of their own for nearly two years, while I healed emotionally, spiritually, and mentally. No one had ever invested in me as they did, and without them, I cannot imagine what my life would be. I thank God always for them, and how they impacted my life, and the generations to come.

Gradually, as I healed, God birthed a dream in my heart, with the promise that, if I would wait for the right time, He would go before me and bless the ministry.

On November 26, 2010, twenty-three years to the day after that Thanksgiving Day in 1987 when I learned of Dodi's divorce, I stood in front of just over two hundred and fifty women and launched our first ever conference for victims of sexual abuse, to acknowledge the crime, but more importantly to open the door to healing. Earlier that year we had established Faith Girls Unleashed, a ministry for women.

Starting with that first conference, gentlemen approached me and asked if we would do conferences for men. At first I said no. But by 2012 we knew that God was moving us into a broader ministry, not limited to women, and we launched Generations Unleashed, and applied for our charitable status. It took over a year for Canada Revenue Agency to grant this request, and in the meantime we planned our first mixed audience conference.

Starting with that conference, they were well received by attendees, with almost fifty percent of attendees being male and many offering emotional thank-yous. By the second conference, numerous gentlemen from my cultural background called, asking questions. Wives, sons, daughters, and even some of the men who called, had suffered sexual abuse. "This has got to end," one middle-aged Conservative Mennonite man said, after registering several family members, "this silence has to be broken."

In 2011 I took a Speaker, Coach & Trainer Certification course, offered through John C. Maxwell, to improve my speaking skills. Instead, when conference attendees approached me with their traumatic stories, I found myself applying what I had learned in the coaching segment, to help victims move beyond victimization, to living full lives. Most of these clients—well over ninety percent—were from the Mennonite community, as were many conference attendees.

That is when my journey back through the Mennonite church started to make sense. By returning to the culture and church of my childhood, I was able to find much good and establish lifelong, meaningful relationships there. I discovered that, while the pain I experienced there was valid, as was the confusion of how I perceived God due to some people misrepresenting Him, there was also much that was right, much I could appreciate, and many who represented Him well. Many remain in my life to this day—sincere believers who love Jesus, face truth, and fight for victims.

Since starting into ministry I have met and befriended hundreds and hundreds of "my people"—the Mennonites—and have had the honour of working one-on-one with many of them, mentoring and coaching them, praying, sharing tears, and finding hope in Jesus together. I am blessed to have mentors among them, as well as family and friends, who encourage and pray for me.

Had God showed me that day in December, I would never have believed all the wonderful things He had planned as a result of the traumatic childhood I had suffered: the redemption of many stories, and the healing of many hearts.

Today I thank God for my story, and I wouldn't go back and change it, even if I could, because it has opened doors and brought purpose to my life, and it has brought hope to others. It has given me opportunity to represent His heart to many who have suffered at the hands of sexual predators, and the control of religiously misguided.

My prayer is that you will find purpose in your life, and in your story. Let your past become a launching pad into greater things. Remember, there is nothing in the world that can happen, no matter how evil, that it cannot become a force for something good. The choice is mine, the choice is yours. Choose well.

Love,

~ T ~

CPSIA information can be obtained at www.ICGtesting.com
Printed in the USA
LVOW04s2050290315

432484LV00012B/141/P